STRATEGY FOR A NETWORKED WORLD

STRATEGY FOR A NETWORKED WORLD

Rafael Ramírez
Ulf Mannervik
Oxford

ICP
Imperial College Press

Published by

Imperial College Press
57 Shelton Street
Covent Garden
London WC2H 9HE

Distributed by

World Scientific Publishing Co. Pte. Ltd.

5 Toh Tuck Link, Singapore 596224

USA office: 27 Warren Street, Suite 401-402, Hackensack, NJ 07601

UK office: 57 Shelton Street, Covent Garden, London WC2H 9HE

Library of Congress Cataloging-in-Publication Data
Names: Ramírez, Rafael, 1956– author. | Mannervik, Ulf, author.
Title: Strategy for a networked world / Rafael Ramírez (University of Oxford, UK) & Ulf Mannervik (University of Oxford, UK).
Description: New Jersey : Imperial College Press, 2016.
Identifiers: LCCN 2016013085 | ISBN 9781783269921 (hc : alk. paper)
Subjects: LCSH: Strategic planning. | Industrial management. | Value.
Classification: LCC HD30.28 .R354 2016 | DDC 658.4/012--dc23
LC record available at https://lccn.loc.gov/2016013085

British Library Cataloguing-in-Publication Data
A catalogue record for this book is available from the British Library.

Desk Editors: Anthony Alexander/Mary Simpson

Typeset by Stallion Press
Email: enquiries@stallionpress.com

Printed in Singapore

To Our Families: Geneviève, Ivan, Louis,
Melvin, and Fabian

Contents

List of Figures, Boxes, and Tables

Chapter 1

Chapter 2

Chapter 3

Chapter 4

Chapter 5

Chapter 6

Chapter 7

Chapter 8

Chapter 9

Chapter 10

Appendix A

Appendix B

Foreword

1. This Book is for Strategists, and for Those for Whom Strategists Work

This book has been written for those that do strategy (strategic management teams, top management teams, strategy consultants); those that strategic planners help (senior managers, board members); and those who learn and study strategy (students, researchers, and teachers).

2. This Book is About How to Do and Think About Strategy in a Networked World

This book is about how to change the way strategy is done. Change is required because the world strategists work in is not only now much more interconnected, but also more uncertain. Strategists require working with an approach that is consistent with turbulent and ambiguous contexts where forecasting is ever less reliable and novel situations arise. We show that conventional approaches embedded in positioning, in value chains, on changing product features, and within established industries are not helpful in such conditions.

3. The Journey of Work and Research that Led to This Book

This book builds on and extends the pioneering work and insights that our late colleague Richard Normann developed working with the authors and other colleagues. This work imagined and developed ways to enable strategists to shift their perspective, and to reorient their attention and focus.

Normann thought of services not as a sector but as a way of creating value, where the actual interaction was what strategists need to understand.[1] This means that the unit of analysis strategists were advised to use was not the firm, nor the position of the firm (in a "chain" or "industry"), but the interactions. While these insights were ahead of their time when they were generated (Schön called the volume "heraldic" in the introduction to his 2005 book), the time has now come for the ideas and the practices they inform to become much less exceptional, better understood, and more widely used.

Normann and colleagues helped strategists to consider how the interactions at the core of strategy might need to be transformed in differing environmental conditions. He also thought that strategists ought to consider their role as designers — designers of interactions, and of the value creating systems (VCSs) these interactions entail and bring forth.

In his last book, before his death at an early age, 60, Normann (2001) put forth the idea that with a different map, strategists could reframe business and change the very landscape their businesses inhabit.[2]

Our journey of working on and with these ideas is a 30 year journey — so the book recounts almost 60 years of professional and

---

[1]He understood this to be valid for products too, and for combinations of services and products.

[2]Research in biology illustrates how this happens in nature. The field of study biologists call "Trophic Cascades" refers to situations where "powerful indirect interactions … can control entire ecosystems. Trophic cascades occur when predators limit the density and/or behaviour of their prey, and thereby enhance survival of the next lower trophic level" (Silliman & Angelini, 2012). A very accessible example of a Trophic Cascade relates how the reintroduction of wolves into Yellowstone National Park in the USA contributed to change various interactions — not only deer behaviour in relation to wolves and what deer eat, but even the actual way rivers flow and how they shape the landscape. A six minute film recounts this in an easy-to-understand manner — see https://www.youtube.com/watch?v=ysa5OBhXz-Q.

research experience if one counts the experience accumulated by both authors. Ramírez was hired by Normann in 1985, while still studying for his PhD. They worked together for 18 years, co-authoring an influential Harvard Business Review article, various book chapters, and a book that was widely translated. Mannervik first met Normann in 1994 when as a research student of design theory he arranged a national hearing on Swedish design, and Normann accepted to be a keynote speaker on the role of design in VCSs. Mannervik was then employed by Normann in 1997 after completing his degree applying design thinking and methodologies to strategy work. Ramírez and Mannervik met the following year, in 1998, when they and Normann together with two other professional services firms (GBN and Wolff Olins) convened a symposium on Business Logics for Innovators in Zurich. In that event, Francisco Varela, Wally Olins, and Richard Normann provided frameworks that led to the work Normann published in 2001, which this book extends.

So, we have been using the concepts and methods in consulting engagements and in research for three decades, and the lessons of these experiences are presented in this book. As strategy consultants, much of our work remains confidential — but not all of it. We are very thankful for the colleagues in the firms and organisations we have worked with, for helping us to test and refine the ideas we present in this book — particularly for those who have allowed us to share their experiences as cases. To support the argumentation we convey, here we also use the research we have carried out on value co-creation, service design, VCSs, and socio-ecological strategy that we have authored and co-authored (or co-authored with others) and published as papers and books since Normann and Ramírez first published *Designing Interactive Strategy* in 1994.

4. Other Intellectual Traditions Contributing to This Book

For over 50 years research (Emery & Trist, 1965; Ramírez *et al.*, 2008; Ramírez & Selsky, 2014) has proposed that conceptions of strategy that seek advantage in a zero-sum competitive struggle can bring forth turbulent environments where one's adaptive capacity falters.

In today's networked world, turbulence, unpredictable uncertainty, and ambiguity are more the norm than the exception.

So, a pertinent form of strategising is called for, one that differs from strategic approaches developed for less turbulent and more stable contexts, where firms are less tightly connected to each other than is the case today. This book explores and explains a form of strategising that is fit for purpose in such conditions.

Companies like Facebook, Airbnb, and Uber (but also well-established firms such as EDF, IKEA, Maersk, Rolls-Royce and Scania) do not have strategic frameworks where it is assumed that customers simply "consume" the value that has been added "for" them in a linear process. Rather, their customers, suppliers, partners, and other co-creators are seen as members of a "VCS", participating in the co-creation efforts that makes their participation worth their while.

The argumentation in this book builds on intellectual traditions that date back hundreds of years and have considered value as co-created. Most recently this can be seen in assessing the specific nature of activities classified as services.

Finally, the book builds on the practice and scholarship of design, and considers strategists to be primarily designers of businesses. The argument we present depicts the design of strategy to be primarily focused on the offerings that relate interactors to each other in ways that enable their values to be reconciled and their value co-creation to be orchestrated effectively.

5. A Succinct Overview of the Argument in This Book

In Chapter 1, we survey the history of a notable failure which manifests the importance of thinking of strategy as VCSs with designed offerings at the core. Myspace seemed at first to have all the advantages for co-productive success. But when it was bought by News Corporation, it lost ground to a rival — Facebook — whose owners were content to let the co-creation it enabled grow. Facebook's development was guided by a focus on enabling its users to connect with each other and help each other to build communities. Facebook did — and still does — very well; Myspace, bought by Murdoch's company for $580 million in 2005, and valued at $10 billion in 2007, was sold for $35 million in 2011.[3]

Strategy is about the practice of creating distinctive value, and this book is about a methodology as well as a theory. The argument focuses strategic attention on the systems that are involved in value co-creation and to implicit designs and assumptions of existing VCS as well as explicit designs for new VCS.

Unlike quantitative and linear approaches to strategising, the offering design approach to strategy enables the strategist to reconsider a rich set of wider possibilities than the narrower set that can be captured when only considering positons within value chains and industries.

The difference between the VCS design approach and conventional strategy is most clearly manifested in the central organising concept of the "offering". This cannot be understood as a simple thing or action linking the supplier with the customer. Rather, the offering manifests a whole system of co-creation. It acts as a code or script that configures the whole designed system of relationships that enable those involved to come together to co-create value. In addition to an overall "configuring" offering that underpins the design of a VCS, we describe the "support offerings" that coordinate the relationships of actors on specific parts of the VCS to support the realisation of the configuring offering as a VCS.

Using the "offering" in this manner enables one to analyse the history of business innovations in EDF and of Shell Global Solutions (SGSI). SGSI has from the beginning been an entrepreneurial enterprise shaped and reshaped within the broader institutional imperatives of Shell International. We also give examples of how SCA has used a VCS approach to extend their leading business of incontinence care products for elderly patients, into wider care system-based "offerings"; and how Scania is expanding well beyond its traditional realm as the world's most profitable truck maker.

Normann and his colleagues imagined and developed strategy thinking and methodologies that were well ahead of their times. These times

---

[3] http://www.theguardian.com/technology/2011/jun/30/myspace-sold-35-million-news (Accessed November 2015).

have now arrived, they have taken place, and they have become commonplace. They have come to business as container and air shipping and ubiquitous mobile devices connect things and people and ideas and information and automated processes more closely to each other. For example, some 70% of foreign exchange trading is now conducted by computers in relation to each other;[4] and some 85% of a car is no longer produced by the manufacturer — instead it is co-created with hundreds of other companies; and the buyers themselves engage with many companies (fuel sellers, insurers, finance firms, garages,...) and organisations (the police, road departments where they live, parking authorities,...) to ensure the vehicle helps them to produce and co-create (with families, employers,...) the values for which it was acquired.

The thinking we convey in this book offers a strategy approach based on the same logic of interconnected value creation that is becoming the norm in business. The argument is for strategy centred on systems thinking, where, assuming that value is co-created, collaboration is at least as decisive for success as competition.

The methodology that this book describes offers a perspective on business as it has become — not as it was.

The book considers that strategising as design works by shifting the strategist's perspective and the focus of what strategy considers. The strategising inquiry starts from the here-and-now and returns to the here-and-now. But it temporarily invites the strategic mind to leave the here-and-now to instead consider its past and possible futures; and to assess and reconsider its context and possibilities, then bringing mindfulness to test the insights in an iterative mode that helps strategy designers to prototype, design, test, and refine the development of better offerings.

For practitioners, the book presents and explains methodologies to assess the design of existing offerings, the VCSs that they entail, and to design new offerings. The methods include "Actor-Network Theory" (ANT), scenario planning for collaborative strategy and design assessment, and offering design. The book is not only about thinking, but also about doing; the final part offers guidelines for practitioners in the

[4] http://www.bloomberg.com/news/articles/2014-02-18/fx-traders-facing-extinction-as-computers-replace-humans (Accessed November 2015).

realisation of VCS designs. For those interested in ideas, we have grounded argumentation in solid scholarship, referenced as relevant; endnotes and appendices expand on the ideas and research upon which the intellectual rigour of the practice is based.

Our overall arguments are more clearly explained in Chapter 1, where the organisation of the book is also outlined.

6. Acknowledgements

We have had the privilege to work with remarkable individuals in world-class firms and public sector organisations, both in our consulting in NormannPartners and in research and teaching at HEC-Paris and the University of Oxford. We are indebted to them, as well as to inspiring and challenging colleagues. They all have contributed to shaping our ideas, specifically those in this book.

Whereas there are truly many that would be worth mentioning, some stand out in particular for this book. Louis Ramírez did the research for the examples in Chapter 1. We thank our WEF colleagues for reviewing and confirming the accuracy of our WEF case study. Our NormannPartners colleagues Gerard Drenth and Bill Sharpe contributed to many rich conversations on value and values presented in Chapter 3 and Appendix A — we thank them for their insight and attention. Chapters 4 and 9, as well as parts of other chapters, benefited from our research on "strategic renewal" at Oxford, done with the European Patent Office and Shell. We would like to express our thanks to those involved there — Eric Allen, Stephane Girod, Peter Lednor, Leo Roodhart, Keith Ruddle, and Marc Thompson. Our former colleague and serial entrepreneur Fredrik Arnander assured that our description of his internet access point innovation Sidewalk Express is accurate. We thank Jeremy Bentham for useful comments on the Shell Global Solutions case in Chapter 5. Chapter 6 was co-written with two NormannPartners colleagues, Shirin Elahi and Fredrik Lavén, as well as two clients from the French electricity company EDF, Claude Nahon and Assaad Saab. Several individuals at our client Scania informed the examples described in the book, especially in Chapters 7 and 8. Of these, we are particularly indebted to Lars-Henrik Jörnving, our client first in research and development (R&D) and then in

Production & Logistics, and Anders Berglund who reviewed the description of their scenarios-based technology roadmap work. A special thank you is also due to Sigvard Orre, with whom we have explored new VCSs for Scania and who has ensured the parts related to the designing of their new logistics systems venture described in Chapter 8 is accurate. Björn Ålsnäs at the global hygiene company SCA — better known for its FMCG brands Tork and Tena — co-wrote the relevant parts of Chapters 8 and 9. A client who wishes to remain confidential allowed us to do the research on Shell Global Solutions, and to share that case in this book.

We are also indebted to the internationally acclaimed photographer Bruno Ehrs, who developed all photographs for the book in a unique style reflecting fresh perspectives of socio-ecological networks.

Our colleague Jerry Ravetz kept our thinking clear and our writing understandable, we are highly indebted to him. Laurent Chaminade of Imperial College Press was both firm and understanding in steering this manuscript towards completion — we thank him for his unfailing support.

Special thanks go to our families, who have endured our taking the time for the writing of the book — you are truly at the very heart of our VCSs.

Author Biography

Rafael Ramírez is a Senior Fellow in Strategy in both the Saïd Business School and in Green-Templeton College at the University of Oxford, where he is also Director of the Oxford Scenarios Programme. Rafael is also a Senior Partner at NormannPartners, which he co-founded with Richard Normann, Ulf Mannervik, and two other colleagues in 2003.

From 2000 to 2003, he was Visiting Professor of Scenario Planning and Corporate Strategy at Shell International in London, and he was Chairman of the World Economic Forum's Global Agenda Council on Strategic Foresight in 2008–2009. Rafael holds a Masters in Environmental Studies from York University in Toronto and a PhD from the Wharton School in Social Systems Science, having worked in the Management and Behavioural Sciences Centre while studying there. He moved to Paris in 1985 to work with Richard Normann, and in 1993 joined the Faculty of HEC in Paris, where he became full tenured Professor of Management. Rafael has worked on interactive strategy and scenario planning since the 1980s, and has acted as advisor to senior professionals and executives in organisations and firms in some 30 countries seeking to produce and design innovative strategies. In Oxford, he co-directed the Strategic Renewal Research Programme carried out by Oxford academics together with European Patent Office and Shell International colleagues, and he has co-hosted four iterations of the Oxford Futures Forum. Rafael is a prolific author and lecturer — this is his 8th book, which builds on and furthers prior work, notably the book *Designing Interactive Strategy* co-authored with Richard Normann, published in 1994.

Ulf Mannervik is a Senior Partner at the strategy consulting firm NormannPartners and an Associate Fellow at the Saïd Business School, University of Oxford. He originally worked as a painting artist for 10 years, and his interest in creative processes led him into business and design research. He met Richard Normann in the mid-1990s, and started to work with him on deploying design thinking in strategy. Since then, Ulf has worked extensively with international clients in strategy, innovation and technology development. He co-founded NormannPartners together with Richard Normann, Rafael Ramírez and two other colleagues in 2003, and has helped numerous executives to think creatively about the future and the business they are in, and to define what to do next. He has led many strategy and business innovation engagements, exploring new growth platforms for large global firms. He has also led Europe-wide initiatives on innovation policy formation. Ulf started to work with the University of Oxford in the mid-2000s as a researcher on strategic renewal in large firms. Today he is an Associate Fellow, teaching senior executives at Oxford's Saïd Business School. He also teaches on innovation and strategy at other universities. Given his expertise in innovation and strategy, the Swedish Government appointed Ulf three times to serve on the board of the Knowledge Foundation, one of Sweden's largest research financing bodies. He earned an MPhil in Design Theory from Chalmers University of Technology, and an MScBA from both the School of Business, Economics and Law at the University of Gothenburg and the Graduate School of Business at Stanford University.

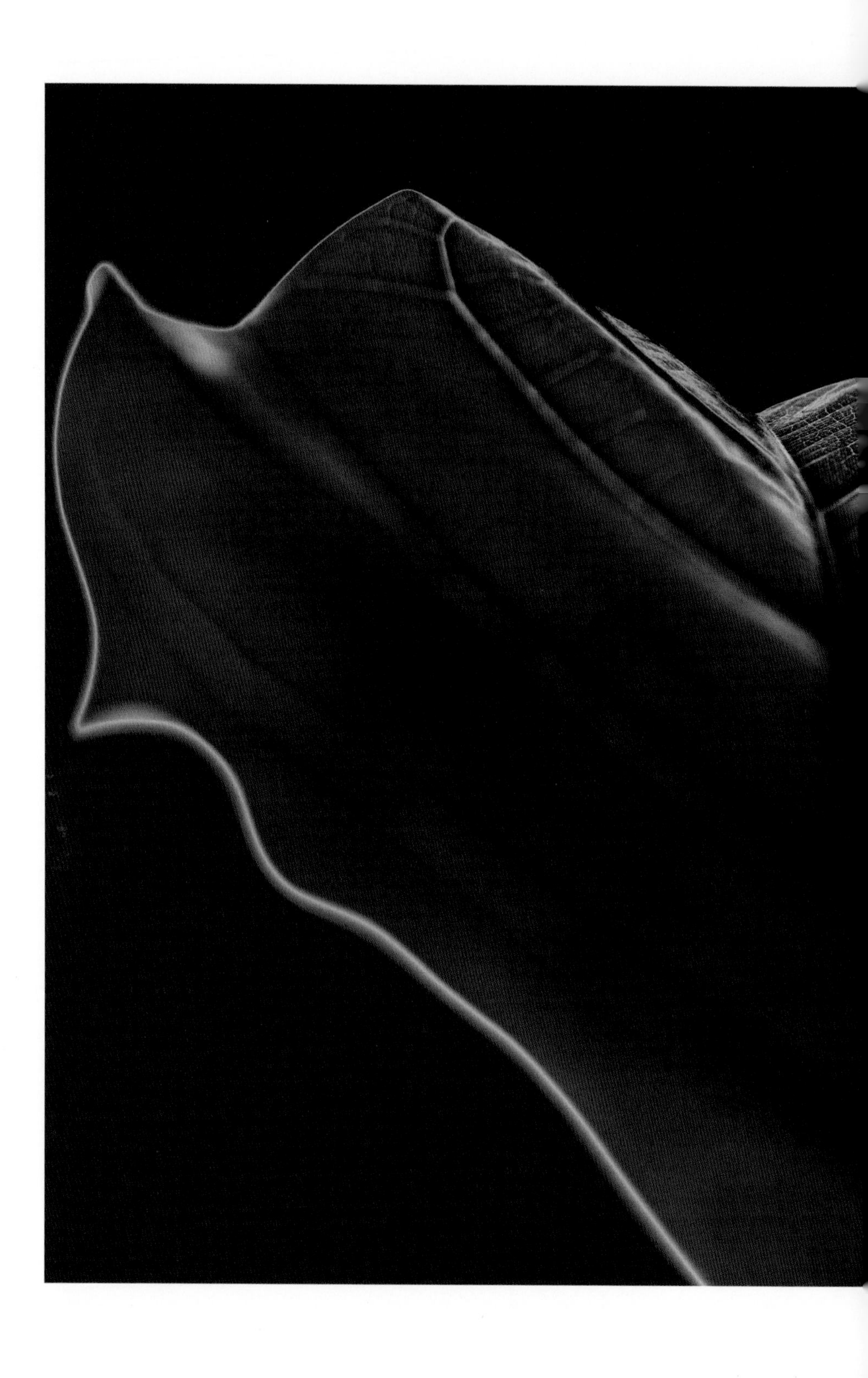

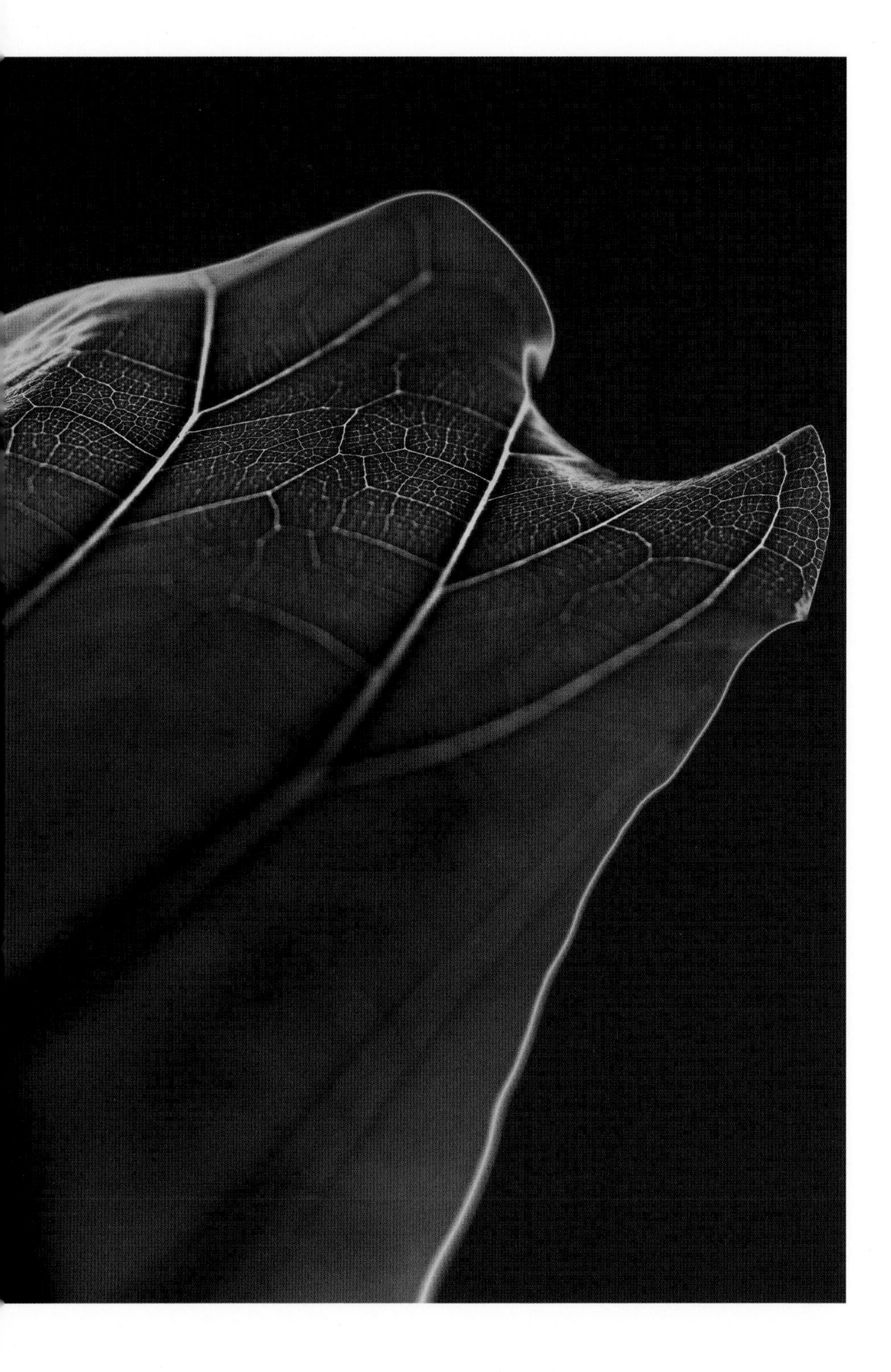

Chapter 1

Introduction to Value Creating Systems

Box 1.1: Chapter 1 at a Glance

This chapter explains how strategy today is about designing effective offerings. The offerings articulate systems of interactions where actors co-create different forms of value. We outline the book's argument — that this calls for a more contemporary strategy framework than that which conventional constructs such as "value chains" and thinking of firms as within given "industries" convey. In the strategy framework which this book is about, value creating systems (VCS), one attends to how value is created, not only by one party in the offering but by all parties in the offering. As opposed to the conventional view of value creation, where a supplier only produces and "offers" and a client only buys and "uses" in the view of value creation offered (*sic*!) by this book, the so-called "users" are taken to have more than one role, and centrally are also seen as value creators. They enter into an offering relationship only if they see the co-creation it entails as helping them to create value, for themselves, and with and for others.

We illustrate our argument with two cases. The first one contrasts Myspace and Facebook. The second case concerns the World Economic Forum (WEF).

This first chapter sets the scene for this book, which is about how designed co-created value, manifested in offerings, enables strategists to bring forth VCS fit for a networked world.

1. A Strategy Framework for a Networked World

This book is about strategy in a networked world.

In today's networked world, conceptualising value on the central basis of two-way exchanges as one did in the industrial era (with the idea of "value-added" products or services) has become very limiting, in fact too limiting, for capturing the full potential of value creation.

Socio-technical innovations that have helped the development of distributed processing, shared services, "platform organisations" (Gawer & Cusumano, 2002), concurrent engineering, and "social networks" (Castells, 2015) have all acted to render value creation more synchronous, less sequential (Warnecke *et al.*, 1997), and more interactive (Normann & Ramírez, 1993a, 1994) than ever before.

Such innovations help to pack in more options for interaction and thus more interactions, and more actors and more possibilities for further action to co-create many more values per unit of time and space than ever before (Davis, 1987).

These novel interaction possibilities in turn change what people value and can trust, as Uber in taxis and Airbnb in overnight accommodation, and Facebook in "friendships" reveal — where one now trusts staying in other people's homes, taking a ride in other people's cars, and leaving one's most loved pet or plant with a friend's friend whom one has not met.

These possibilities for interacting are now bundled in ever denser packages ("denser" meaning more functions per space and time unit, and thereby also per person or interactor). These possibilities help people and their organisations to co-create value in ways that were unimaginable a few decades ago. For example, the browser on one's personal device (personal computer, smartphone, tablet etc.) forms connections (and is formed by the nexus of many links) that are activated in real time as one browses, with "cookies" keeping track of one's interactions and influencing the information that is presented from many different actors. As one interacts, one's trail modifies these preferences in real time, and will further influence one's future interactions, not only with providers of goods and services, but equally with other interactors.

As business becomes more system-like, with "business ecosystems (BE)" such as Android becoming the norm and not the exception, value and its production requires more system-like, networked, and emergent conceptual frameworks. Value co-created by two or (typically now) more actors, with and for each other, with and for yet other actors, is an invitation not only to rethink organisational structures and managerial arrangements for value creation, but also to rethink value creation itself. This includes rethinking what is now meant by "value" and how it is becoming reconnected to what one means by "values" and it also involves moving these concepts from "nouns" to "verbs" (John Seely Brown, personal communication). It involves thinking of value and values as contingent, always located in a setting — no longer as isolated in things or individual bodies or groups of bodies.[1] Value and values here become dependent on those with whom one connects, and in connecting, who co-create value. Value and values also matter in terms of whom this co-creation affects positively as well as negatively.

Patterns of interactivity arise or can be designed. These patterns connect those we term "actors" as co-creators, and their designed interactions support or may even constitute their roles and identities. In turn, these actors' roles and identities interact with each other, and in doing so form interconnected patterns; so these roles and identities in turn thus maintain the interactions. This may appear very abstract here, but below — in this chapter — we illustrate how this is what makes Facebook and Davos work so well.

We consider this configuring of interactions to be the result of a design activity. We use the term VCS for the pattern of interactions intentionally configured by the strategic planning carried out by an organisation.

The designed interactions become manifested as ("designed") offerings: configuring offerings that set the overall design of and integrates a VCS, and supporting offerings between any two actors in such systems.

As Normann and Ramírez (1993a) put it: if the key to creating value is to design and co-create offerings that mobilise others (who may have the role in the interaction of customer or supplier or partner or employee or investor, etc.) to co-create value, then the key source of success is to conceive the VCS and make it work. We suggest that this designing of offerings is a key task for strategists and managers engaging in strategy work today.

---

[1]That is, among many people in, and as, cultures.

In this book, we use many examples of VCS, and help the reader assess how these can be understood, explored, redesigned or designed, and realised. We start out by analysing how Facebook overtook Myspace. Then we survey how the successful VCS of WEF has been designed and evolved.

2. How the VCS of Facebook Outperformed Myspace

The year 2004 saw the launch of two similar websites that would come to dominate the social networking landscape of the early 21st century.

In January, ex-employees of an internet marketing company, eUniverse, opened Myspace to the public. A month later, undergraduates from Harvard University launched the facebook.com, a campus exclusive social networking system. By the end of that year, Myspace had 5 million members, and Facebook had opened up its access to all Ivy League students.

By 2005, media mogul Rupert Murdoch's News Corporation bought Myspace (which had attained 35 million users) for $580 million in July. The website, it had seemed, was unstoppable and had even beaten Google and Yahoo in its number of unique visitors in the USA. Facebook (with its recent name change)[2] at that time trailed far behind, despite having opened itself up to also include high school students.

Between 2005 and 2009, Facebook reinvented its offering at least five times, whereas under new ownership Myspace's actions were far less dynamic. As Murdoch later accepted, his company "screwed up in every way possible".[3] By 2010, internet blogs and analysts widely claimed Myspace had been surpassed by Facebook. It is our contention that

[2]While Myspace was bought by a large corporation, Facebook was backed by venture capital — Peter Thiel, the founder of PayPal, saw potential in the company and bought a stake, earning him a place on the board. The difference of such ownership has been the subject of recent research. See Emily Pahnke C., Katila, R. & Kathleen M. Eisenhardt (2015). Who Takes You to the Dance? How partners' institutional logics influence innovation in young firms. *Administrative Science Quarterly*, 60, 596–633, first published on 17 June 2015.

[3]https://twitter.com/#!/rupertmurdoch/status/157719858904174592 (Accessed October 2015).

Facebook overtook Myspace because they were far better at designing VCSs. The writings in this book explain the differences involved.

Originally, Facebook and Myspace had similar offerings. Myspace's founders understood the problematic rigidity of the preceding "friendster" offerings and opted for a more "fun" and flexible layout, appealing to young people. Originally Facebook's owners opted for exclusivity, restricting access to Harvard students. Both websites basically offered integrated blogging platforms where users could post photos and other content, send each other messages; and, crucially, "add each other" into the system, therefore developing networks of friends. This is graphically depicted in Figure 1.1. More people brought more interest, which brought more people in.

Following its corporate takeover, Myspace found itself under pressure to become profitable. Still capitalising on its original buzz and having become the most popular website in the US, its 2005–2006 configuring offerings (see Chapter 5) were principally advertising deals. Notably, it secured a $900 million contract with Google. While Myspace started posting advertising generated content onto its user's profiles, Facebook started posting user-generated content onto user's profiles. At this point, Facebook not only gave users a place to post photos, statuses, etc.; it also

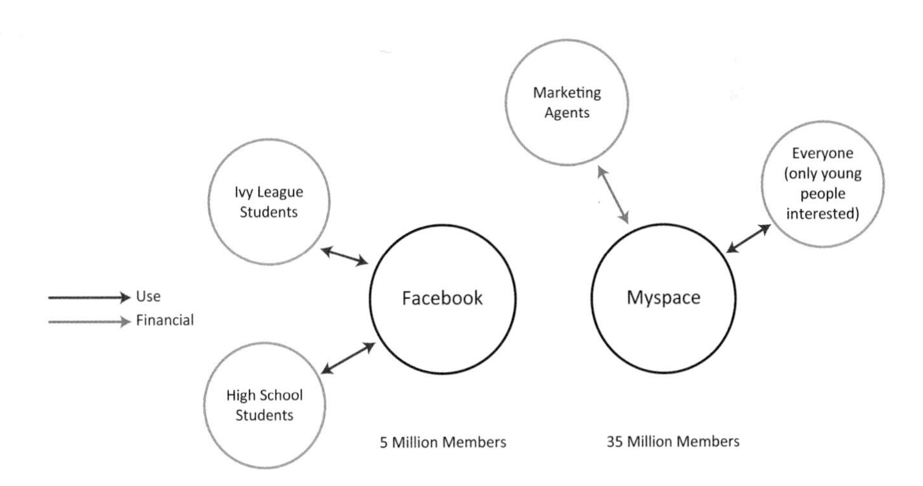

Figure 1.1: VCS of Facebook Versus VCS of Myspace 2004–2005

created a synthesis of users' friends' content and made this the centrepiece of the Facebook experience. This was called the "Newsfeed", a ground breaking innovation in social networking.

Facebook developed its configuring offering by building on its competence of providing an online platform where its members could express themselves by posting content, enabling them to connect with and build various communities of friends, family, and colleagues. Instead, Myspace started an altogether new offering, enrolling (see Chapter 6 and Appendix B) different interactors. So while Facebook remained focused on the experiences of its users in relation to each other and how to improve these, and on enhancing their ability to build their communities, Myspace was focused on how to make the relationships profitable — even at the expense of user experience quality. This is graphically depicted in Figure 1.2.

In the digital economy, within business ecosystems such as the ones in which the designs of the Myspace VCS and the Facebook VCS arose, the more effective priority for strategic attention is on inventing and reinventing and evolving the configuring offering. This attention on the

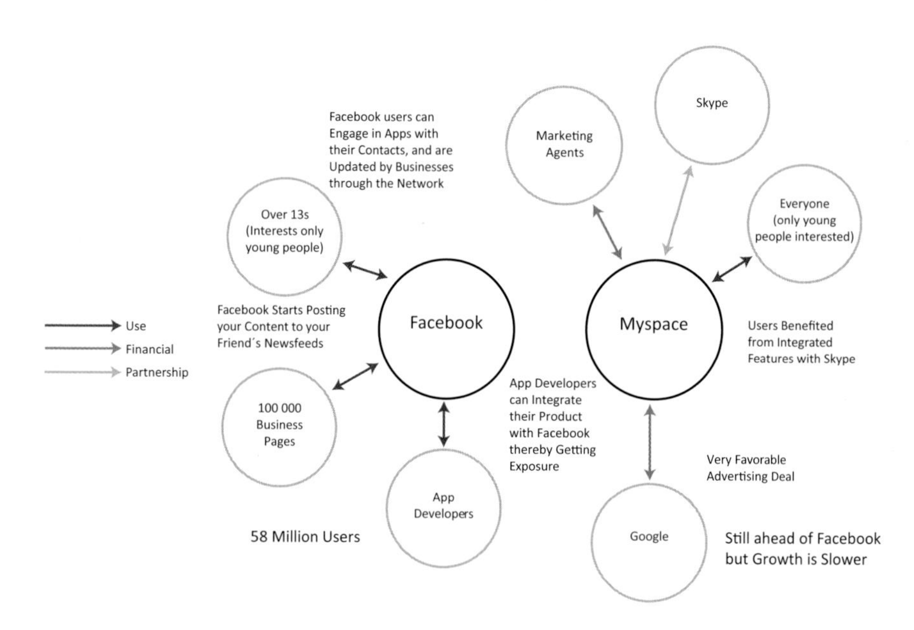

Figure 1.2: VCS of Facebook Versus VCS of Myspace 2006–2007

configuring offering design is an attention for, and with, those whose interactions matter most. Facebook showed that those it collaborated with most were the users to whom it helped to connect better with other users; Myspace's corporate owners forced Myspace users to collaborate with the owners, and thus with advertisers, at the expense of helping them jointly build better quality value and values with other users.

Our research suggests that the reconfigurations in Myspace's VCS were driven by profitability; Facebook's reconfigurations were driven by improved co-creation with users — moving numbers up to 58 million in one year. Facebook developed an integrated platform that allowed its users to partake in value co-creation applications such as games and the now famous Instagram photo uploading and sharing platform. Facebook also went on to enable organisations to get an online presence by developing and offering bespoke features. For example, "facebook pages" became user-controlled pages that allow individuals to publicise their organisations online. Profit later followed from this — and not the other way around, as Myspace's new owners had assumed.

Myspace did upgrade its offering by teaming up with Skype, then another up-and-coming media company started in Sweden, that offered internet-based (free if one had a broadband connection) telephony, allowing users to converse with each other (video was available, but initially at an extra price). While one can think of such efforts as a commitment to improve the offering, it does not appear to have been derived with users and with real insight into its users' value creation logics or systems. Users were apparently seen first and foremost as social networkers, and for them face-to-face video conversations were a world apart from what they wanted to do to communicate via Myspace. We contrast this with Facebook's continued striving to increased "networking" and community development, and individualised experiences based on one's own specific set of interactors, which it called "friends". But when Facebook expanded to include businesses in one's social network, it was not only friends that popped up on "one's newsfeed", it was also companies.

Facebook showed that it understood that value was not created by one party in the offering, but by all parties in the offering. As opposed to a traditional view of value creation, where a supplier "offers" and a client "uses", the so-called "users" were also seen as value creators, who enter into an offering relationship only if they see this as helping them to create value, for themselves and also with and for others. Facebook understood this way better than Myspace did. As we finish this book in November 2015, Facebook lists 1.55 billion users worldwide.[4]

While Facebook focused on creating a platform that allowed outside developers to build new applications that enhanced user co-creation, Myspace built almost everything in-house.[5] Facebook thus became a far more adept collaborator, and helped many more outsiders to co-create value and values than Myspace. Focusing on "product improvement" rather than enabling users and other actors to become more effective co-creators of value (as Facebook did) was a terrible mistake. As Shawn Gold, Myspace's former head of marketing and content, said

> "Myspace went too wide and not deep enough in its product development. We went with a lot of products that were shallow and not the best products in the world…. The products division had introduced many features (communication tools such as instant messaging, a classifieds program, a video player, a music player, a virtual karaoke machine, a self-serve advertising platform, profile-editing tools, security systems, privacy filters, and Myspace book lists, among others). However, the features were often buggy and slow as there was insufficient testing, measuring, and iterating."[6]

By the end of 2008, Facebook's users benefited from integrated instant messaging with one another. MSN messenger, which had become a huge player in the online communications ecology, was about to lose its expansive network of users to Facebook's superior VCS. In effect, what had been MSN messenger's focus became enrolled by Facebook's superior offering redesign capabilities as a mere feature in the wider offering of social media.

Meanwhile, Myspace attempted to increase profits by selling rights to divulge its users' contents, thus accelerating the exodus of users. Myspace

---

[4]Comment made by Simon Milnere, VP of Policy for Europe, Africa, Middle East and Turkey of Facebook, Reuters Institute of Journalism, Oxford, 23 November 2015.

[5]https://en.wikipedia.org/wiki/Myspace#2008.E2.80.9311:_Decline_and_sale_by_News_Corp (Accessed October 2015).

[6]Felix Gillette (22 June 2011). *The Rise and Inglorious Fall of Myspace.* Bloomberg Businessweek. *Retrieved 23 June 2011* — cited in above Wikipedia entry.

also teamed up with major record labels in a bid to offer its dwindling number of users more access to music, attempting to reinvent itself as an entertainment platform. But again, this was somewhat inconsistent with the value creation of users — listening to music and social networking were seen by them as separate areas of their activity even if bloggers do blog while listening to music. So while Facebook improved the quality of social networking by facilitating instant communications, Myspace tried to incorporate other features from the growing online business ecology into it. By 2008, this type of poor strategic offering design and redesign decisions for Myspace meant Facebook surpassed it in terms of numbers of users.

To further the growing gap with Myspace, in 2009, Facebook added another feature in its offering — the ability to "like" — which allowed users to almost instantly give positive, standardised feedback about the contents they received. This feature allowed those offering anything to these users to modify content and to tailor it to any one user's unique "liking" profile, enabling bespoke targeted advertising to be delivered at an unheard of scale. That same year, 2009, saw Myspace lose many key executives and lay off over one-third of its workforce.

It was only then, once it understood its users' value co-creating priorities well, with user numbers skyrocketing, that Facebook started thinking about profitability. The "like" feature allowed Facebook to engage the world wide web as an integrated Facebook feature. More and more web pages invited users to "like" their content directly, making the opinion of the millions of Facebook users an attractive proposition for would-be advertisers to join Facebook. As a result, the demographics of Facebook users expanded to include many well beyond the youth to which Myspace had confined itself. The result of the 2008–2010 period of development of each VCS is graphically depicted in Figure 1.3.

With Myspace's tumbling user numbers and its Google advertising deal expired, Myspace found it more difficult to generate profits. By 2010, its postings could be posted in Facebook; in 2011, it was sold, reportedly for $35 million.[7] Facebook had a far more effective understanding of their users' networking and of its role in helping them build communities.

---

[7]Laurie Segall (29 June 2011). *News Corp. sells Myspace to Specific Media.* CNN. *Retrieved 29 June 2011.*

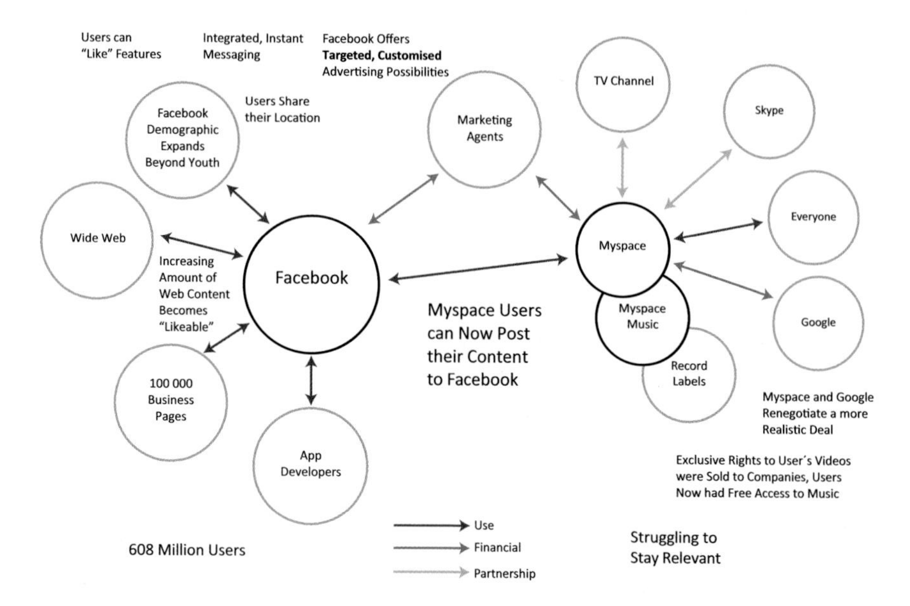

Figure 1.3: VCS of Facebook Versus VCS of Myspace 2008–2010

Facebook succeeded in enrolling users and other actors in co-creating the offering, which enabled value creation. That Facebook eventually could enrol Myspace's users' contents for its own users is the ultimate accolade of its superior VCS and offering design capabilities.

Firms such as Facebook in social media, Airbnb in accommodation and Uber in transportation are current exemplars, as we write this book in 2015, of designing VCSs by focusing on the offerings that help those involved to co-create value and values. It is such designs of offerings to co-create value and enrol different parties into a VCS that this book explores. The second example of an effective and innovative VCS we offer in this introduction is the WEF.

3. How WEF's VCS Engages Leaders in Co-Creating Strategic Agendas

Today, the WEF organisation attracts thousands of participants each year to its flagship event in Davos, Switzerland, as well as quarterly regional meetings and the "summer Davos" event held in China. WEF is widely acknowledged to have become a world leader in setting up and hosting cross-sectoral, international, forward-looking dialogues.

The WEF grew by inventing and reinventing what it offers, which is to help members and stakeholders to offer co-creation to each other and to others; expanding and revising its network of stakeholders and the interactions among them.

The WEF staged its initial "congress" as the European Management Symposium in 1971. It was attended by 450 participants from 41 countries, joined by 50 faculty staff and media representatives[8] in Davos "to discuss a coherent strategy for European business".[9] To make this event possible, its founder and designer, Dr. Klaus Schwab, secured support from the Swiss government and the European Commission. This first design of what became the WEF is graphically illustrated in Figure 1.4. In the design of the symposium, those attending met with each other, and

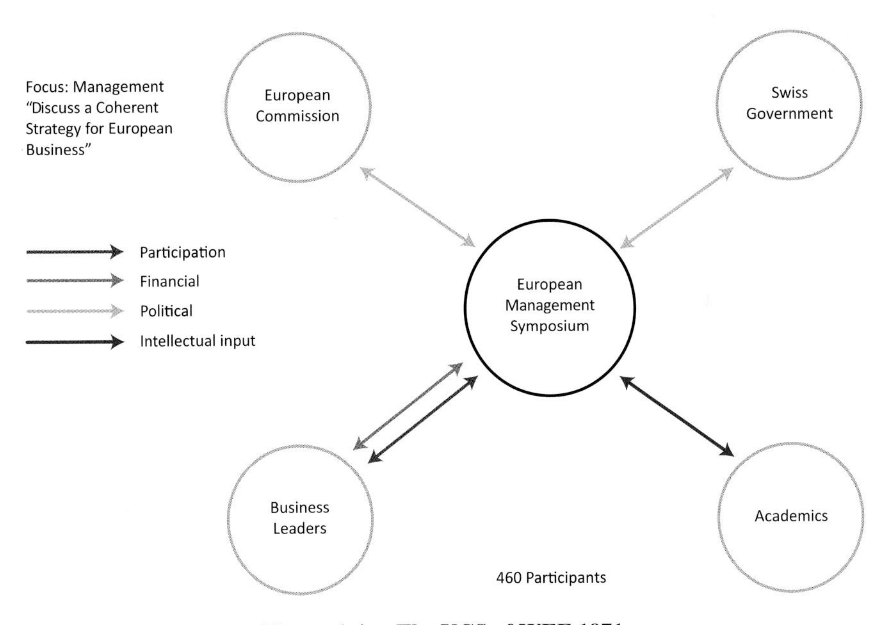

Figure 1.4: The VCS of WEF 1971

[8] WEF, *The First 40 Years*, 2010.

[9] www.wef.com (Accessed June 2014).

in so doing, European business leaders created value for the European Commission through fostering European cooperation. The Swiss government benefited from hosting an event on its soil that fostered international cooperation. With Schwab's design, the European business leaders managed to meet in a novel informal setting with actors in their networks and slightly beyond; allowing unminuted, semiprivate dialogue on key issues such as strategic challenges of the future. The European executives were also enabled by the WEF to meet with members of the American management intellectual elite, thus better equipping themselves to compete in areas were non-European companies acted (Pigman, 2007: 1). The event also raised funds that became a part of the endowment for a new foundation: the European Management Forum (EMF).

In 1973, the EMF expanded the content of the dialogues from managerial issues to also include broader socio-economic issues, with the oil crisis as a catalyst; thus beginning the invitation of political leaders to directly take part in the dialogues it hosted (Pigman, 2007: 11).

As is shown in Figure 1.5, the shift to include public figures entailed a broadened offering with new interactions and more roles for participants, for instance, with the introduction of round tables. The European

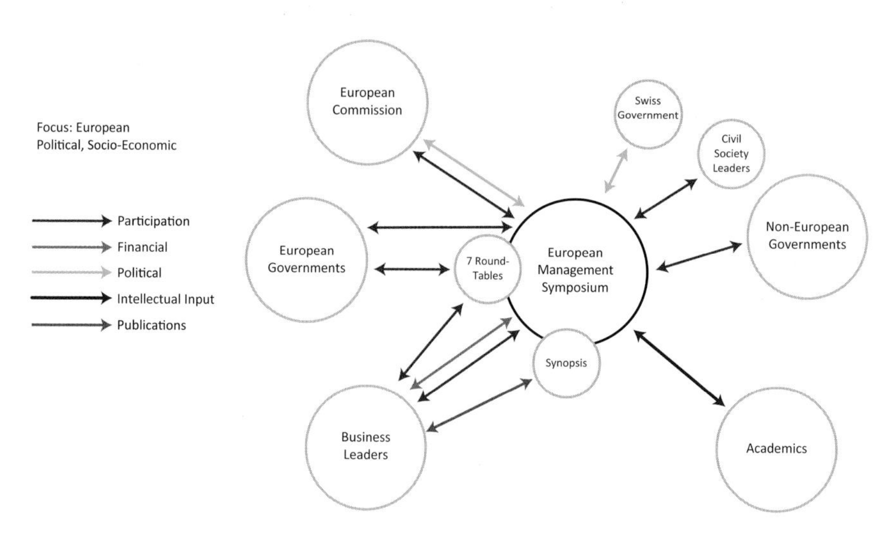

Figure 1.5: The VCS of WEF 1975

Commission expanded its involvement from patronage to become an active participant, and the EMF added to its role the publication of information for its participants through the publication of synopsis.

By 1975, seven round tables such as the one held between European governments, the Commission, and leaders of business had been set up. Governments also began taking part in the dialogues beyond these round tables and became involved in the forum itself. This included the government of Mexico, a first step to acquiring a global, or at least extra-European dimension.

In the language of this book, the WEF is a good example of a well-designed VCS that grew by creating an offering, which it redesigned and developed to enrol new interactors — giving them co-creation roles that they and others valued — in the evolving WEF VCS.

In 1976, the Forum entered into a partnership with United Nations Industrial Development Organisation (UNIDO) to create the Cooperative Exchange Program, providing an official channel for developing country delegations to pitch investment opportunities to Forum participants. It also organised the first Arab–European Business Cooperation Symposium — a separate event that furthered its internationalisation. In 1976, it also became a membership organisation. This is seen graphically in Figure 1.6.

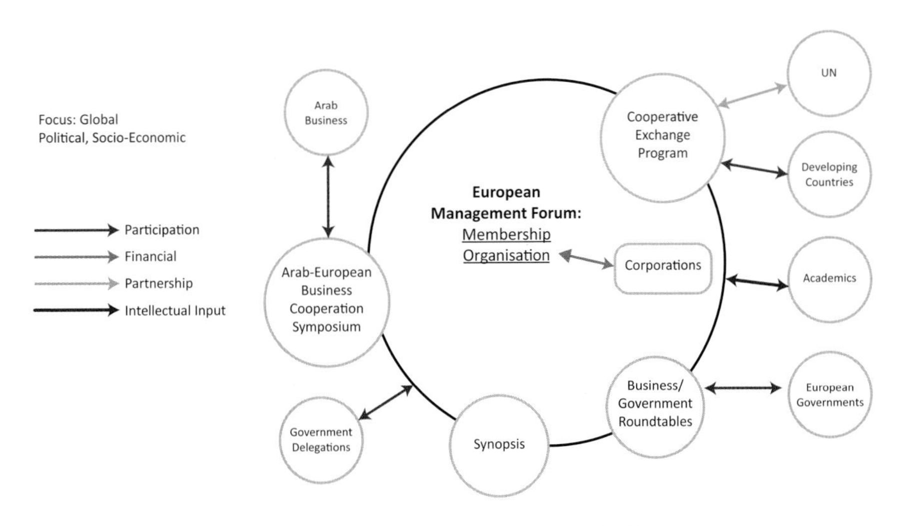

Figure 1.6: The VCS of WEF 1976

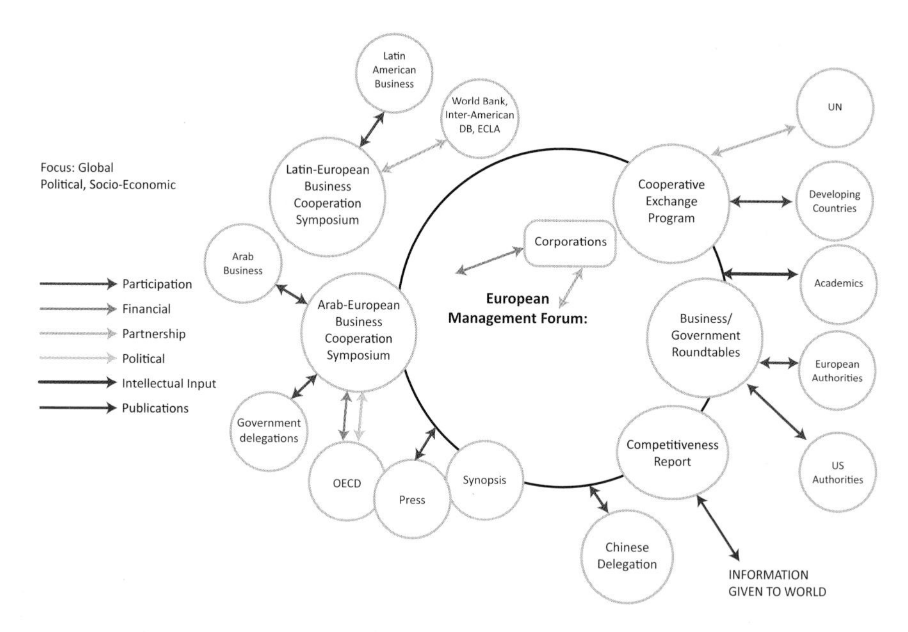

Figure 1.7: The VCS of WEF 1979

The Forum went on to replicate the Arab–European summit success by creating the Latin–European Business Cooperation Symposium, also enlisting the support of the World Bank. It also attracted the United States government to a round table and invited the press to participate in the symposium.

As seen in Figure 1.7, in 1979, WEF started publishing its competitiveness report (which over the years became increasingly influential), shifting its role from facilitating knowledge co-creation through dialogue to also include the generation of assessments.

By 1982, the Forum created the Informal Gathering of World Economic Leaders (IGWEL), allowing leaders to more fully meet "off the record" in an informal, but very well organised and structured setting that allowed them to get to know each other. This secured participation as a "must attend" event for corporate elites — for example, a CEO in just three days could meet 40 key contacts, saving hundreds or even thousands of hours of travel time each year.

To deal with growth, between 1982 and 1987, the Forum started hosting "industry specific" summits. It was when India and China joined that it changed its name to WEF. By 1991, with many landmark diplomatic achievements on its hands such as the first ministerial-level discussions between North and South Korea, the Forum expanded its offerings to also include cultural values and so launched the World Art Forum as an umbrella organism. The 1990s were a time of growing globalisation but also entailed a backlash against the world view that the Davos meeting had come to embody.

In 1997, the Forum changed its configuring offering from the socio-economic and political focus it had before to a broader one that enrolled more values, manifested in the phrase "committed to improving the state of the world" which it attached to its WEF brand.

This broadened offering paved the way for enrolling of a new set of co-creators, such as the Forum's humanitarian platform and the creation of a Schwab Social Entrepreneurship Foundation. Young "global leaders" and "global shaper" communities as well as educational programmes for these with key universities were added as well.

Partnerships with consultancies that competed with each other to second high potential employees to the WEF enabled world-class professionals to work on Forum initiatives and studies, such as foresight and scenario planning assessments on countries such as Mongolia or Russia and industries such as financial services or mining and metals.

By inventing and prototyping, and refining and broadening its core offering and developing and enhancing novel support offerings, time and time again over its history, WEF brought in new members to co-create new forms of value and new values in new ways. The new offerings enrolled members and co-creators into new partnership roles, mixing both informal meetings with confidential meetings (e.g. among leaders in their exclusive hotel suites in Davos) with educational events and good food and skiing in a well-protected and beautiful setting.

WEF's development thus illustrates how a design to bring different actors together to co-create value in a system of interactions — with different motives and values enabled and co-created — can succeed.

Designing ways that help users to come together to create value, as WEF and Facebook have done, by designing and redesigning offerings to that effect (not by adding features to a "product", as Myspace did) is what this book analyses. It is in this way that this book offers strategists a framework and a methodology to produce more effective strategy for today's networked world.

4. How this Book is Organised

This section outlines the remaining chapters and appendices in the book.

Chapter 2*: *Why a socio-ecological approach to strategy

Chapter 2 explores how and why business environments and opportunity spaces are becoming more interrelated, and how the relations occur in ever shorter time frames. It proposes that the construct of "industry" as a focal area for strategy is today giving away to inter-industrial blurring, where systems thinking becomes a more helpful framing to understand what is going on. In such situations, many strategists feel that their business environments are becoming increasingly complex. To more productively engage complexity and to better access resources, collaborative business models are becoming more important for success.

This chapter assesses not only why but also how a more system-based view and framing for strategy today is becoming more effective for strategists' work. The transition from chains to systems, in turn, calls for a shift from a strategic frame centred upon conventional "neoclassical" economics, focusing on predictable uncertainties and "neat" solutions. Strategists realise that these do not work when the very definition of a "problem" is elusive and the situations are "wicked" in the sense that the over-simplified so-called "solutions" may worsen the situation.

In such circumstances, strategists would be well advised to let go of dangerously limiting models of stable sectors or industries; shifting their stance to a "socio-ecological" view of strategic planning. The focus with such a strategy frame is on engaging complex systems and unpredictable uncertainties, by reframing and redesigning value and value creation.

The socio-ecological stance for strategists also allows them to work with a frame that seeks to reconcile multiple values that cannot be given a single metric, so strategy moves well beyond securing just financially calculable value. The socio-ecological systems frame also invites dropping increasingly outdated, increasingly inapplicable, and increasingly irrelevant conceptual constructs such as the "value chain", the "industrial sector" or "industry", or the "end" or "final" customer — all derived from neoclassical economics.

Chapter 3: Reframing the idea of value

Chapter 3 surveys a better alternative to the familiar, inherited, idea of value. In this chapter, we review the history of how value has come to be thought of, as well as of an alternative conceptualisation of value as interaction, as co-created, and as plural: comprising many types of values.

We critically review notions of value inherited from the logics and metaphors of industrial manufacturing. We contrast those with the view of value as co-created that is used in this book.

In reviewing the history and the implications of viewing value as co-created, we consider how value is designed by strategists in an era of complex networks of interaction.

We find strategists situated in contexts exhibiting highly distributed access to information with substantial powers to analyse it and deploy it, becoming capable of interacting more effectively.

Chapter 4: Effective VCS designs

In Chapter 4, it is explained how the VCS view offers a useful way to understand how value is co-created in business and societies today. As we saw in Chapter 3, the VCS strategic framework considers value and values from an outcomes in use (and also, expected outcomes) perspective, a perspective that is always from the point of view of an actor who is acting to create value — for the self, and for and with others — and who is using what other actors do to help create value. This chapter on effective designs for VCSs presents the VCS strategy framework as a conceptual construct, and explores what constitutes effective designs of such systems. Also, the chapter describes the methodological approach to strategy that has emerged based on use of the VCS framework, and which makes VCS a distinctive strategy approach. Lastly, the chapter suggests when the VCS framework and approach to strategy are timely and effective to use, and under which conditions other strategy approaches might be more suitable.

Chapter 5: How offerings link co-creators in VCSs

The offering is the core unit of analysis in this book, and this is the focus of Chapter 5. The offering is a rich construct, both conceptually and in terms of practice, and it is also paradoxical.

The offering manifests the relationship of co-creation between actors, and in joining them, distinguishes them from each other in terms of roles and — typically — also in terms of values. In the VCS approach to strategy, strategists design, create or change offerings that act as the organising "links" that manifest how interacting actors co-create value.

With an offering, an actor is linked to another, and they act together in concert to mobilise resources in ways that enable the creation of both value and values. In VCSs, there are two kind of offerings; configuring offerings that organise the VCS, and support offerings between two actors within the system.

Offerings can be static or more dynamic and open to change by their co-creators. In a networked world, this poses challenges (and also new offering design tasks) for strategists.

We describe five elements required to be designed into an offering: people, process, technology, information, and a risk sharing formula. This chapter is centrally concerned with defining, describing, and analysing how offerings work and the choices involved in designing them.

Chapter 6: Analysing the designs of existing VCSs

Chapter 6 articulates our thinking on how to use Actor-Network Theory (ANT) — actually, more a methodology than a theory — to "reverse engineer" an existing VCS to determine its design, so as to become capable to redesign it and transform it. ANT is described in detail in Appendix B: its history, development, and use as a methodological approach to understand the original designs of VCSs and their development.

In Chapter 6, we show how the use of the ANT methodology helped the French energy utility EDF to distil common elements in many different situations it had experimented in, to be able to develop a coherent strategy for electrifying the billion inhabitants of the planet not connected to the electricity grid in the late part of the 20th and early part of the 21st centuries. The complex web of interrelations that were brought together to design and create different alternative electric VCS by EDF professionals in many parts of the globe were analysed with ANT. These designs were compared using the same VCS configuring and support offering design patterns we discuss in this book; and conclusions were drawn from this experience.

Chapter 7: *Assessing the future contexts a VCS design might inhabit*

In Chapter 7, we assess two of the key roles scenario planning can hold when assessing the viability of existing VCS designs and as a support in a stage of designing of new VCSs. We very succinctly review the thinking and practice of scenario planning, and we relate it to the business idea and to the design of offerings.

Scenario planning redirects attention to contexts — which is particularly useful when these might become uncertain. We articulate our reasoning as to why, in the uncertain contexts where scenario planning is of help, collaborative strategy becomes at least as important as competitive strategy.

We review two applications of scenario planning. The first is to design collaborative new inter-organisational forms with the express purpose of decreasing the turbulence (particularly, the aspects pertaining to unforecastable uncertainty and complexity) that would buffet the organisations if they did not come together. The second application is the use of scenario planning to support the design of technology and competence roadmaps and the new VCSs that these investments allow.

Chapter 8: *Designing a new VCS*

This chapter outlines methodological guidelines for designing new VCSs in ways that — as relevant — can benefit from both ANT and scenario planning.

Sometimes, as a result of a comprehensive and more extensive design process, a VCS design is entirely new (such as the one that put a human being on the moon, and returned him home safely), but often a new VCS is set up to capture newly understood opportunities, or to address threats or shortcomings that an existing VCS cannot engage, but which can include aspects of an existing VCS design.

The argument in this chapter follows and develops the business design approach described by Normann in his 2001 book *Reframing Business*. After overviewing this background, five main components are described. The first is a historical overview of the shaping factors of the VCS context and distinct competences of the organisation that aims at designing the new VCS. This is followed by analysis of existing VCSs, including all co-creators, whether they are denominated "customers" or hold other roles, and assessing what potential invaders (typically from other fields or "industries") might enter that space. The next stage involves exploring opportunities as well as challenges for the VCS design to define the strategic intents and the first version of the configuring and enrolling offerings manifesting these.

The chapter uses several references to the global companies SCA and Scania, which are leaders in their fields, and users of VCS approaches to continue pioneering these fields. Chapter 9 describes the fifth stage — building strategic pathways and preparing for governance.

Chapter 9*: *Guidelines for realising new VCS innovations

This chapter recounts the main challenges that have been experienced by people we have worked with in attempting to think about, analyse, design, prototype, pilot, and realise new VCSs — or changes to existing ones. It also offers guidance on how strategists can effectively handle these challenges.

We discuss seven different challenges to realise a new VCS:

1. Letting the design vision guide, but not define the design.
2. Redirecting management attention into VCS thinking.
3. Creating organisational ownership of VCS changes.
4. Step-by-step realisation of a new VCS.
5. Understanding value creation as multiple and contingent.
6. Learning as a stepping-stones process.
7. Avoiding value chain push backs.

Chapter 10*: *The growth of VCS thinking

In Chapter 10, we review how VCS thinking is steadily growing and replacing the obsolete value chain thinking. Although the early optimism of Normann and Ramírez (1994) has taken some time to be realised, some of the obstacles are now being overcome. We can understand the delays by analysing why the older system could persist. First, the value chain idea is still useful in many situations. Also, the new forms of business practice have come to widespread importance only quite recently. Even now, most managers have been trained on the old tools and do not easily abandon them. But now is the time to change thinking, from structure to process, and from chains to systems.

Appendix A: Origins of VCSs

This appendix is concerned with the fact that many of the ideas we present and relate to each other in this book have long pedigrees, often stretching over several hundred years. We believe it is of help to readers who want to use these ideas to know where they came from, and what "baggage" in the forms of connotations and relations they carry with them.

So this appendix overviews the historical development both of VCSs thought and of offerings. In doing so, the appendix proposes to situate the book as another step in an unfolding story — a story that is still being written alongside several other intellectual initiatives such as those described and analysed in this book. Thus, another purpose of this appendix is to acknowledge the building blocks from which our thinking is derived, and to help practitioners who want to use our proposed approach to develop business to be capable of relating them to other practices, traditions, and approaches.

Appendix B: ANT

This appendix gives a more extensive description of Actor-Network Theory (ANT), which we use to explore the emergence of an existing VCS design, as described in Chapter 6.

ANT started out in France as the so-called "sociology of translation" (Callon 2001; Latour, 2005; Law, 2009). Its proponents sought to understand how the manager in one company (or "actor" as sociologists would call it) attempts — and often succeeds — to "translate" the role of any one other "actor" with whom it interacts to develop what these sociologists refer to as an "actor-network" — composed in effect of many such enrolments with several actors. Their "actor-network" in strategy terms is a VCS.

Chapter 2

Why a Socio-Ecological Approach to Strategy

Box 2.1: Chapter 2 at a Glance

Business environments and opportunity spaces are becoming more interrelated, and the relations occur in ever shorter time frames. The construct of "industry" as a focal area for strategy is giving way to inter-industrial blurring, where systems thinking becomes a more helpful framing to understand what is going on. In such situations, many strategists feel that their business environments are becoming increasingly complex. To more productively engage complexity and to better access resources, collaborative business models are becoming more important for success.

This chapter assesses not only why but also how a more systems-based view and framing for strategy today is becoming more effective for strategists' work. The transition from chains to systems, in turn, calls for a shift from a strategic frame centred upon conventional "neoclassical" economics, focusing on predictable uncertainties and "neat" solutions. Strategists realise that these do not work when the very definition of a "problem" is elusive and the situations are "wicked" in the sense that the oversimplified so-called "solutions" may worsen the situation.

In such circumstances, strategists would be well advised to let go of dangerously limiting models of stable sectors or industries, shifting

(*Continued*)

Box 2.1: Chapter 2 at a Glance (*Continued*)

their stance to a "socio-ecological" view of strategic planning. The focus with such a strategy frame is on engaging complex systems and unpredictable uncertainties, by reframing and redesigning value and value creation.

The socio-ecological stance for strategists also allows them to work with a frame that seeks to reconcile multiple values that cannot be given a single metric, so strategy moves well beyond securing just financially calculable value. The socio-ecological systems frame also invites dropping increasingly outdated, increasingly inapplicable, and increasingly irrelevant conceptual constructs such as the "value chain", the "industrial sector" or "industry", or the "end" or "final" customer — all derived from neoclassical economics.

1. A Networked World Calls for Systems Thinking in Strategy

Already back in 1993, Normann and Ramírez argued that the "value chain" and the thinking behind it was becoming outmoded, primarily as it was built on an increasingly obsolete notion of the meaning of value. It was designed and suitable for analysis and strategy in stable environments with little complexity and change — and not for the then emerging and now contemporary uncertain, complex, networked and faster changing business realities, in which sets of distinct competences and collaborative relations are decisive for success.

> *Our traditional thinking about value is grounded in the assumptions and the models of an industrial economy. According to this view, every company occupies a position on a value chain. Upstream, suppliers provide inputs. The company then adds value to these inputs, before passing them downstream to the next actor in the chain, the customer (whether another business or the final consumer). Seen from this perspective, strategy is primarily the art of positioning a company in the right place on the value chain — the right business, the right products and market segments, the right value-adding activities.*
>
> *Today, however, this understanding of value is as outmoded as the old assembly line it resembles and so is the view of strategy that goes with it.*

> *Global competition, changing markets, and new technologies are opening up qualitatively new ways of creating value. The options available to companies, customers, and suppliers are proliferating in ways Henry Ford never dreamed of (Normann and Ramírez, 1993: 65).*

Systems thinking and collaborative value creating systems (VCSs) ("value constellations", as they called them then) have come to have more importance in the business realities of today, and increasingly so since Normann and Ramírez published their first article suggesting this. It is spurred by the emergence and spread of social media, of data intensity, of communication networks, of connectivity, of IT platforms and services — but also of more and more containerised and air freight traffic for goods, e.g. allowing tropical fruits to be displayed year-round in Montreal and Helsinki supermarkets at affordable prices for the many.

The current reality is one of collaboration among different individuals and organisations and of cost-effective, often digitalised connections of ideas and processes and things, arranged in relation to each other in more complex systems rather than in linear chains. This increasingly networked ubiquity has given rise to recognition of the apparently inexorable rise of systems, such as so-called "business ecosystems (BE)", in which strategists can design and realise systems of value creation.

Another extensive phenomenon of our times that calls for systems thinking and its approaches to strategy is the increase in the numbers and influence of what Ahrne and Brunsson (2008) called "meta-organisations". These are entities whose members are entirely or mostly organisations (such as industrial or professional associations) that are incomplete compared to organisations[1] and require different forms of governance, as an important part of their job is to get their member organisations to collaborate and do the large parts of the work that organisations typically would be expected to be done by individual members; and to do this work among them in a reasonably coordinated manner. Because this coordination can never be perfect, Ahrne and Brunsson suggested that those running meta-organisations have to put up with an inevitable level of "necessary

---

[1]Incomplete because the work done in "traditional" organisations for individual members is partly done by the members of meta-organisations, which are themselves organisations.

hypocrisy", where the espoused theory and the theory in action will always inevitably be partly misaligned (see Argyris & Schön, 1974).

Paradoxically, this "systemification" of business has also made what had been thought of as "monolithic" organisations come to recognise themselves as actually being more pluralistic. In 2008, the HEC Montreal Business School created a Chair of Strategy in Pluralistic settings, held by Anne Langley. Her work stresses that in "pluralist settings" there are many different sources of legitimacy and power, with multiple objectives and metrics that cannot be resolved by single metrics or solutions. These pluralistic settings are present in many parts of society — be it universities, inter-governmental agencies, or hospitals (or, as we argue in this book) complex VCSs.

2. Moving the Strategy Field Beyond the Construct of "Industry"

When business realities are becoming more systemic and complex, ideas or constructs such as stable sectors, industries, or linear value creating become less relevant and unhelpful for strategists.

The idea of a firm being in "an industry", or of industrial "sectors", exhibiting similarity in what firms sell as products and services, was already shown by Normann and Ramírez in the 1990s to be increasingly problematic. They argued that such aggregations are built on what they considered outdated ideas of how value is created and organised.

The increasingly outdated notion of "industry" unduly and artificially narrows the frame the strategist uses; and thus the strategic focus of attention with regard to opportunities and threats. Since the 1990s, it has become increasingly apparent that the product-centric view of traditional strategy approaches manifested especially as competitive strategy (more about this later) can be dangerously limiting. For example, positioning oneself as a firm within the "music industry" would typically lead to thinking of one's business as selling records or CDs, rather than enabling access to and sharing of streamed music and entertainment and community building in the various situations where one likes music to be part of one's life. Instead, what is occurring is an increased complexity and blurring of categories: for a while it was the telephone device maker

Nokia, not Sony or Panasonic, that became the world's largest seller of MP3 music digital players; and then Apple, nominally a personal computer maker, entered this field and took it by storm.

Collaboration and competition among units within and across system fields call for involvement of competences and resources from many other actors than those in one's traditional "industry" — ones that can no longer be arranged or described or analysed in simplistic linear chains of activities.

An automotive manufacturer is increasingly less able to only think of its business as selling cars. Many are moving their business to enabling mobility for people who are conscious of not only costs and image and convenience, but also of limiting their carbon footprint, and who exhibit societal values that now make car ownership more irrelevant for determining or manifesting one's identity or status — and hence reframing what is value and what is valued.

The multi-industry spaces — be they for citizens in a given geography, or for moving liquefied natural gas across oceans — call for a wide set of competences and resources to become involved and coordinated into distinct VCSs that help those involved in their design and use to create various values.

As we see in Chapter 10, even though business realities have transformed into systems, several tools and models that strategists use are stuck in old conventional patterns of thinking. It is into "industries" that economic activity is classified by national statistical offices, and intergovernmental entities, such as the OECD, and financial analysts use these "industry" categories to compare the performance of one firm with another.

Like the "value chain", the concept of "industry" was popularised by Harvard strategy Professor Michael Porter in 1985 as the "important" set within which "competitive" strategy should be determined. Being in the right industry was taken to be as important as having the right firm level strategy. The notion of industries, just as the notion of value chains, is becoming ever more outdated and hinders strategists from understanding their changing business landscapes and identifying threats and opportunities for realising value potentials.

The construct of "industries" does not allow the strategist to consider uncertainties in the broader contexts that can transform existing playing fields, or that give rise to new ones — such as "nutraceuticals". Focusing strategic attention on industrial sectors, such as the automotive one, instead of considering oneself in a set of broader (and not necessarily technology-specific) systems, such as mobility or accessibility, prevents considering or seizing enhanced value creating opportunities. As we see in Chapter 5, General Electric (GE) brought in activities from many "industries" to redefine its offering in medical imagery based core.

Our research and experience suggests that redesigns of systems that help value to be created, rather than product- and industry-specific competition strategies (and optimisation within existing product and technology categories) is called for if something substantial is to be done about opportunities and threats linked to the inefficiencies that we see in business and societies at large today. Transport is one such area. If one looks upon transport as an industrial sector, and one deploys neoclassical value chain thinking, one is invited to look at how to seek out and defend positions in parts of an imagined value chain, where one might be led to focus on car models competing against other car models. If one instead looks upon transport as part of larger systems that are supported in different ways, such as systems of logistics and of mobility, or as goods- and people-accessibility systems, then other opportunities for enabling greater system efficiencies and spaces for creating value open up. New questions arise that offer new opportunities for creating value. These could include questions such as — What values are sought by different actors in the system? Can freeing up time for other work, enabled by shortened commuting times or not needing attention for driving with the help of "car platooning" work out as a net enabler of values in some situations? Can more sustainable and less congested urban environments be obtained by more effective mobility systems, with car sharing and with different means of public transport combined with and enabled by changes in technology, urban planning, fuel infrastructures, communication technologies and behaviours? Would better fill rates of trucks become the norm if route planning can be made to better align with goods flows, saving fuel consumption, and better meeting sustainability challenges? Where might inefficiencies be identified and reduced, different values created, and how might these be reconciled and compensated and monetised into profits? We explore how Scania undertook such inquiries in Chapter 8.

The system thinking and approach to strategising in a co-socio-ecological manner (Ramírez & Selsky, 2014) thus opens up new collaboration opportunities. It also brings in new implications for what a company and linked actors in such systems might require in terms of capabilities. For vehicle makers, this may involve becoming involved in urban planning, vehicle movement system design, orchestrating systems of users, or passing some of the old activities to specialised vehicles providers.

Not using system approaches to frame strategy in a networked world could involve keeping the substantial costs of preserving existing and inefficient solutions — be it in energy, health, welfare, mobility or other fields. An indication of these inefficiencies is the waste that legacy systems entail, where according to Lawrence Livermore Laboratories,[2] more than half of the energy produced in the USA is not actually used.

But the potential of thinking of value creating in system terms is not only a matter of avoiding legacy system inefficiencies. Value chain models and their neoclassical strategy approaches also risk unduly limiting the strategic opportunity space for companies and organisations which — despite themselves, perhaps — are already operating in larger systems that typically do not follow conventional industry definitions and demarcations. These firms come under increasing pressure to change when their business models rest on unsustainable trends such as increasing GDP/capital spending on healthcare or food subsidies. As broader changes encroach on old established business models, changes enabled by technology development, digitalisation and connectivity, new behaviours and values of people, it is new players unencumbered by past legacy positions or incumbency or path dependency who can act on opportunities and design offerings better suited to the merging landscape. Yet established or incumbent players, such as some we review in this book (EDF, GE, SCA, Scania, Shell), are also capable of inventing novel offerings and realising entirely new VCSs.

[2] https://flowcharts.llnl.gov/content/energy/energy_archive/energy_flow_2013/2013USEnergy.png (Accessed December 2015).

Energy systems provide another example of how the notion of "industrial sector" can limit understanding of how to unlock new value potentials. Much of the formal energy production is still today dominated by centralised large scale generating plants linked by high powered transmission lines to far away users with the help of local distribution networks. This field has traditionally been characterised by large capital investments and fixed or sunk costs in production capacity, upstream-downstream linear energy flowing in one direction, and a clear distinction between who is supplier, transmitter, buyer, consumer, etc. It has employed well-defined sectors, such as turbine producers, power plant builders, plant operators, grid operators, metering companies, etc. Under historically stable conditions, the field has arguably been well served by theories of value chain strategy models. But today the model of centralised energy production is undergoing substantial and dramatic change in many places, giving way to more decentralised energy production VCSs. The traditional roles of being only a customer, provider or supplier — just to mention a few roles involved — do not fully apply any more when energy users in households place solar panels on their roofs and become producers, and also suppliers when they start to sell energy back into the grid. Furthermore, new business systems and new business system architects emerge into networked energy communities and jockey for being the ones to most effectively enable actors to generate and have access to energy and take on roles in the system (see the examples of efforts in this regard that EDF has been involved in Chapter 6). Actors from outside the energy field such as car makers start to produce hybrid and electric vehicles that can also tap into the energy systems and store solar generated power at night. Appliance manufacturers also matter as they start to reflect on providing small power plants for the house, just as they previously introduced washing machines and dishwashers. Such appliances were just as inconceivable a century ago, as is today the idea of having small power plants in one's home. In addition to this, lots of other actors collaborate with each other and compete to figure out who can take a lead in defining and integrating smart home offerings that include and depend on energy, including telecom operators, and even home security companies such as Verisure, who wants to broaden its platform-based business system for home security into one that also enables better energy management at home. Indeed, the whole notion about what energy "supply" and "demand" is and what the various actors' roles could be is undergoing change beyond the recognition of what a "customer" is or what "demand" involves. The whole system is up for redefinition and reconfiguration as it becomes more widely clear that conventional "neoclassical" definition of industries as areas of related products and services do not apply in this complexity, and that these definitions are misleadingly limiting strategy frameworks. It is because of these developments that the applicability of the linear value chain model becomes ever more limited.

3. The Time Has Come for a Collaborative and Systems-Based Approach to Strategy

Following Normann and Ramírez's publications in 1993 and 1994, Ramírez and Selsky (2014) contrasted what they described as the "conventional" view of strategic planning, based on neoclassical economics, with what they termed the "socio-ecological" view of strategic planning — which informs how strategy can be considered if one thinks of value creation as VCSs.

They proposed that "conventional" strategic planning assumes that competitors are rational and all have access to more or less the same information, and that the type of uncertainty that strategy is taken to focus on in this view mainly comes from different competitors' moves — basically within four choice vectors — cost-quality, timing and know-how, entry barriers, and financial resources (D'Aveni & Gunther, 1994). Based on such a conventional view, a company would seek a strategy that optimises its position among the others within its industry to maximise its own profits. The focus of strategists here is on their own company and maximising its profitability, rather than on changes or indeed uncertainties beyond its immediate industry. In this conventional view, strategy is a competitive game much more than a collaborative one.

Ramírez and Selsky (2014) showed that this view of strategy may be argued to be suitable for stable conditions, where change follows and repeats old patterns. But they argued that it is not so good in unstable, complex, uncertain or fast changing business environments that are subject to sudden jolts. They did allow for the fact that there are more nuanced versions of the conventional view, versions that recognise issues such as path dependencies or information asymmetry as Selsky *et al.* (2007) suggested. Yet, Ramírez and Selsky argued that even these nuanced versions still follow — and suffer the shortcomings of — the neoclassical approach to strategy:

> *...all emphasise competitive activity among a group of peers (usually firms in the same industry), and to be played as a zero sum game (Denning, 2012). Moreover, efforts toward strategic renewal and the development of dynamic capabilities tend to be directed toward each focal firm's profit maximisation and market share goals. Yet in a number of sectors today, strategy comes from players across a range of industries, in which they both collaborate and compete. For example, Sempels and Hoffman (2013) describe how in the "city services business" companies like Cisco, Siemens, IBM, Veolia, Bolloré, Peugeot, and JCDecaux compete for a bigger share of city budgets.*

A consequence of the neoclassical approach to strategy is that it focuses on what Ramírez and Selsky (2014) defined as predictable uncertainty, rather than unpredictable uncertainties arising from the wider context firms are embedded into:

> *In neo-classically based strategic planning, the single firm focus on commercial and competitive challenges, even when these lead to hypercompetitive (d'Aveni & Gunther, 1994; Hanssen-Bauer & Snow, 1996) or game-changing possibilities (Christensen, 1997), implies a rather predictable kind of uncertainty. Decision theorists know that much of this can be assessed as risk. Responses tend to be "more of the same" leading to more intense competition as if nothing had changed or could change — which as Christensen showed, in most cases leads to the firm disappearing.*

This view does not imply that such intra-sector uncertainties have gone away in the contemporary business and strategy landscapes, but it instead highlights that these predictable uncertainties may be subjected to more fundamentally unpredictable uncertainties from outside such sectors.

4. The Last (?) Defenders of the "Value Chain", "Industry", and "Industrial Sectors"

Even if the current business realities call for systems thinking and collaborative strategy with broader notions of what value is and how it is created, the outmoded ideas of value chains and sectors have got stuck, and maintain their framing grip of strategists' thinking. In the same way, "value-added" taxation (VAT) remains in place, and — therefore, possibly thanks to how these accounting notions frame valuation — so does the calculation of value considered as "added" within firms and across them. Value "chains" remain the primary mode of mapping value creation used by the engineers and MBA's who run companies. So relations with suppliers are called "supply chains" — though (mysteriously) relations with consumers are not called "demand chains". So, for many reasons, there is continued persistence of value chain — framed thinking and practices. Indeed, what Normann called "the world of business" or WOB (denoting the actual creation of value) is housed in, and not always well supported by, a "world of management" or WOM. In many places, the WOM changes slowly — slower than business. Many parts of the WOM become institutionalised by society in the forms of tax laws, accounting practices, financial reporting rules and codes that frame how we think and act, and which are very difficult to shift. They are subjected to intense political pressure that does not always reflect the way value is actually manufactured in an evolving WOB.

Also, the value chain methods taught in all MBA courses have become a "standard" way for assessing value, which in becoming institutionalised in company practices and the law and accounting professions then become locked-in like the QWERTY keyboard on which we are typing this book. This lock-in becomes the standard way of doing things and of teaching people to do these things. Standards that gain this virtuous (or vicious) circle of lock-in are hard to exit.

In spite of all these considerations, in more recent years, we have started to see shifts away from the value chain model, even if some of the alternative approaches suggested still share some of the assumptions behind the neoclassical view of strategic planning. The strategy thinking of competing linear value chains invites to competing and fighting over existing volumes with diminishing returns — "clawing to the bottom" and zero-sum games — be it from a single company perspective or from economy-wide perspectives. For example, in their book *Blue Ocean Strategy*, Kim and Mauborgne (2005) referred to this way of strategising as leading to "red oceans", in which sharks lock in on each other in destructive competition within existing product categories. They instead advocated that companies should seek "blue oceans", where introduction of new product functionalities can lead to new categories where there is less competition. We believe such contesting of the competitive strategy model is a good step in the right direction. However, the Blue Ocean Strategy view of redesigned functionalities is still confined within a value chain strategy model, focused on products and services offered by a supplier to a buyer.

In this book, we argue that seeking and defending a position in a value chain unduly limits the possibilities to redefine the larger VCS of which one is part. Normann and Ramírez (1993) suggested that under contemporary business conditions, it is not companies that compete, but offerings, in which various firms from different industries as well as within any one "sector", and other actors such as NGOs and municipalities user communities can be contributing to a VCS — sometimes as competitors and often as collaborators. They proposed that the winning systems would be those that best enable each party, whether in any one configuration they hold primarily the role of supplier or that of customer or partner or producer or supplier, to create value, at a profit for both the actor that organises the system and the other actors that have roles in it. This is something we explore in the following chapters of this book.

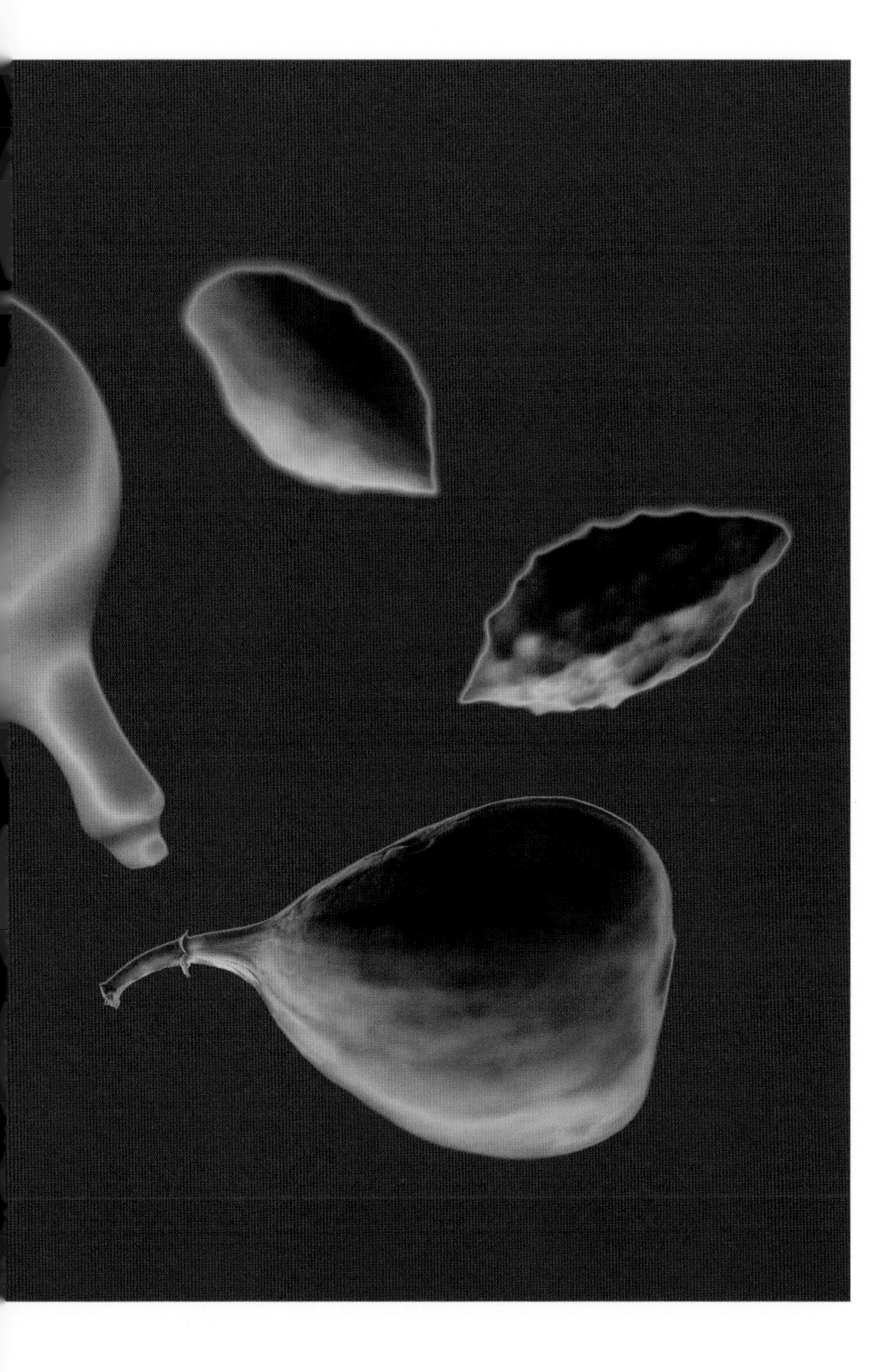

Chapter 3

Reframing the Idea of Value

Box 3.1: Chapter 3 at a Glance

There is a better alternative to the familiar, inherited idea of value. In this chapter, we review the history of how value has come to be thought of, as well as an alternative conceptualisation of value as interaction, as co-created, and as plural: comprising many types of values.

We critically review notions of value inherited from the logic and metaphors of industrial manufacturing. We contrast those notions with the view of value as co-created.

In reviewing the history and the implications of viewing value as co-created, we consider how value creation is designed by strategists in an era of complex networks of interaction.

We find strategists situated in contexts exhibiting access to highly distributed information with substantial powers to analyse it and deploy it, becoming capable of interacting more effectively.

1. Value: Many Aspects Carried by One Term

It is important to realise that while for many decades value has been thought of as "added", sequentially, by one economic actor linked in a linear manner to another one, and then to the next one in "value chains", this framing is by no means the only way that value has been thought of. This diversity is fully explained in this chapter as well as in Appendix A.

Thinking of value as co-created — not added — by two or more actors in a relationship, synchronically as well as sequentially, sweeping in and reconciling many values (not just economic value) helps to relate the thinking on which this book's ideas are based to other "schools" of thought[1] that enrich strategic thinking.

Various nuances relate personal values with interaction values. It is helpful in an interactive world for strategists to recognise that there are very different ideas on what "value" is and what roles it can play. What any one point of view means by "value" at any one point in time or in any concrete situation is a central factor guiding activity, determining priorities, shaping expectations, forming behaviour, and defining strategies. But many such points of view matter in any one situation or time and indeed across situations and over time.

One important way in which value becomes visible is in interactions, and thus in transactions. As such value has been manifested as the stock market valuation of companies based on interactions. Indeed, even today, as a remnant of the history of how the terminology of "value" has evolved (surveyed in Appendix A), in colloquial French *une valeur* means not only a value but — in that transactional context — a stock traded in the stock market.

The views on value and its co-creation in strategy offered in this book are in some ways similar to those offered by other approaches, and in some ways distinct. We outline some of the more well-known similarities and differences here. As we see in Appendix A, some of the differences can be explained by the fact that several of the other approaches have arisen in fields such as marketing with its roots in psychology and social psychology; in biology, chemistry, and ecology; and in computer science and operations research; but not in strategy.

Research has demonstrated that what value is at any one point in time for someone depends strongly on circumstances — a person will value a million pounds of diamonds more than a litre of water if the person lives and works in London, but water is of higher value if that person just parachuted in, and is all alone in the Atacama desert. One such circumstance that has changed valuation priorities considerably in the last few decades

[1] See Appendix A.

Box 3.2: Not Calculation of Financial Value or Pricing

We would like readers to note that the views on value that we cover in this book do not include financial techniques for calculations of value — such as determining the worth of a company in terms of shareholder value, price-earning ratios, value-at-risk, nor guiding marketing decisions such as the pricing of something offered in the market. These quantifications of value are of course very important, but they relate more to the fields of finance and marketing than to strategy. Thus, in our view the monetary value of shares of a publicly traded firm should result from strategy, rather than guide strategy. Also, our research and engagement experience makes us believe that thinking of value first qualitatively (i.e. in design terms) and only thereafter in quantitative terms, not the other way around, is a more helpful way to consider how to increase profitable topline revenues, and to find distinctive ways to generate new such revenues.

is the technology that is used in manifesting, producing, or communicating value. We survey this after reviewing some of this history of thinking about value as co-created. To do so, we review the history of three important notions (1) value, (2) consumption, and (3) value co-creation. We do this by following Ramírez's (1999) analysis of the historical development of each term as a manifestation of how we have come to think, with these terms manifesting our thinking, about the issues we explore in this book.

1.1 Value

The notion of "value" has had a long and complex history.[2] Value was studied in moral philosophy until the 18th century, when economics became a field of study in its own right. Since then, much debate has taken place on the relationship between the economic and ethical aspects of value (see, for example, Bucki & Pesqueux, 1995; Klamer, 1995; Rothbard, 1995).

[2] Part of this section is derived from Ramírez (1999).

Etymologically, "value" originally denoted both (i) how people acted, what they could become, and (ii) how they traded goods with each other. Over time these meanings separated. *The Dictionnaire Historique de la Langue Française* tells us that in French, *valeur*, first appearing in 1080 and having derived from the classical Latin term *valor*, meant both (i) "*the esteem a person receives according to merit and qualities*" and (ii) an "*assessment of the quality & interest of things*" (Ramírez, 1999). The first meaning by 1155 denoted the "importance" of a person and, as of 1172–1174, personal acts of valour.

The second meaning of *valeur*, the *Dictionnaire* tells us, denoted that something had value upon its "*being appropriate for a certain use*". Thus, what later became known as "utility value", as opposed to "exchange value", is some 900 years old.

"Value" became associated with being measurable during the 13th century, where "exchange value" was first applied to traded assets. By the 16th century, "value" became commensurate with a measurable unit; this paved the way for the notion of price to represent this measure, which appeared at the end of the 17th century. So, as we saw above, by the beginning of the 18th century, *une valeur* was the generic name given to negotiable securities; the term *valuta* for currency is common in a great variety of European languages. Early in the 20th century, *valorisation* and *devaluer* respectively denoted the enhancement and decrease of market, or exchange, value. The modern industrial view of value creation is achieved by joining the industrial concept of the added value being "in" the product with the concept that this value is measured by the price.

1.2 Consumption

While in the industrial view the customers "consume" the product and thereby destroy the value created by producers, in the alternative frame we present in this book, the customers also create value. More exactly, those who hold the central role of a customer co-create and even co-invent value, both with those who hold the central role of supplier and then with those who hold the central role of "producer". As a result, when thinking of value as co-created, there are no "final" or "end" customers. The history of the term "consume" clarifies this.

The French verbs *consumer* and *consommer* suffered semantic hesitations until Vagelas clarified their sense in 1647 (*Dictionnaire Historique de la Langue Française*: 480, 483). These difficulties were also present in the English "consume", for it was derived from the French usage (*Webster's Dictionary*). According to *The Oxford English Dictionary*, "consume" in Middle English was derived from the Latin *consumere*, and meant, (i) "*to make away with, to destroy*"; (ii) as of 1460: "*to waste or squander*"; (iii) as of 1527: "*to use up*", especially "*to eat or drink up*"; (iv) as of 1533: "*to take up, spend, waste time*"; and (v) as of 1526: "*to waste away*", or "*burn away*" as of 1591.

A second definition of "consume" from 1483 was derived from the Latin *consummare*, and by 1541 this second sense meant "*to accomplish, complete*". This sense survives in the term "consummate" in relation to marriage.

These definitions imply that by 1541 at the latest two contradictory senses of "consume" came to be accepted in English.

The confusion was exacerbated by Christian religious teachings and the use of "consumption" to denote tuberculosis, starting in the first half of the 17th century.

In economics, this confusion led authors in the mid-1800s to distinguish between "*productive or reproductive*" consumption and "*unproductive or non-reproductive*" consumption (*Littré dictionary*: 719). Adam Smith's 1776 distinction between productive and unproductive work is its most famous manifestation (Rothbard, 1995: 444–448).

There is a paradox hidden in the traditional economic sense of "consume". The objects are not merely destroyed as by waste, fire or disease, but they are put to use in the process. Thus, the French *consommer is the employment of things which get destroyed as they are used* (*Littre* 720, translated by Ramírez, 1999). If things are employed and used, then some sort of value is created in the process. Some sort of happiness is brought into the world. But in the traditional model, made explicit in the industrial era, that value was definitely left outside of the formal monetised economic system. If it existed at all it was purely subjective, and could not be sold on as another commodity. Not being counted, it did not count. It was to be realised only in the private sphere, and was left there, invisible and outside the realm of the economy — and of business. Thus, the paradox of value being created while its carrier is destroyed became firmly hidden from the view of economists and accountants.

1.3 Value Co-creation

When business became interactive there was no longer a precise point at which the value moved away from the formal, quantified, and monetised sector, to the informal and private. A person downloads an item from the Internet, perhaps paying for it only by viewing some advertisements (thereby increasing their value). The person likes the item, and shares it on social media. That sharing action is recorded and goes into the profiles of the person, the item, and those who also like it. The transaction increases the person's value as a potential purchaser of other relevant items, and that information itself can be sold on a market for contacts. For some purists, this commercialisation of private pleasure seems intrusive and corrupting. But it demonstrates very clearly how — when information becomes a commodity of equal significance with material artefacts — the economy and cultures of sharing of production and of consumption are transformed. One's values (shared in social media) become measured, become commoditised (made into a commodity to be traded) and can be and are traded; one's sharing and one's commercial exchanges in turn shape one's values; at least as those values are assessed by others.

With the networked economy, the value associated with the object is not "in" the object "itself". It is also not embedded in, or only the result of, the activities that have made it possible for the object to come to be, as is implied in Smith's, and later Marx's labour theories of value. Interestingly, while some resource-based strategy authors argue that a resource's value rests on the difficulty of replicating it, Bowman (1996: 4) showed that other resource-based researchers such as Barney (1986) held views compatible with value as co-created. Value in this second sense resides in the actions — and more particularly the interactions — which the acquired resource makes possible or supports. Strategically, this alternative framing is crucial: Simmel went as far as suggesting that it is exchange, or interactivity, which is at the origin of both the rarity and utility (1977: 82) upon which economic value rests; not the other way around. It is this focus on exchange, on links, and how they are designed that underpins the conceptual frame of, and the argumentation in, this book.

Offerings, which we analyse in greater detail in Chapter 5, are as Normann and Ramírez (1989) pointed out, the locus of design for co-creation. A designed configuring offering defines the whole value co-creation system (VCS), and support offerings make it possible for all co-creators to work together in the VCS.

The conceptual framework of value co-creation that we use has, as seen above and as is also outlined in Appendix A, a long history. It is the technical breakthroughs that have enhanced the liquidity of all resources and assets (Normann & Ramírez, 1993a, 1994) — meaning that they can be broken up, moved, and reunited with unprecedented ease — that have made this strategic framework come of age.

2. Notions of Value Inherited from Industrial Manufacturing

While assembly work actually represented less than 10% of industrial labour (Hirschhorn, 1984: 9), something about assembly lines captured the imagination of management and the broader public. Henry Ford became an American icon in the 1920s. In Huxley's *Brave New World* (1931), people said "Ford" instead of "Lord". Car assembly lines, which had first appeared in the dictionary in 1930 (*idem.*), were argued to be the "keystone to prevailing 20th century concepts of human management" (Emery, 1976). Hence, industrial value production was conceptualised in terms of the value chain.

With the chain concept, value creation was taken to be not only sequential, but also as "added" by the manufacturing process to the raw materials and was then "in" the finished product. The taxation system developed at that time (still with us in the form of value-added tax, VAT) reflected this. Unfortunately, the norms and systems that the value chain depiction of value spawned — such as taxation, and as we see below, accounting — both limit and confuse the role that value can play in strategy. An important intention in writing this book is that we wish to liberate the notions of value that we consider important for strategists to use in developing new business from the legacy of regulatory and accounting systems that arose in industrial value production.

We saw above that up to and including industrial value creation, customers were seen as "consuming" the product, and thereby destroying the value that producers created for them. Even for longer-lasting products, the accounting systems emerging at that time would "write down" the value of what was acquired, eventually making the value equal zero in the books of the client or consumer or customer or user, over a shorter or longer "depreciation" period. Consumption in other words was equal to destroying value.

The so-called "end user" in this industrial era representation of how value is created and destroyed thus equalled that which in value chain terms was called the "final" customer. For producers, value was "realised" in the transaction, which simultaneously joined and separated them from customers. In this context, value was equated to the price that the customer paid: "*...in competitive terms, value is the amount buyers are willing to pay for what a firm provides them*" (Porter, 1985: 38); or, "*value is what customers are willing to pay*" (*idem*: 3).

Consistent with this understanding of value, Hirschhorn (1984) specified that in industrial manufacturing, value creation was characterised by:

(i) economies of scale;
(ii) large, physically and temporally concentrated production facilities;
(iii) long production runs;
(iv) mass markets;
(v) task specialisation; and
(vi) standardisation.

Although much of manufacturing is still of this pattern, large parts of the economy and even important parts of industry have been increasingly moving away from it. First with the increase of the importance of activities that were catalogued as services, and now with the rapidly growing importance of data and information in an evolving networked economy, new forms of value creation that are not industrial manufacturing production have grown to significance. The appropriate conceptions of value production change with them, and the industrial era is seen as a special case (Normann & Ramírez, 1993b).

3. Post-Industrial Value Creation

Considerable parts of how value works in business are increasingly depicted in ways that can no longer be modelled on the assembly line production of material objects for sale. From the perspective of the managers of a typical firm, value is no longer something that is simply "added" in a linear sequence of production processes but is increasingly becoming "co-created" and "tested and contested" through a complex network of relationships, with the co-creation in turn sustaining the network. "User-generated content" is an outstanding example of value co-creation. Thus, for some years, reportedly (Ouzeau, 2014; Brantley, 2008) the author of Dilbert has encouraged users to modify his cartoons with their own content and to distribute them. This type of user-generated material now constitutes the majority of uploaded online content.

Appendix A outlines how the conceptual foundations for co-creation were laid long before the value chain production line model of industry was established. Yet, in practice, value seen as co-created became visible for strategists only when value co-creation was used to understand the growing number of commercial activities labelled as "services". Yet, as Normann and Ramírez (1993, 1994) argued, since then the distinction of assembly line specific rules and concepts as "manufacturing" from another set of activities labelled as "services" — originally thought of comprising a separate category — has become increasingly blurred, with each losing its distinct identity. For example, is a service quality function supporting manufacturing a part of the manufacturing or is it a service supporting manufacturing? Is it useful strategically to settle this only on a make/buy contractual choice, where something that is bought is considered a service, and if it is done in-house as part of the production function of a good? This book argues that the networked co-creation of value view has become the dominant strategic reality, and that thinking of value as added is losing its range of applicability. We explain why this is so in this chapter.

An important reason for arguing that thinking of value as co-created is gaining ground over thinking of value as added is that the way in which value is manufactured and valued has been changing profoundly over recent decades.

Figure 3.1: Radio Shack Advertisement 1991[3]

The advertisement presented in Figure 3.1 above illustrates an aspect of this transformation. The ad shows the number of possibilities for action

[3] Source: http://www.huffingtonpost.com/steve-cichon/radio-shack-ad_b_4612973.html, (Accessed December 2015).

and interaction, which have been shrunk into a smart-phone since the RadioShack advertisement appeared in 1991.[4] All of what was featured then as embodied in many different objects is held within one hand-held device now.

These possibilities for acting and interacting are now bundled in ever denser packages ("denser" meaning more functions per space and time unit, and thereby also per person or interactor). They help people and their organisations to co-create value in ways that were unimaginable a few decades ago. For example, the browser on one's personal device (personal computer, smartphone, tablet, etc.) forms (and is formed by) the nexus of many links that are activated in real time as one browses, with cookies keeping track of one's actions and influencing the information that is presented from many different actors. As one interacts, one's trail modifies these preferences in real time, and will further influence one's future interactions (and the interactions others that these networks compare one with), not only with providers of goods and services but equally with other actors.

Could Wikipedia, Linux, Twitter, Facebook, Instagram, Airbnb, and Uber have come alive without involving a fundamentally new view of value and value co-creation? How can business strategists make good sense of social media and other interactions and of the myriad ways they are reconfiguring news/data/information/opinion creation and distribution? Technological innovations allowing work practices such as distributed processing, shared services, "platform organisations" (Gawer & Cusumano, 2002), concurrent engineering, and "social networks" (Castells, 2015) have all acted to render value creation more synchronous, less sequential (Warnecke *et al.*, 1997), and more interactive (Normann & Ramírez, 1993a, 1994) than ever before. Socio-technical innovations help to pack in more options for action and thus more actions, and more actors and interactions, and more possibilities for further action to co-create more values per unit of time and space than ever before (Davis, 1987). These interactions in turn change what people value and can trust, as Uber in taxis and Airbnb in overnight accommodation and Facebook in

[4]Source: http://www.huffingtonpost.com/steve-cichon/radio-shack-ad_b_4612973.html (Accessed December 2015).

"friendships" reveal. Would one have considered leaving one's dearly loved pet cat with a total stranger while on a long weekend away in Vienna (with a friend of a friend of a friend) before such media "vetted" the trustworthiness of this person? Trust maps have been changed, as have been roles — a "friend" is not exactly the same online as in person. Through the digital joint manufacture of trust, they actually enable new service technologies and innovative co-creation arrangements where very different values such as convenience and safety can be reconciled anew.

In such a networked world, conceptualising value on the central basis of two-way exchanges as one did in the industrial era (with the idea of value-added products) has become very limiting, in fact too limiting, for the understanding of value creation in many-to-many, complex settings.

As business becomes more system-like with "business ecosystems (BE)" such as Android becoming the norm and not the exception, value and its production requires more system-like, networked, and emergent conceptual frameworks. Value co-created by two or (typically now) more actors, with and for each other, with and for yet other actors, is an invitation not only

Box 3.3: Linking Different Values

As we see in Chapter 4, the views on co-creation we explore and articulate in this book also imply that what is now meant by "value" is becoming reconnected to what one means by "values". An example as we write this book in mid-2015 is the killing of a lion in Zimbabwe by a dentist from Milwaukee who thought he was doing this hunting "legally". The lion had previously been tagged for scientific research by Oxford University scientists and had been coaxed away from a reserve at night time to be killed. The interaction was discovered and shared widely across the web and social media, and this put the predator (dentist) who had tracked and killed the prey (lion) into another role — the dentist found himself in the role of prey (through the online campaign to vilify both him and his values). Unknown to him at the time of the hunt, the lion had been given an all too human name, Cecil, by the researchers. The resulting celebrity on its demise then radically transformed its value for the hapless dentist, whose values were also made public and questionable.

to rethink organisational structures and managerial arrangements for value creation, but also to rethink value creation itself.

In the strategy frame we use in this book, we place interactivity as the focus for where value is created and assessed. Interactivity is, of course, also a major source of risk as well as of value. For example, Edward Snowden revealed spying and surveillance of data communication. Another example is how hackers exploit the networked world to bring whole information systems down, be they those of airlines or stock markets.

Our argument is that this central concern with the interactivity that has become so ubiquitous inescapably leads strategists to rethink value creation and strategy.[5] Attending to interactivity involves moving many concepts relating to value from "nouns" to "verbs" (John Seely Brown, personal communication). Attending to interactivity also involves thinking of value as contingent, always located in a setting — no longer as isolated in things or individuals or groups — and dependent on those whom it connects and who co-create it as well as in terms of those it affects positively as well as negatively.

4. Designing Systems to Create Value

As we demonstrate in this book, patterns of interactivity that enable the production or co-creation of value and values arise or can be designed.[6] But as we see especially in Chapter 6, even a pattern of activity that arose (and was not explicitly designed as it arose) through several rounds of exploratory iterations, through compromises, and through accidental or happenstance innovations which came together over time and managed to work together to help co-create value can be analysed to find the value creating designs that underpin it — and with this explicitated understanding can be copied, emulated and indeed improved or redesigned.

These patterns connect those parties termed "actors" with each other, where the relations allow them to interact. Their interactions support or may even constitute the actors' roles and identities — this is explained in terms of Actor-Network Theory (ANT) in Chapter 6, and in Appendix B. In turn, actors' roles and identities interact with each other and in so doing

[5] And indeed the firm and its boundaries, as The Economist of 24th October 2015 explored.

[6] We thank our colleague Bill Sharpe for helping us make this important distinction.

form interconnected patterns; so these roles and identities in turn maintain the interactions. One of the core things we explore in this book is — how can value be articulated and described in terms of these ongoing complex and reflective patterns of interaction, which have designs or have been designed? And how do these articulations and design possibilities inform the work of strategists?

So as we said above, patterns of interactivity can emerge without explicit design intent. For example, an apple has value for someone as food regardless of anyone's intent or otherwise when planting the tree from which one can take it (and the tree might have not even been planted). Or a mountain might be appreciated as a place to walk, or be seen as a resource for mining — both are intentional perspectives that reveal value for an actor, but neither need assume intentional design in the mountain having arisen geologically. Victorian England was driven by the debates on whether the many examples of apparent design in Nature were the result of intention, as at the Biblical Creation, or had arisen spontaneously through "natural selection". So perceived patterns of interactivity do not therefore require any intentional design on the part of any particular actor, though they might arise in part because of such intent — and often do arise in this manner in business. More famously, the architect Christopher Alexander (Alexander *et al.*, 1977) showed that medieval town layouts arose from interactions without any one urban planner designing the town. Related to this we note also that the notion of "value" was not always required for the mapping of those patterns, though Darwin himself freely used the value-laden terms "favoured" and "races" in his great work (Darwin, 1859).

An important way to understand how value works for strategists as proposed in this book is based on the idea that the notion of value arises for the strategist when one takes the perspective of an actor within a pattern of interaction. A pattern of interaction seen from a stance taken as being "outside" or external to the pattern might not hold the same values for the observer than if the observers consider themselves part of that pattern.

Of course, many patterns of interactivity arise through the explicit intent — realised in design — of actors. In particular, organisations arise through intentional purpose, however fluid or historical or even malevolent, and it is strategy of organisations that we are analysing in this book. We are therefore anchoring the language we use in this book to assess the intentional life of strategic managers in organisations, and the views on value that these strategic managers possess, in the context of design and designing. This is a "hot" topic today; see discussions of Michlewski (2015) and Bason (2014) in *Ashgate* (2015a, 2015b).

Considerations about value and values lead to questions such as — is a group of trees in the Amazon of bigger value to mankind when it is absorbing carbon from the atmosphere supporting the vital ecosystem, slowing down global warming; or when it is cut down and refined into luxury furniture in a hotel lobby or even if it partly becomes chips for making toilet-paper? These questions on values help to assess how actors choose which interactions to privilege over others, and how they relate one interaction to another.

An organisation's managers express its intents — and thus its values — by configuring interactions to establish (more or less) continuing patterns of activity with other actors. Are interactions with employees more important than those with customers? Are interactions with shareholders more important than those with employees? For which of these interactions is the strategy primarily constructed? These senior managers take views on what possibilities for value co-creation their organisation is providing for which actors, and make choices that reflect and reinforce their values: for example, determining what possibilities of preserving water, for food production, for recreation, or for mining finite resources in a particular location they favour or block — and how do these do and might relate to other interactive patterns already in play. These are not just lofty conversations, they affect very tangible aspects such as healthcare packages in employment contracts or even what appears for customers in a health provider organisation's website: does it aim to offer information of high integrity for users to self-manage a medical condition, or is it meant to advertise and promote certain products or therapies — or can it do both?

We consider this configuring of interactions as a design activity. We use the term Value Creating System (VCS) for the pattern of interactions intentionally configured by the strategic planning carried out by an organisation. The designed interactions become manifested as "designed" offerings (see Appendix A for a history of the term): financial offerings such as shares or bonds; job offers; commercial offerings; offers for neighbours or analysts or journalists or NGOs to meet the top management; offers for scientists to come together to monetise their research. As Normann and Ramírez (1993) put it: if the key to creating value is to design and co-create configuring offerings that mobilise others (who may have the role in the interaction of customer or supplier or partner or employee or investor, etc.) to co-create value, then a key source of success is to conceive the VCS and make it work.

5. Co-Created Value

Socio-technical advancements (Trist, 1981) have been liberating businesses from the constraints of the industrial manufacturing mode of value creation; rendering value creation synchronic and interactive. Yet, the institutionalisation in practices such as VAT taxation, value added calculations taught in business school MBA programs around the world, accounting standards, and so on, render the prevalence of the inherited view more durable than might have been expected. The old view has been "locked in" (or into) accounting and financial reporting practices and is difficult to displace.

Reconsidering this "central role" for a designer of the configuring offering of a VCS is what makes it possible for us to propose the fundamental change in value creation as described in this book.

Box. 3.4: The Time for Value Co-Creation Has Come

As we have described, the alternative view of value creation we use in this book, "value co-creation", has been available to us in one form or another for over 300 years. Just as Leonardo da Vinci imagined the helicopter long before technical innovation enabled its actual production; so too technical breakthroughs now allow strategic managers and researchers to take advantage of the options offered by this alternative view of value creation.

In industrial manufacturing, each individual firm held only one central role, and was thus catalogued as (primarily or exclusively) being a "supplier", or "producer", or "customer". Sometimes, other central roles were attended to as well in strategy — roles such as "investor" or "distributor" or "partner" or "competitor". The central roles were one-at-a-time roles that any one holder held, and which were held for longish periods of time and in mostly stable conditions. These single central role attributions allowed other constructs to emerge: in comparing oneself with other parties holding similar "production" roles to oneself one could term these comparable others "competitors", and putting them all together allowed a configuration construct of an "industry" to arise — perhaps, throwing in all of the relevant "first tier" links of firms these producers called (only) their "suppliers".

The view of value creation described in this book is that with networked co-creation the situation has now become more difficult to pin down in simplistic terms, and more fluid. Any one actor now recognises one's self as holding many roles simultaneously: a firm is a buyer and producer and partner and competitor and investor and distributor all at the same time, and the stability of configurations such as "industries" is irrelevant in determining new value creation possibilities.

In this alternative view of value as co-created which we use in this book, the roles of producer, supplier, or customer are just this — a role to be assumed in relation to another in a given time and place, that can be readily discarded in another relationship. We have moved on from the world of static roles embedded in rigid institutions with their own exclusive cultures. Now, any one party can hold that role (and any other) in relation to another party — and some other role, at the same time. I may be X's customer, Y's partner, Z's supplier, and at the same time a producer. In job A (in New Zealand) I may be X's customer, while in job B (in New Orleans) I am X's supplier. In job C (in New Caledonia) I am X's partner, and in job D (in Sao Paulo) I am competing with X. X and I hold all of those roles at the same time.

Take as an example the recent changes in the role held by those who used be depicted as "customers". A pioneering conception of IKEA was that "customers" could be treated as full partners in value creation — and their role changed to becoming "prosumers" (Toffler, 1970) or as Eiglier and Langeard (1987) put it, to participate in "servuction". Now, in ever more cases the so-called customers actually (co-)create a bigger and bigger share of the value involved, as one can see in Facebook, LinkedIn, Airbnb, etc. Without customers producing the "user-generated content" the services would be almost worthless and the businesses would collapse: as someone once put it, "online, if something is "free", it is likely that you are the product". In these examples, customers are not only customers but co-creators who repeatedly co-create value. Now, in any area where the proficiency of users is important, notably but not exclusively in ICT (Information and Communications Technology), the fund of information supplied freely by volunteers on websites, and easily accessed by Google queries, becomes a vital part of value creation of almost any offering. Here, one can see producers, users and co-creators all blended together.

In this view, value is not simply "added", but is mutually "created" and "recreated" among actors with different values. These multiple values are "*reconciled*" (Hampden-Turner, 1990: 2) or "*combined*" (*idem* : 3) in co-creating value, and as we shall see below, cannot be reduced to a single metric, like the sale price of a commodity. For example, imagine someone cooking a meal for family and friends. They might look up a cooking website, reviewing evaluative comments from other people who have tried the recipe. They prepare the meal taking account of their own capabilities, the likes and dislikes of the people coming, and the kitchen equipment that they have. The meal itself is the occasion of social interaction of which the food, taken from a raw state of individually valued goods to a newly-created offering, is just part of the value created, but which affords the occasion of a convivial event.

6. Some Implications of Co-Created Value

Here, we overview how the conceptual framework discussed above helps to understand value creation practices in ways that are consistent with designed VCS. This is at the core of the strategy framework this book describes.

We characterise VCS as designed activities that are part of much broader business ecosystems or business ecologies ("BE").[7] These

[7]We again thank Bill Sharpe for clarifying this distinction with us.

BE are "higher order" unit of analysis than VCS: a VCS is almost always part of a larger BE. In current business writing the distinction is not always very sharp, and failing to distinguish clearly confuses what can be designed (the VCS) from that which cannot be — the BE. Google, Android, Facebook, Twitter, LinkedIn and iTunes are variously considered VCSs, or BE, or VCSs fitting into a larger "social media" or "IT" or "ICT" BE. The point is that in this book we are concentrating on cases manifested by a designed VCS, not a BE that might be the result of myriad VCS designs coming together.

Of course, one can have a VCS designed to connect other VCSs: Oracle's owners, for instance, have made a fortune by designing interfaces among unconnected VCS to make them compatible with each other. In this sense, Oracle has acted as a "meta-VCS", setting its own VCS design so that it renders other VCSs to be incompatible with one another. One can argue that Android has done the same among the VCSs of app suppliers, advertisers, mobile phone operators, device makers, and users and web surfers.

In this book, we consider strategy as entailing reconfiguring roles, actions and interactions among economic actors (Normann & Ramírez, 1993a, 1994; van der Heijden, 2005) through designed configuring offerings that result in a given VCS. At the risk of repeating this too much — the distinctive aspect of this book is that it attends to the fact that all of these relationships are manifested as designed "offerings", which both distinguish and join economic actors within the VCS.

It is important to emphasise that we do not pretend that we are saying that something "new" is happening. What we are saying is that it is time for us to accept that "another" way of thinking of value takes its due place in the world, and that this other way of seeing yields possibilities for value creation to which the value chain (industrial assembly) view of value is blind. Ciborra (1996) suggested that the reason complex relations had not been more readily researched in the past, was that our methods of observing organisational life arbitrarily and artificially "slice" or "carve out" elements of an infinitely interconnected set of dynamic relationships into static, limited "cases" or examples. His research implied that co-creation has actually been there all along. We also suggest that thinking of value as VCS also may correct some of the costly by-products of thinking of value as produced — such as conceiving unwanted by-products like industrial accidents, pollution, and the unsustainable proliferation of waste as "externalities".

6.1 If Value is Co-Created, How is it "Manufactured"?

Co-creation asks one to reconsider the nature of value creation. From a management and research perspective, it requires that one considers how to reconcile a multiplicity of values, held in relations with multiple actors, which cannot be reduced to a single metric (Dean *et al.*, 1997: 423).

In co-creation, it is the co-created offerings and the relationships these manifest, not the "business unit" actor, which become the central unit of (competitive and collaborative) strategic analysis.

A lot of co-created value "manufacturing" exhibits some the following characteristics:

(i) Scope is as important as scale in economic calculations, and it allows smaller units to compete against big ones: Skype and WhatsApp, when they were small startups could take on large established incumbents such as Deutsche Telekom, Orange, and AT&T.
(ii) Short product life cycles and production runs are economically viable, enabling, for example, print-on-demand book publishing to emerge as a viable business.
(iii) Enhanced asset liquidity and reconfigurability render "fixed" or "sunk" costs risky. Instead, there is a move to re-allocate as many fixed costs as possible and render them more flexible — activity-based costing, customer-centred analytic accounting, and other battles to eliminate "average" costs are signs of this.
(vi) Stakeholders (Chevalier, 1968; Freeman, 1984) are made to have more important roles in value creation (c.f. Weiszfeld *et al.*, 1993). Interactively involving them enhances positive return economics (Arthur, 1996), but also requires their multiple values to be reconciled (Hampden-Turner, 1990). Even Michael Porter (Porter & Kramer, 2011) has acknowledged that it has become important for business to "share" value with other stakeholders. In resource rich extractive firms such as mining and oil, attending to local stakeholders has come

to be seen as a worthwhile investment to retain the "license to operate" that society informally as well as formally grants to their operations.

As customer self-help became a recognised production factor (Fuchs, 1965, 1968; Gershuny, 1978), organising and managing "beyond" the organisational boundary became necessary. Co-creation as a point of view explains that customers appearing to be difficult, inefficient, or otherwise "troublesome" may well behave in these ways (even being unprofitable) because the interfaces (offering), which their suppliers have developed with them, allow them — or even invite them — to behave in such ways, and even make it rational for them to do so. Thus, such a relationship is not without difficulties: In the 1990s, some RATP (Paris bus and metro system) customer groups did not want to be thought of as co-creators as, in the context of French public service culture as it was conceived then, this would have meant that they would not be able to complain about the producers' failings.

6.2 No "End Customer" or "Final Customer"

When value is understood to be co-created, "end" customers no longer exist. Hotel guests endorsing the hotel they stayed at have become part of the hotel's marketing machinery, electricity customers with solar panels on their homes' roofs are becoming co-creators with the grid or utility company and in effect activate demand control plans to support peak energy sharing or can store energy when connecting the battery of their car to the system to produce backup power etc. Retailers of manufactured consumer products provide customers' evaluations online as part of their offering. Evaluation websites for consumers, as Yelp or TripAdvisor, are a growth field. Skype and LinkedIn use the users' PC and their WiFi connection to power the system (no infrastructure expense), the user's network to market the service (no marketing or sales expense) and make money on the "premium" service to which only a subset of users subscribe. In such increasingly common cases customers are aware that they also act as a *de facto* (if not official) member of the production team, or of the infrastructure, buyer or the marketing departments. In such roles, they are not "end" customers, they also act and interact in ways that extend the VCS to their own counterparts whose interactions they value. So the multiple roles we alluded to of the "customer" are also multiple roles for others: someone whose central role was that of "supplier" may now also simultaneously be a "customer" of its client in receiving training about a new standard they need to manufacture for. As a classic pioneering case, Benetton systematically engaged others in multiple dialogues as an essential leitmotif structuring its corporate development (Lazzarato *et al.*, *op. cit*; Benetton & Lee, 1992), even deliberately seeking controversial dialogues (Toscani, 1995). Lazzarato *et al.* showed how Benetton internalised the social logics of those it engaged in co-creation, and then got these to internalise its own logics.

Designing co-creation requires the strategist having the role of ascertaining and ideally defining the engagement (Trist & Murray, 1990) and the dialogue that underpins designing novel and distinctive value creation. Normann and Ramírez (1994) suggested that a critical dialogue is that between the marshalling and rendering accessible of capabilities and resources on the one hand, and of those who will access these capabilities and resources to create value on the other. This does not mean that the "client is always right": If IKEA in the early years would have asked their customers if they want furniture that they would have to assembly themselves the answer would probably have been "no!". But in hindsight, designing for enabling the unskilled customer to be an integral part of the production process has paid off. In the same way, individuals would not have dreamt of accepting payment for complete strangers to stay overnight in their spare room until Airbnb devised a system allowing them to do just this, conveniently and safely by the creation of digital communities.

So in VCS every party holds multiple roles. In using WhatsApp or Skype or LinkedIn, individuals get invited to link to another; and they may in turn invite another to link in to themselves. They are lending their PC and internet power to the "social media" provider. By accepting the legal terms, they are entering into contractual work and risk sharing and risk-management arrangements not only with WhatsApp or Skype or LinkedIn but to many other individuals. Through WhatsApp or Skype or LinkedIn the contractual arrangements extend to all those that supply them with insurance, auditing, legal services, software, equipment, and all other capabilities and resources that WhatsApp or Skype or LinkedIn have marshalled and rendered accessible. In this way, their users/marketers/suppliers of information along with other users are enabled to co-create value.

6.3 What Organisational Arrangements Support Value Co-Creation?

The complexity of holding multi-role relations poses several managerial challenges. As opposed to "complicated" systems, where (a) components and variables, (b) their dimensions, and (c) their purpose in a given system are known; "complex" systems are those in which one or more of (a), (b), and/or (c) is not known (Atlan, 1979).

Managing complex systems thus requires managing ignorance, which may even include the system's objectives (Fogelman Soulié, 1991). This is — almost by definition — different from managing knowledge. For example, the strategic planning manager of one firm told one of the authors: "*we need to know what we do not know*" about a geographical area they were expanding into.

One way to address the ignorance that complexity entails is to "engage" counterparts (Morgan, 1983: 13; Trist & Murray, 1990: xi) with whom one co-addresses this ignorance. Such engagement connects the managers of these organisations together, and as we saw above, such organising takes on networking characteristics. In "engaging with" (as opposed to one actively studying and the "other" being a passively studied), both parties co-explore something as well as each other and each other's way of engaging. In working together, they discover how the differences of how each would engage alone, and when compared, can help each party to ascertain the blind spots it would otherwise keep about a given issue. When this works well, as in the "wisdom of the crowds" (see Wikipedia), the results can be extraordinary.

In the management of this multi-relations and multi-role complexity, it must never be forgotten that counterparts themselves have their own agendas. When one reads about a hotel in an online evaluation website, one should not assume that the customer only wants to share her experience for the benefit of the guest community. She might have accepted a lower room rent in exchange for a good review; or she might be working for a malevolent competitor! Systematic fake evaluations have become a significant problem in the evaluations field. Asking "Who guards the guardians?" is elementary prudence in many areas of social life; and in the management of complex systems it is foundational. This is recognised in the digital-internet consumer systems like eBay and Airbnb. where a community of trust is created digitally through the published profiles of participants (including records of their previous activities). Thus, the co-creation of value, systematically carried out, recreates some of the attributes of the "community" or *Gemeinschaft* of pre-industrial societies, while retaining the freedom and flexibility of modernity.

In summary, we suggest that value seen as "value co-creation" has a long intellectual history that is becoming ever more obvious with recent socio-technical breakthroughs. This mode of seeing value now lives alongside the industrial view that became established through the 19th and 20th centuries. Some of the main differences between both views, as have been examined in this chapter, are summarised in Table 3.1 below.

Table 3.1: Two Views of Value Production

Industrial view	Co-creative view
• Value creation is sequential, uni-directionally transitive, best described in "value chains"	• Value creation is synchronic, interactive, best described in "VCSs"
• All managed values can be measured in monetary terms	• Some managed values cannot be measured or monetised
• Value is added	• Values are co-invented, combined and reconciled
• Value is a function of utility and rarity	• Relations as a key source of utility and rarity
• Values are either "objective" (exchange) or "subjective" (utility)	• Values are "contingent" and "actual" (established interactively)
• Customers as consumers destroy value	• Customers are relieved or enabled to (co-)create values
• Value "realised" at transaction, only for supplier (event)	• Value is co-created, with customer, over time — for both co-creators (relationship)

Following Ramírez (1999), considering value as value creating systems, strategic planners are helped to design new offerings that commercially join actors through innovative co-creative relationships. These new offerings, when strategically effective, reconfigure the roles that each co-creator holds in relating to others, and this design work becomes manifested in new VCSs.

Chapter 4

Effective Value Creating System Designs

Box 4.1: Chapter 4 at a Glance

The value creating system (VCS) view offers a way to understand how value is co-created in business and societies today. As we saw in Chapter 3, the VCS framework considers value and values from an outcomes (and also, expected outcomes) perspective, a perspective that is always from the point of view of an actor who is acting to create value — for the self, and for and with others — and who is using what other actors do to help create value. This chapter on effective designs for VCSs presents the VCS framework as a conceptual construct, and explores what constitutes effective designs of such systems. Also, the chapter describes the methodological approach to strategy that has emerged based on use of the VCS framework, and which makes VCS a distinctive strategy approach. Lastly, the chapter suggests when the VCS framework and approach to strategy are timely and effective to use, and under which conditions other strategy approaches might be more suitable.

1. The VCS Framework and Approach to Strategy

Value co-creation takes place in systems.

In the VCS view, the value related to a medical technology device has not been "added" to it in layers of activities involved in producing it, nor is the value of this technology "in" it, nor is it just its price minus the cost of producing and distributing it, nor is it its technical performance. Instead, the VCS approach attends to the fact that when the device is used it enables values to be created. In the contexts of care, for example, such values might include improved health, cost effectiveness, freed up time that can be used better for other care, pleasant experiences or less painful ones, feeling less distress for elder relatives who are given care, etc. The values are in the interactions between actors; the actors are in a specific system. Importantly, in the VCS view, the (co-)creation of all of these values also involves and is dependent on one or more system(s): the other actors and their activities and interactions — as helped by the device. Thus the "value" in an offering arises from the organisational or personal "values", which in turn enables the offering to be co-created.

Box 4.2: An Example of a Designed VCS

A further example of viewing values as co-created, where values have been established in use, is the "power by the hour" invention by Rolls-Royce in the jet powered airplane business (Baines *et al.*, 2007). An airline owning — say — a 747 Boeing jet, instead of having to buy five engines (the four on the plane plus a spare one in case one of the others fails or is offline for major maintenance), and investing to finance and amortise and maintain and repair these; with "power by the hour", it has a deal with Rolls-Royce where Rolls-Royce keeps ownership of the engine and installs it. Rolls-Royce charges for the power delivered by only four engines, with the airline paying only for the use it gets from these engines: per hour flown, not per planes bought or leased. The previous engine centred offering was a good with service support that often included what manufacturers often refer to as "after market" (!) services; whereas "power by the hour" is a service. Although the buyer and seller are the same, and the engine used is identical in both offerings, the "power by the hour" offering involves different work sharing and risk sharing for each party than selling engines offerings do. The "power by the hour" offering involves different co-creation, and different risk taking by each party. Thus, it is a different offering, and it implies a different VCS than is the case when the engine is bought and operated by the airline.

The VCS framework lends itself well to a strategy approach for understanding and exploring value creation happening in, being supported by, and in turn supporting systems. It invites and allows those who use it to reframe what their business is, what it could be, and to explore how more and better values can be created, and how system effectiveness can be improved.

The VCS framework, and its approach to strategy and its practices have continued to evolve over more than 20 years since 1994 when the Harvard Business Review (HBR) published an article on designing interactive strategy. It has some distinct features and assumptions about strategy and about strategy methodology (see Table 4.1). This table outlines the contents of the rest of this chapter.

2. VCS Strategy Framework Features

In the section that follows here, the distinct features of the VCS framework (the left part of Table 4.1) are described in more detail.

Table 4.1: Features of VCS Strategy Framework and Methodology

VCS strategy framework	VCS strategy methodology
• Value is (co-) created in systems of use, with intended or un-intended designs • Value creating systems are part of larger business ecologies and/or ecosystems • Focus on distinct competences, not on core ones • Strategy is about design of offerings, these link value co-creating actors • Collaboration in systems is at least as important as competition • Value co-creation seeks to make assets less dormant and reduce waste	• Qualitative analysis is at least as important as quantitative analysis in understanding a value creating system design and/or how its design emerged • Use of scenarios to explore context of the strategy helps to surface and test design assumptions • Design thinking and methodology are effective in strategic innovation where the focus of design is on designing the offering • Decision on how much co-creation to design and what to leave out is an essential aspect of effective VCS design, as is distribution of roles

2.1 Value is (Co-)Created in Systems of Use, with Intended or Unintended Designs

The VCS framework suggests that value is created in systems of use. Or rather, value is co-created in interactions between actors in such systems. As we argue in Chapter 6, where we explain work done with the international electricity utility and energy group EDF, any form or manifestation of a value creating can be described as a system that has a design — regardless if the design was explicitly intended and created or if the value creation "arose", happenstance as it were, with no one party claiming to be a designer.

2.2 VCSs are Part of Larger Business Ecologies or Ecosystems[1]

Any VCS is embedded in, and forms part of larger business ecologies (BE), with actors and their interactions that are more or less directly or indirectly linked to the VCS itself, with its configuring offering. For example, as Normann and Ramírez (1993, 1994) documented, IKEA has created a complex VCS with component manufacturers, distributors, inspirational catalogues, digital services, stores, furniture, its customers, manuals, financial services, and other actors interlinked in interactions and given specific roles and process scripts. In so doing, IKEA redefined the business of home furnishing products into one enabling a better everyday, by home to home accessible furnishing service affordable to many people. Yet, this VCS in itself is part of larger business ecologies, with other actors offering banking and road infrastructure to IKEA employees, suppliers and clients; as well as electricity and water, to their homes. This relation between the VCS and the broader business ecologies is of special interest for strategy and innovation, as an important strategic decision is what part of the wider business ecology is to be included — or excluded — from the VCS. To use Normann's words (2001), the VCS is placed in larger games that one is part of.

2.3 Focus on Distinct Competences, not on Core Ones

Building on the work of Selznick (1957), Normann argued that organisations emerge and exist if they stand for a purpose that is meaningful in the larger

[1]We thank our colleague Bill Sharpe for his precious help in clarifying this distinction between business ecosystems and VCS.

world, embodying this in its structure. Selznick called this fit the "distinct competence" that an organisation had within the larger context in which it played a role and upon which it depended. Normann pointed out that distinct competence is thus a systemic concept, based on fit between elements in a system, which is a contrast with the core competence school (e.g. Prahalad & Hamel, 1990). We — as Ramírez and Wallin (2000) did — take this argument further, suggesting that in the VCS paradigm, distinct competencies enable other actors in the system to create values, and in a way that allows the organisation to make money or generate other value from this enabling.

2.4 Strategy is About Design of Offerings, These Link Value Co-Creating Actors

Strategy is designed through offerings. Offerings link value creating actors. The focus is on interactions at least as much as on actors and actions — and often more so. A further feature of the VCS approach to strategy is the centrality of the notion of "offerings". As we saw in Chapter 3, and we see again in Chapter 5, offerings are not seen only as products or services, but as the integrating mechanisms that relate actors into a co-creative relationship system, and thereby enables them to create value and manifests how they do so together.

The offering is the script for how to mobilise and bring forth the enablement that otherwise is just "frozen knowledge" (capabilities encoded into and packed into technology, skills, processes and information), so that such capabilities can be made available to be used, "thawed" and made to flow into the situation of use where using them will help to create value.

The offering[2] is the encoded script for the organisation of the value creation. As script, the offering tells those it joins what roles they will play and hold to enable resources to be deployed in the value creation. An IKEA customer, as part of the interaction with IKEA, is instructed on how to assemble and assure the quality of the furniture she has bought at their

[2]The offering is related to but distinct from the business idea, which — to use Richard Normann's words — is "a unique, historically evolved set of factors related to each other in a pattern" (2001, p. 148) that enables the organisation to make money. The offering is to the VCS, what the business idea is to the organisation — and the orchestrating of the offering is part of the business idea.

store. The script for this is the carefully designed role for her, both in terms of expectations of what she should do, and the manual instructing her how to do that. The full script includes also other interactions, such as how she takes on some of the otherwise IKEA in-house logistics roles, as she physically identifies the location of her furniture in their warehouse — or can look for it on their online system — and bring it from the warehouse to the check out.

The offering can be dynamic, in the sense that it might include a platform, onto which others might link extensions of their VCS, just as for instance Apple's iPhone and App Store enables a myriad of app providers to link their own apps and their offerings and VCSs, in gaming, mindfulness, communities, etc.

2.5 Collaboration is at Least as Important as Competition

With the above views on systems and offerings it follows that in the VCS approach to strategy, collaboration is at least as important as competition[3] (see Ramírez and Selsky 2014, for a fuller argumentation). The decisive strength lies in how well the interactions within the VCS enable values to be co-created, i.e. on how well the actors collaborate, and how capable they are to attract and keep actors to collaborate with. This means that the roles they are offered in a VCS have to be attractive (see Chapter 6 and Appendix B). The IKEA example above illustrates this. It is the complex set of interactions, which IKEA defined, that sets its VCS apart, it is this that makes it unique and difficult to copy — and to compete against it. Yet, the system in itself will come to nothing if IKEA cannot enrol the other actors into taking on these roles and help each other to interact to produce values that suit each.

It follows that the ability to invite, interest, enrol, and mobilise others into one's VCS is more important than focusing on competing with opponents who provide similar products or services and have designed competing VCS. So, for example, an important Apple strength lies in its capacity to attract and enrol others into the Apple VCS. This includes attracting and delighting mobile device users through Apple's design thinking, but Apple also attracts a myriad of

[3]VCSs can compete with other VCSs; as well as collaborate with them.

app designers and service providers into their VCS. All these actors interact in ways scripted by Apple. Their interactions strengthen and help develop the VCS.

Another aspect of the importance of collaboration is manifested on how competing organisations also can engage each other in collaboration to achieve a common value. An example of this is how in the Premier League of English Football teams compete but they also very much collaborate not only with other teams in the same "business" but also — and importantly for this book — with many actors in other businesses and in non-businesses to keep their overall game more attractive than other sports. They thus collaborate with advertisers, TV stations and broadcasters, sponsors, owners, fans, journalists, football academies, and city authorities. If they stopped collaboration their team-to-team competition would become impossible to sustain.

Both collaboration and competition thus play roles in effective VCS designs; yet the ability to compete is dependent on, and mainly derived from, the ability to collaborate. In VCS collaborations with others — including from other fields or systems — is at the forefront of strategy, competition in the background. Collaboration helps the pie to get bigger for everyone; competition is about what size of a given pie one might take.

Of course, different VCSs often compete with each other, just as Apple competes with Google and its Android VCS in the broader business ecologies of communications, entertainment, and technology they both form a part of. Yet, both need to collaborate with each other and the authorities in terms of formats (Robles, 2015), patent reform (Levine, 2014) and security, for example. However, as we see in Chapter 10, legal issues limit how far the collaboration can extend before becoming an anti-trust case (Cheng, 2009).

The VCS framework invites and allows a focus on how to come together to "make the pie bigger", enabling better, and more varied types of value to be co-created among actors, by actors, and with and for other actors — jointly. This sets the VCS framework in stark contrast to the traditional competitive strategy school (e.g. Porter (1995) and Prahalad and Hamel (1990)) with their focus on how to take a "bigger slice" of the existing pie. As we saw in Chapter 1, Facebook and the World Economic Forum created co-productive pies and helped those they co-created these with to make them bigger.

3. Features of the VCS Strategy Methodology

After describing some of the distinguishing features of the VCS framework, we now turn to some specific aspects of VCS strategy methodology that has evolved with the use of the VCS framework. As we argue later in this chapter, these methodological characteristics are particularly useful in contexts where the ground is moving and uncertain; where neoclassical economics based strategy approaches are less effective or even potentially harmful.

3.1 Qualitative Analysis is at Least as Important as Quantitative Analysis in Understanding a Value Creating System Design and/or How its Design Emerged

Analysing strategy in qualitative terms typically precedes quantitative analysis in terms of methodology because one is considering the plausible (and not probable) pattern of co-creation fit of the interaction that makes up the design in terms of values and not only value.

Plausibility (Ramírez & Selin, 2014) helps to assess whether something might happen, not whether it will. Qualitative assessments help offering designers to create systemic understandings, to surface and challenge assumptions that existing businesses and strategies rest upon, to identify and question roles, to dig out underattended values and dormant resources, to explore potential moves of and roles for existing or new actors, and to reframe strategy and the interactions one is in.

The open system model — in contrast to the linear value chain — of thinking (Emery, 1969) both requires and allows one to let go of conceptual or emotional attachments one may have to existing, linearly arranged structures and roles. Yet, it does so iteratively and tentatively. This is one of the strengths of the VCS methodology, but also one of its challenges, as the approach is more nuanced, less step-by-step-like, less directive and self-instructive; possibly initially also less intuitive than analyses related to the value chain, such as five forces and positioning in the chain.

When using the VCS in strategy, of course, one also uses quantitative analyses to estimate potential market sizes, costs, revenues, etc. But in contrast to competitive strategy's quantitative approaches, such as the popular "waterfall" models with estimates of how much costs can be squeezed out from specific activities, the VCS-based strategy approach puts more emphasis on qualitative analysis, including such issues as what values enable co-creation in a specific system.

The VCS methodology enables and invites reflection, disagreeing perspectives, and dialogue. It involves a more genuine and courageous strategic conversation (van der Heijden, 1996, 2005) about values, about relationships and collaborations, about roles, about enrolment, about bundling and unbundling in offering design, about contradictions, about perceptions and forces at play and the businesses one now is in and could be in, and what values one could enable others to create; rather than setting off early on with unleashing number-crunching in various quantitative analyses of the existing system. Ratios and spread-sheets play a role — but only later in the analysis, to quantify implications and test viabilities.

Another aspect of the use of VCS methodology in strategy involves recognising, attending to and understanding how the existing VCS has emerged (see Chapter 6). This involves both the organisation itself and its relations with its context (the business idea, as defined both by Normann (1977, 2001) and by van der Heijden (1996, 2005)), and the configuring and support offerings that together form the VCS (see Chapter 5).

The historical understanding of how the system arose (as Christopher Alexander so elegantly analysed in his 1997 *Language of Pattern Design*, when seeing how village architectures evolved) and developed, helps one to expose and understand system dependencies, forces at play, what might be very difficult to change, neglected values, underutilised resources, etc.

As we see in Chapter 6 and in Appendix B, we have adapted and deployed Actor-Network Theory (ANT) as a good approach to map and understand the roots of VCS designs, their dependencies, and potential. As pointed out by one of its originators, Bruno Latour (2005), ANT is in spite of its name not (just) a theory, but (also) a method to explore interactions and dynamics between actors in relation to each other and at different stages of the evolution of the system that they both constitute and which constitutes them.

3.2 Use of Scenarios to Explore Context of and Assumptions in the Design of the Strategy Helps to Surface and Test Design Assumptions

The open systems inquiry and nonlinear VCS framework are particularly helpful in unstable business landscapes with contexts that are turbulent, uncertain, novel, or ambiguous ("TUNA", as per Ramírez & Wilkinson 2016), imposing both unprecedented threats and unheard-of opportunities for established or new actors. Unsurprisingly, we thus also use scenario planning in designing such VCS conditions. When using the VCS framework in TUNA environments, scenario methods are effective for exploring what business conditions the designed VCS might find itself in within a certain time-horizon, as we see in Chapter 7. Indeed, a small set of plausible scenarios consider possible contexts that the intended future business the VCS enables in a "transitional" (Amado & Ambrose, 2001) mode.

In the engagements of our consulting practice, NormannPartners, where we use the VCS approach to strategy, numerous large organisations have been supported by scenario planning in exploring plausible and different futures. They have been thus better able to test the strength or challenges of existing or new strategies and their VCS, enabling the organisations to proactively initiate VCS changes — to stay ahead in collaboration or mitigate competitive threats. We offer examples in Chapters 8 and 9.

3.3 Design Thinking and Methodology are Effective in Strategic Innovation When the Focus of Design is on Designing the Offering

VCS methodology manifests a strategy practice that has a long history of deploying design thinking and design methodology.

Design thinking in business and strategy has started to gain attention lately, following from the current emphasis and importance given to innovation and innovativeness. At the time of writing this book, the consulting firm McKinsey has recently bought the design consultancy Lunar in an attempt to bring a more creative stance to its strategy practice. In the same way, the Chinese communication group BlueFocus acquired the brand and product design consultancy Fuseproject; the US bank giant Capital One bought the products and service design consultancy Adaptive Path; and Accenture bought both Fjord and Chaotic Moon to strengthen their in-house design capabilities.

The strategy approach founded by Normann has used design thinking and methodology for more than 20 years, and its roots go back even further. VCS strategy methodology is thus unsurprisingly intimately linked to design thinking, with its focus on systems of use and its broad meaning of value as created with and for actors in the system; and to design methodology, as is described in detail in Chapter 8, with its focus on methodology for designing new VCSs. Furthermore, Chapter 6 describes how VCS design is focused on designing offerings — the offering designs manifest the VCS design.

3.4 The Decision on How Much Co-Creation to Design and What Co-Creation to Leave out is an Essential Aspect of Effective Design

When Nokia included music in its phones it became the biggest seller of MP3 players in the world. When it included cameras, it was also the world's biggest camera seller. Then — after Nokia got into trouble — it was acquired by Microsoft. In all of these examples, the bigger VCS acquired a smaller VCS. These acquisitions allowed them to make offerings available for larger numbers of co-creators, helped by lower unit prices, which in turn aided to build volumes further. However, this is not always successful. Microsoft wrote down the price of the Nokia acquisition by more than $7 billion within 15 months: the scenario for making the acquiring of the Nokia VCS financially viable was unavailable once the deal was completed.

How does one know whether one's offering and implied VCS is not about to be included — possibly against one's wishes — into a more extensive one? We saw in Chapter 1 in the case of Myspace's acquisition by News Corporation that the larger VCS logic can destroy the smaller ones, if the system has not been upframed in a way that continues to enable values being co-created by the relevant interactors — such as jointly building communities, by which Facebook continued to enable people and organisations to do together for many years thereafter. Part of the art of successfully taking on another VCS thus depends on how well one can respect its specific mode of joint value production.

Unsurprisingly then, the VCS-based design methodology can be a very effective strategic innovation process. It can be used both for assessing and for reinterpreting a business; it can be deployed for exploring the opportunity space of what it could be, and it can be used for prioritising and focusing on what it should be. Neither the process nor the realisation of strategic innovation is strictly linear, so the VCS methodology is an iterative process of disciplined imagination and enacting change; each — imagination and trying things out — informing the other.

4. How the VCS Framework is a Distinctive Strategy Approach

The VCS approach to strategy is distinctive in that it does not focus on production or "goods" or "products" or "services" as such, but on the systems in which interlinked actors co-create value.

As we saw in Chapter 2, competitive strategy has traditionally focused on maintaining or improving the strategic position of a firm and its product or service. It focused on activities and assessed strength in zero-sum games involving only others catalogued on historical criteria (now often irrelevant) as being in an existing given "industry" and/or market. Competitive advantage was said to be reached through differentiation, through superior functionality, or cost and price advantage — with any one player focusing on only one of these. There was an underlying assumption that value is economic only, created and added in steps or layers of activities structured in a value chain, in which the product or service is refined up to the point where it is transferred to a customer. As we already mentioned, the customer was in effect considered to be a value destroyer after paying for what is bought — the goods were then amortised, depreciated, written down and eventually turned into useless waste. But in this age of systems and of ecological awareness, such linear thinking exposes itself as obsolete.

What we conceive of as the "offering" was for competitive strategy manifested only in a narrower construct — the product or the service. For competitive strategy, its value was assumed to be only built up by the producer or producers (never by the client) along value chains. Locating oneself in the value chain was a big strategic decision. That approach has been a powerful and highly regarded one, and has been suitable for what is today considered to be "non-TUNA" (Ramírez & Wilkinson, 2016) contexts — that is, stable, unambiguous, and predictable business environments.

What if the potentials of creating value involve not only the producer and customer, but also other actors in the customer's context, as well as the customer as co-creators? What if there is an opportunity to redefine and redistribute roles among many actors, and that each can play multiple roles that cannot be neatly decomposed into dyadic relationships without affecting the relations with others? This is what the new owners of Myspace (in Chapter 1) misunderstood, whereas those financing and developing Facebook understood. What if it is systems of co-creation, not actors or activities that are the key to defining and designing and shaping an entirely new way of creating value, which enables more effective value creation for several interacting actors — together making a bigger and better pie?

With the VCS framework, a strategist's perspective of the business landscape is inherently taken to be a more complex setting, where the legacy industry borders and distinctions are blurred by new technology, new values and behaviours in society, by changing demographics, by new business models emerging elsewhere and by rising expectations. For instance, once people became used to not buying and keeping their own CDs but could have a much larger music selection available digitally for their access and use, CD sales diminished but a larger variety of music could be listened to in more places and shared with more people than before, enhancing the values derived from these activities and the sharing.

The same replacement of one VCS by another is visible and ongoing in myriad domains: in city transportation by Uber, in accommodation by Airbnb, indeed, in car ownership. Studies indicate that car ownership in the US may have peaked in 2006, with fewer young people who take driving licenses (Sivak, 2013). This both opens and calls for new ways of rethinking transportation and mobility. For example, Sempels and Hoffman (2013) discovered that many companies from many industries both collaborate with each other and compete to redesign mobility in Paris.

The VCS approach helps to understand, design, and redesign value co-creation, especially in networks that are fluid and dynamic in TUNA contexts. The applicability of competitive strategy on its own is limited in such situations.

A fundamental aspect of VCS is the notion that value is created in relations with counterparts, and thus the counterparts own context must be "swept into" the design of the business.

As we see in Chapter 8 with Scania, the client of someone who offers trucks creates value when using the trucks — and there will be a whole set of actors involved in this: drivers, service and workshop staff, managers of transport and mobility companies, or of retail or other companies to whom things are being transported; authorities; tax collectors; fuel suppliers, and so on. These clients may include a city governor, serving residents and consumers and workers in the city, where trucks are but an aspect of how they co-create value in terms of transport and mobility flows that can be minimised and optimised, perhaps also enabling better air quality, less time wasted in traffic jams, and enabling more time with family or at work. Understanding of the value creation — or rather the creation of various values — in these larger contexts cannot be done by adding one 1:1 relation (between a supplier and a customer) to another; it has to be studied as interactions manifested in offerings. Engaging such situations with VCS designs holds more opportunities for improving value creation, for exploring opportunities to improve efficiency, and for the orchestrating of incommensurable values in the larger system as a whole, than focusing on those who are buying a truck at a customer organisation.

Depending on how the larger system is defined, ever wider types of different actors may be included, and different opportunities — and indeed threats — may open up. Just think about how, from a truck company's perspective, a logistics VCS may be different from a transport VCS or a leasing VCS, or a retail VCS, or a city distribution VCS, or a city mobility VCS, or a quality of life VCS, or a city sustainability VCS. The VCS approach does not limit itself to the product or service category, nor to the supplier and customer relationship. It looks beyond these, and instead explores the wider context of uses and of co-creation.

5. When and Why the VCS Framework and Approach is Timely and Effective

So why, and if so when, should strategy practitioners embrace and use the VCS framework and VCS methodology? We have already illustrated this in several ways in this chapter, and round up this overview with some concluding remarks on why we think the VCS approach is gaining attention now. We also suggest reasons to use it and also when it might not be effective and thus unadvisable.

In stable business environments, with well-defined actor positions where actors can be considered to play one (or a major single) role; with little change, complexity and uncertainty, the value chain is still an effective strategy model. Dominant firms can focus on maintaining their position, and might successfully compete for power with other firms and stakeholders in zero-sum games where it is share of pie that matters.

But many of today's business environments are far from stable; they are in TUNA contexts.

As social media and digitalisation continue to transform our societies, consumers are changing behaviours, preferences, partners, suppliers, tastes, priorities, and their ability to take on new roles. More and more aspects of business and of life in our societies, such as personal transportation and mobility, goods transportation, holiday accommodation, books and storytelling, social media and games, energy production, power distribution, and many other business fields show more focus on access and use rather than on ownership. Bigger proportions of what is sold has been bought in rather than manufactured in-house[4]; though perhaps much of what is made by others is still designed by the seller and the design is licensed.

An ever more connected and interconnected society opens up new possibilities for reshaping the VCSs. These are located in broader but also ever more tightly interconnected business ecosystems or ecologies. With

[4] This applies even to material commodities, where the "service" elements matter more and more — as quality assessment, warranty management, timeliness, insurance liabilities, assuring contractual terms, and sharing all matter much more now than when it was only tonnes that were bought and sold.

such interconnection, things do not "go away" easily; so values that before could be relegated as "externalities" such as the safe disposal of materials with possible longer-term, health and environmental and social consequences, now also need to be managed. Thus, corporate social responsibilities have become more significant in corporate strategy.

As spending moves from person-to-person interfaces and analogue media to more digitalised interaction, this interactivity becomes more manifest and more visible, although the movement towards a more networked world has been arising for decades — arguably at least since 1956, when the container was invented, allowing things to be sold and bought at prices that were unimaginable before shipping networks could — with the help of the container — bring the cost down so far. This growing interconnectivity is an important part of the explanation of why strategy frameworks such as VCSs, value networks and business ecosystems are gaining ground in strategy practices today.

The VCS strategic framework as a way of articulating what design can do to intervene and shape such value co-creation is well suited to explain how value is created in such business environments. The VCS methodology offers strategists effective tools for designing the value creation in them, as we describe in the coming chapters.

Chapter 5

How Offerings Link Co-Creators in Value Creating Systems

Box 5.1: Chapter 5 at a Glance

The offering is the core unit of analysis in this book. It is a rich construct, both conceptually and in terms of practice, and it is also paradoxical. The offering manifests the relationship of co-creation between actors, and in joining them, distinguishes them from each other in terms of roles and — typically — also in terms of values. In the value creating systems (VCSs) approach to strategy, strategists design, create or change offerings that act as the organising "links" that manifest how interacting actors co-create value. With an offering, an actor is linked to another, and they act together in concert to mobilise resources in ways that enable the creation of both value and values. In VCSs, there are two kinds of offerings; configuring offerings that organise the VCS, and support offerings between two actors within the system. Offerings can be static or more dynamic and open to change by their co-creators. In a networked world, this frame poses challenges (and also new offering design tasks) for strategists. We describe five elements required to be designed into an offering: people, process, technology, information, and a risk-sharing formula. This chapter is centrally concerned with defining, describing, and analysing how offerings work and the choices involved in designing them.

1. Offerings as Value Co-Creation Relations

An offering is much more than a "product and service bundle", which is how conventional strategy considers that which is bought and sold. Rather than being only "something that is offered from a seller to a buyer", in the VCS framing of strategy, an offering is instead also the very core of the design of the VCS. Offerings are thus not reducible to "a thing" or "a service" but instead manifest a design of the relationships or interactions that enable value to be created — and they also depict the interlinked and enabled activities that a strategy brings forth.

The term "offering" was coined by Normann and Ramírez in 1989 to free the mind from the "product" versus "service" distinction, which they found obsolete and misguiding. They found it unhelpful that if a car was bought it was considered a "product" by national statisticians, whereas renting it was catalogued by them as being a "service". In the same way, if the cost of the quality control for that car was kept in-house by the manufacturer it was taken to be part of the product's production cost, but if it was bought in from a supplier it was classified as a business-to-business (B2B) "service". Instead, Normann and Ramírez proposed that all services required products to be of value, and all products required services to be of value. They called the combination of products and services "offerings". In their 1989 publication, they added "information" to the product-service make-up of offerings, and proposed that in redesigns, more service or more product or more information could take the roles any one element had performed in an established, given offering.

So how do offerings join and distinguish co-creators of value? A ticket to attend a concert is a good example of an offering joining a concert goer and a concert organiser. For the concert goer, the ticket states the conditions for attending — when to arrive, where to sit, when the concert ends, etc. For the concert organisers the ticket manifests the conditions of who is to pay for seating in each place in the theatre: better places have higher prices. So the ticket offering implies work sharing between client and supplier. The conditions on the ticket also state who takes what risks: the ticket conditions will indicate what happens if the concert goer is late or cannot come; or indeed if it is the musicians who are those that fail to show up. When coming together as specified in the ticket, the concert organiser and the concert goers co-create the concert — of course, also co-creating the concert with whomever is playing — with whom the concert organisers will have another offering joining them and specifying terms for co-creating the concert.

Box 5.2: Offerings in Business

Offerings are well accepted as a term in business language. One accepts a job offer. Firms that want to go public make public offerings (of shares) in stock markets, and firms that want to buy another "offer" a given amount for it, which the board of the potential acquisition may accept or reject. Thus, for owners of a firm the offering their firm makes for them as owners may be shares and dividends and profits and shareholder meetings; for investors the offering may be shares or bonds and returns; with employees the firm enters into work contract offerings; with customers and suppliers it relates by offering the goods and services and payment terms and warranties; the firm offers press releases and interviews with its key executives to the press, which then writes articles about the firm; and the firm offers analysts and NGOs presentations, strategies, conference calls and Q&A sessions.

Depending on the role that any one offering provides for it, a given actor may be labelled to be (primarily) a "partner", "producer", "supplier", "client", "customer", "distributor", "retailer", "middleman", "transporter", "insurer", and so on. It is important to note that it is the architecture or design of the offering that designates this role, not the intrinsic nature of an actor. It is also important to note that any one actor may have multiple roles when participating in multiple offerings — one may be a customer when buying bread, and a supplier when coaching an executive, and a partner when playing doubles in badminton. In fact, one may have two roles in relation to one counterpart: one may be a coach to the bread maker and a customer when buying her bread. This multiple role reality happens all the time in business: Verizon may be a competitor with AT&T in some offerings, a partner in others, and a supplier in yet others.

The Normann and Ramírez notion of the offering that we use here focuses both on value in use and on value as expected, not on value as an end result of historical activities (i.e. "value added").

2. Two Types — Configuring and Supporting Offerings

Offerings are designed, organising conditions of the interactors' value creating activities. We distinguish between two types of offerings. The "configuring" offering is the main offering that configures a given VCS; it is called "configuring" because it is the one that sets the conditions for the other offerings that together orchestrate the value creating in the VCS.[1] The "supporting" offerings support the configuring offering and together enact the co-creating in the VCS. So, for example, for the fourth violinist in a symphony orchestra, the contract she has to play in a given concert may be — for her — the main offering (and it may well configure her family's activities around her practice and playing schedule, including that evening); but for the symphony orchestra that entered into an agreement with the concert organiser to play that evening, the contract with the fourth violinist is a support offering.

Typically, it is the configuring offering that defines or contains the conditions for the support offerings. But as we will see in several examples such as those of EDF in Chapter 6, a given configuring offering can be replaced by what had been a support offering — for example, if economic imperatives frame a political arrangement as no longer viable; then the economic relations offering becomes the configuring one, and the political one — say transforming a given set of relations with local officials because of the economic changes — the support offering. In the same way, if a public outcry brings politics back to the fore; what had been a technical or commercial configuring offering defining the VCS takes on the less important role of being a support offering — as happened to British Petroleum (BP) in the Deepwater Horizon offshore platform disaster, where legal and political offerings become the configuring ones. How actors are linked in VCSs to co-create offerings is illustrated in Figure 5.1.

---

[1] Normann and Ramírez (1993, 1994); Ramírez and Wallin, (2000); and Normann (2001), where the firm that designed the configuring offering is called the "prime mover".

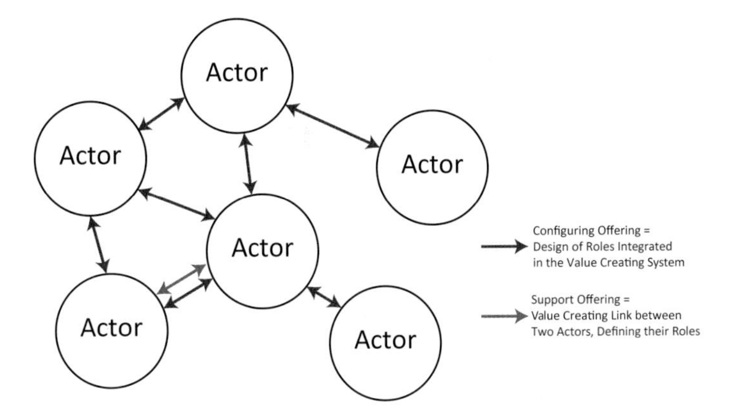

Figure 5.1: The Configuring Offering and Support Offerings

The focus of the configuring offering is not limited to the narrow transactional linear relation of the buyer–seller, but also brings in and mobilises the larger context of any counterpart — regardless of whether in the VCS they hold the role of "customer" or "supplier" or "partner"; or other roles or several of these roles simultaneously. The support offering organises the specific value creation and roles between two interlinked actors.[2]

The design of the offering helps strategists to understand how comparative advantage is deployed to organise more effective VCSs.

Comparative advantage matters in offering design because it is not good to spend time and resources doing something badly that someone else can do well at a lower cost.[3] The growing ease of buying in the resources one needs to co-create value, only when needed, was taken to be the prime reason for why the very nature of a company is being profoundly "reinvented" by entrepreneurial organisations like Uber and Airbnb (Anderson, 1995).

Offerings thought of as redesigns for more effective value co-creation enable exploration of new ways of organising existing interactions; as The

[2]The offering manifests the relationship of co-creation between actors. In joining the actors and their interaction, it also distinguishes them from each other in terms of roles installing and often in terms of values.

[3]This (obviously) must include transaction costs — the cost of finding, choosing, buying, and installing that which is bought.

Economist put it, this redesign efficacy allowed "WhatsApp to persuade Facebook to buy it for $19 billion despite having fewer than 60 employees and revenues of $20 million" (*op.cit*: 11).

Understanding the offering as the designed organising of co-creative relationships between and among actors can help open up new opportunity spaces for value creation; it can also help free the executive's mind from falling into the trap of deploying the usual suspects for the "next" strategic planning cycle: the first usual suspects that can be gotten rid of often are the existing product or service categories or definitions.

To illustrate the offering as a designed organising of a VCS, let us consider the example of internet cafés, and the Scandinavian company Sidewalk Express, started in 2001.

The traditional internet cafés introduced back in the 1990s used to be a place one walked into, and where one could pay for using a computer to access the internet for a specific time. This offering was attractive to travellers who did not want to lug a heavy PC with them. The company running the café bought or leased computers, which they made available for customers for prepaid timeslots of 30 minutes, 1 hour or more, paying typically around 6 euros per hour. After some time of use, the computers were gradually replaced by new computers, or it was the furniture that was replaced. The main costs for running this offering were the capital cost for the computers and the furniture, the broadband and connection costs, the store rent, insurance, and personnel. It was a production and product-focused business; perhaps a "productified" service, but still with a product logic at its core offering — the product being a standardised, generic service.

Then after a while, internet cafés became a bit more service oriented, looking upon the business not just as renting access to connected computers, but more as a service business. Those in that business learned more about the people coming into the café, and saw that they could provide other services and products too, linked to communications or to what one might want to do when communicating: faxing, printing, or even having a coffee or taking a quick meal. These entrepreneurs started to shift the business logic to seeking knowledge about the customer and treating this knowledge as a source for new value creation opportunities, developing their offering to involve a greater density of activities and values (i.e. per hour in the café, or per square meter of rent) in the relations between the organiser of the café and its activities and the people entering the cafés.

The creators of the company Sidewalk Express took this development further by designing and making available an offering that redefined the VCS. Having worked with Normann and later also co-founding NormannPartners, the serial entrepreneur Fredrik Arnander has a profound understanding of the VCS logic. He "unbundled" several elements that had made up the offerings of the prior generation of an internet café, and instead rearranged the offering by mobilising a number of underutilised resources. He did so by deploying a superior understanding of the temporal and spatial aspects of the use situations affecting potential users — realising that people in the age of broadband access and widely available Wi-Fi may still want to access the internet with larger screens when not at home or at work — which had been the traditional turf of the internet cafes.

The new offering he designed responded to what people valued as access when they were on the go and when they had a bit of time to spare or use productively when they were in underutilised spaces, where the physical flow for these people is temporarily slowed down. Sidewalk Express does not have any traditional internet cafe spaces. Instead, it operates a chain of internet access points in busy places where people wait, or where they take a break. In Northern Europe, Sidewalk Express changed what an internet café had been, by inhabiting small spaces in other shops or waiting halls — at gas stations, burger chains, convenience stores, train stations, airports; thereby creating an new kind of offering that enabled activation of a set of underutilised resources (e.g. under-used spaces, and people having "free time" in waiting places) and new revenues for actors such as the space owners.

Sidewalk Express attracted people into those otherwise under-used places, or made it logical and attractive for them to stay longer at places which would be otherwise unattractive (think of a wide, under-used, secondary airport corridor), so they could use larger flat screens and very easy to use systems. The space uses can be traded in the Sidewalk Express offering — a ticket allows access that can be used in another Sidewalk Express site located elsewhere too.

The VCS of Sidewalk Express was based on bundling in three components into its innovative offering design — the location, the quality of the service (good computers with broadband access), and the price.

Sidewalk Express' novel offering organised the relations among relevant actors (space owners, real estate companies, hardware suppliers, broadband infrastructure providers, and advertisers) to make available an attractive service that enabled the users to create value (check flights, communicate, share documents), in the best locations and with a very low price, around 1 euro per hour, thereby quickly outcompeting the traditional internet cafés.

As Sidewalk Express attracted consumers into existing venues such as coffee shops, where they bought an extra coffee as they stayed a bit longer to use the internet; so in many of these venues, Sidewalk Express got access to the spaces for free or at a very low fee.

The computers and other equipment were leased, and serviced by sub-suppliers. Gradually other activities and actors were integrated into the VCS, such as advertisers with a pay per click advertising business model.

Sidewalk Express designed and orchestrated the VCS that it had envisioned. It was not competing with traditional internet cafés, but had a new and fresh perspective on the context of use and it created a new offering that configured a new VCS. The VCS strategy manifested in the Sidewalk Express novel configuring offering design made the pie bigger for the actors involved: internet users "on the go" got access to large screens in convenient locations and more effectively and productively used their time available at waiting spots — making them better employees, consultants, and family members. City centre cafés and restaurants with unused or underutilised space attracted more customers, and kept them in their premises longer — increasing turnover of their other offerings. Computer equipment and service providers increased their business and grew it into a new niche, as did the leasing company that benefited from carrying the capital expense. Pay per click advertisers more effectively reached out to more potential customers in their target groups. Airport corridors got rental income. Sidewalk Express and its pay per click advertising sister company were rewarded with different and new profitable revenue streams at low fixed costs.

Sidewalk Express created a new configuring offering that enabled a new business that was not competing with any existing businesses, and that was built up by the unique configuring offering and the support offerings organising co-creation of value and values between individual actors.

Sidewalk Express is a brilliant example of a configuring offering design that redefined co-creation and unlocked new value potentials, in a newly designed and orchestrated a VCS.

Then in 2007, the rise of mobile broadband and wider penetration of smartphones led Sidewalk Express to transform itself into a digital outdoor advertising chain, offering advertisers an attractive advertising channel through its more than 2,000 installed large screens across northern Europe — while offering consumers internet access for free. By changing the configuring offering yet again it again transformed its role and its VCS, and moved its business development to a next stage in its evolution.

Sidewalk Express is an example of an actor who designed and orchestrated a VCS; and then redesigned it. The configuring offering defined roles and interactions that help those who participate in the VCS to create value and values, as we explore in the next section.

3. Configuring Offerings as the Design of the System of Interactions

A crucial competence in a networked world is to be able to design configuring offerings that organise systems of value creation. The configuring offerings set out the interactions and resulting roles that mobilise, and in that sense activate and engage interacting actors supported by capabilities and resources to jointly create value.

The design of successful configuring offerings like those of Facebook and WEF seen in Chapter 1, or those of IKEA in Chapter 4, or Sidewalk Express as seen above, manifest an imagined and realised set of interactions that help value creators to access untapped or underutilised resources that they use to co-create innovative value because they are better organised to do so by that configuring offering.

Designed configuring offerings join several interactors to reallocate capabilities and resources, getting them to work together more effectively, as Sidewalk Express illustrates so well. They can also mobilise capabilities and resources that were previously unavailable, such as helping people to meet other people more effectively as Facebook and WEF have done; in so doing they are ensuring that as many interactors as possible benefit by becoming more effective value co-creators.

Our notion of configuring offerings has similarities with Eisenhardt and Martin's definition of dynamic capabilities: "A firm's processes that use resources — specifically the processes to integrate, reconfigure, gain and release resources — to match and even create market change" (Eisenhardt & Martin, 2000: 1107). However, Eisenhardt and Martin's focus is on individual firms, not on systems of interactions that extend beyond a singular firm. Our understanding of capabilities is closer to Blois and Ramírez (2006) who described capabilities as "repeatable patterns of action in the use of assets to create, produce and deliver offerings" (p. 1027). As both configuring and support offerings extend beyond the singular organisation, we see offerings as constituted by elements that include capabilities as well as resources, helping co-creators to organise and utilise both. We return to this later in this chapter, in particular, when describing offering elements.

The design of a configuring offering can be rather "static", with relations fixated for long times, as happened with the invention of the typewriter. That stability is something valued in many contexts. Our colleague Bill Sharpe has argued that stabilising the design of calculators so teachers could teach their students to use them every year was a key to success, even as the calculator's prowess was developed year on year.

Or the offering can involve more of a "learning" interaction[4] such as that offered by eBay and PayPal to help individual, commercial, and NGO sellers and buyers to trade ever faster and more securely with trustworthy payments, enabling more and more efficient market behaviours with more choice and speed for trading goods and information, adding enhanced value creating density in terms of more actors who can co-create more value with yet more other actors across time and space gaps.

---

[4]Ramírez and Mannervik (2008) called these learning offerings "enclaves".

Ramaswamy (2009) similarly argued that value is a function not of products, but of experiences — such as those found upon using web platforms for consumer interactions in communities with others. He, like us, also suggested that value is created in interactions between individuals everywhere in a system, and thought that organisations would be well advised to become organised to function around them, suggesting that thinking of value in this manner calls for a shift of mindset for the leaders of such organisations.

Google, as described in the book *In the Plex* (Levy, 2001), has designed many support offerings. Its search engine configuring offering enables a clear and straightforward individual user experience, which helps to attract many other actors into its VCS. Google adjusts its interface and interaction according to users' behaviours and learns from this exchange: its algorithm tracks interactions (in the language of this book, it relates offerings to each other) and links interactions — not events or actions or actors or users. The Google configuring offering is very much an interactive learning offering design, and as such is what we call a dynamic configuring offering. One can thus say that Google's VCS is designed to co-evolve with the behaviour of the actors it has enrolled in its value constellation — people searching the web, advertisers, those who want to be known, suppliers of infrastructure and software, app writers, etc.

Ramaswamy and Ozcan (2014) described how organisations like eBay, Google, and Apple design and build what they called "co-creation platforms of engagement". These platforms were designed so that various stakeholders can come together to co-create value. Each brings in their own individual domain of experience, comparative advantage, resources, networks, and capabilities to co-create value — often new value. Enterprises (which can be public, private, or social) participate and gain learning and new strategic capital; stakeholding individuals participate and gain increased experience of value and wellbeing, which can include increased wealth and welfare.

4. The Design of Dynamic Offerings in the Networked World

In their chapter "Designing VCSs", Ramírez and Mannervik (2008) described how the role of design has changed as the character of offerings has changed over time. They outlined how in the complex, networked world that characterises 21st century business so far, companies like eBay and PayPal combine to help sellers and buyers to benefit each other — in their case, with widely available secure payments. The design of this co-evolution configuring offering design masters two fundamental design challenges of the networked world: to help others navigate the complexity; and to design stability enclaves that help control or reduce the complexity for those in the enclave. In that world, Google has designed a clear and straightforward user experience that, as seen above, is adjusted according to their behaviour as it learns from changes in the interactions and links among the interactions. Google helps people searching the web to better "surf" the universes of complexity, connectivity, risks and potential new VCS for which its users provide links. Its configuring offering design also helps many others to make the dynamic and learning support offerings that help users to create value together stable enough so that all concerned can profit from them.

Over time, the design of offerings has involved shifts in both the view of the customer as a value creator and of what is considered as a distinctive capability. As we illustrate with Figure 5.2, the focus has shifted from the product-focused business strategy approach that characterised the neoclassical view of strategic planning (Ramírez & Selsky, 2014), to then

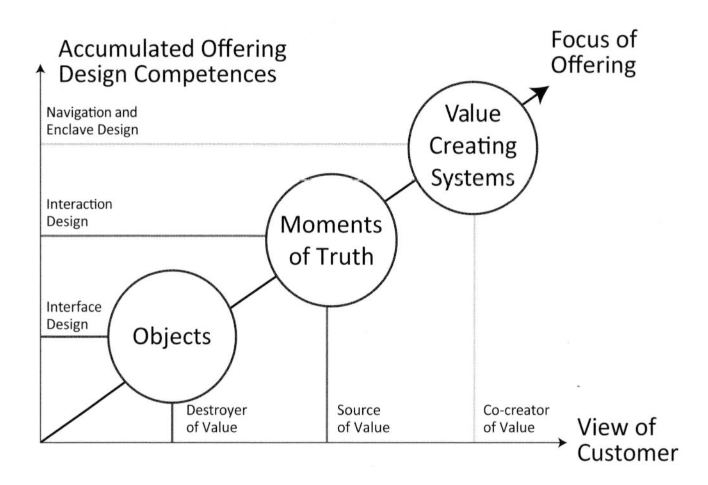

Figure 5.2: Evolution of the Design of Configuring Offerings

move onto a second stage where customer relations became a focus when service thinking and management emerged (initially in Scandinavia and France the 1980s, as is seen in the Appendix A), exemplified with the notable SAS configuring offering invention of Business Class, which enrolled support offerings such as premium lounge and in-flight services, unique deals on rental cars and hotel nights, and so on.

At the core of the service focus of the SAS business class as a configuring offering design was the guiding notion that value was created in the "moment of truth" where the customer and supplier encountered each other as the service was executed. Each "moment of truth" involved a support offering — like dedicated checking-in lines at the airport.

Prior to the service era, the key offering design competence had been to shape the interfaces between the objects, processes, and people, provided by the supplier. In many cases, the customer was relegated to an anonymous and underattended category, which was "the market" or "the end user". The implicit view of customers was that they destroyed the value built up by the producer or supplier in the production process of the object (Ramírez, 1999). A big advance in the "service decades" that followed was to instead view the customer as the source of the value that the service provider was to enable. Yet, even today customer bases do not appear on the balance sheet of companies — and are only valued as assets during a merger or acquisition in terms of "installed product" base or "footprint".

Service-centric configuring offering design thus moved the focus from the product onto the "moments of truth", the series of well-defined but only episodic interactions that enabled the promised value to actually be co-created by client and supplier (Normann, 1985; Eiglier & Langeard, 1987).

Yet now, this too is becoming obsolete in the networked world and its co-evolution of connections and interactions. The interactions in the era of ubiquitous computers, where users can interact with computing in many different forms such as laptops, smartphones, tablets, terminals in everyday objects, all connected to each other and data centres with 4G and Wi-Fi broadband, involve a denser set of co-creating possibilities. This makes the context exhibit greater complexity, and connectivity can be both an asset and a liability or distraction. Here, an important challenge for designing configuring offerings are navigation (or sensemaking) and enclave (or stability) so that customers and other actors can not only co-create value, and jointly learn to co-create it better with dynamic configuring offerings; but also hold reasonably stable roles and identities (see the description of Actor Network Theory (ANT) in Chapter 6 and Appendix B).

In other words, in this world the customer and the supplier want to join the producer not only in co-creating but also in co-designing.

All counterparts are now brought together to participate actively and positively in the co-design and co-construction of their VCS — and indeed, in their redesign and change.

Design of dynamic configuring and support offerings in the networked world encompasses co-evolving, partially overlapping, sets of VCS. It also involves multiple values, which need to be reconciled rather than optimised — very much in "pluralistic settings" (Denis *et al.*, 2007) where no one objective, priority, metric, or parameter can be used to assess and organise the others.

In a networked world, co-designed configuring offerings imply that strategy is as important in terms of collaborative advantage as it is in terms of competitive advantage — perhaps even more so. It is a world of business where those who design offerings with others create better design and value than others who do not collaborate in the designing.

5. Good Offerings Address Strategic Challenges

In his book *Good Strategy/Bad Strategy* (2012), Rumelt suggested that one of the hallmarks of a good strategy is that it is clear about what challenge it addresses. Good strategy also helps those that use it to make choices on how to address the challenge. We consider that this is also valid for good offering designs.

Good offerings address strategic challenges that have hitherto hampered the efficacy to co-create value for the offering designer and its co-creators. A good offering design does so by deploying and activating resources, by rearranging relationships and roles in such a configuration that the resulting VCS can overcome that which had hampered the efficacy. The resulting offering design is built from insight into strengths and weaknesses, opportunities and threats, underutilised resources, comparative advantage, accessible capabilities, and especially the relations among these — so that the design brings forth (and in that sense creates and manifests) strategies that interlink actors and their activities in new and better ways.

An important task for the strategist, business developer, and (of course) the CEO or head of a division who is a configuring offering designer is thus to clarify what challenges the offerings are seeking to address, or enable their organisation to do so — possibly "interactively" with others as Normann and Ramírez (1993a) suggested.

In this book, we consider how such challenges can be defined and how in VCS terms they are considered business development opportunities. For the purpose of offering design, we mean one and the same thing with these terms.

As we have seen in earlier chapters, the challenges need to be framed at a higher logical typing (upframed, see Chapter 3) than had been the case prior to redesign coming into action. How one chooses to up-frame the VCS — that is, to consider the current VCS from the perspective of a broader context than is done on everyday operational (or short-term strategy) work — is one of the core design choices to succeed. We illustrated this in Chapter 3 using the example of Scania, whose customer's user system and challenges were different whether the issue was to be up-framed as a consumer of trucks VCS, as a transport VCS, as a logistics VCS, as a retail VCS, or a mobility VCS. We explore this further in Chapter 8, providing methodology guidelines for understanding the historical roots and dependencies of a VCS, for exploring its future context, and for the designing of offerings that bring forth strategic VCS innovations.

6. Five Offering Elements

In 1989, Normann and Ramírez suggested that an offering is built up by three elements: people, physical goods and information. The three elements could be thought of as dimensions, and the total potential offering design space as a cube, as is seen in Figure 5.3.

With the simple example of an offering that allows one to listen to live music, there is oneself, the others in the audience and the players plus the ushers and the technicians and so on ("people"); the programme and the music sheets and the fire exit signs and the "knowledge/taste/

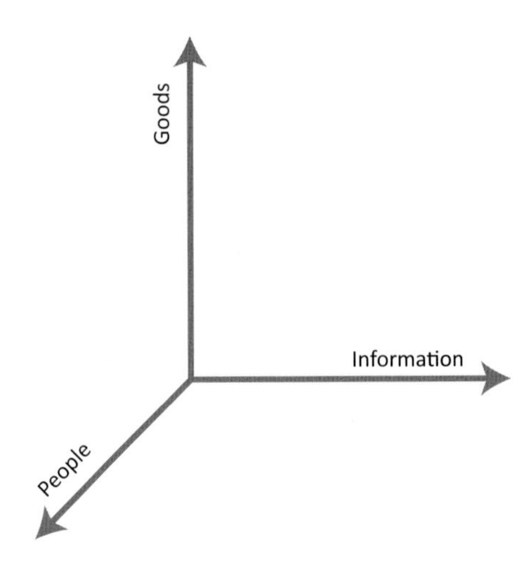

Figure 5.3: The Offering as a 3D Space of Potential Designs

appreciation" in every ones' minds ("information"); and all kinds of physical entities such as musical instruments, chairs, the stage, the theatre roof, etc. ("physical goods") that have been orchestrated together into the offering. In 1989, Normann and Ramírez suggested that a new offering design could unbundle some of these features and separate them from each other, as Arnander did with Sidewalk Express. Or in another offering design these elements could be bundled anew, as with the invention of the CD player.

The authors argued that a lot of offering redesign involved exchanging the role done by one of the components so it could be done by another; the vacuum cleaner (the good plus information as instruction manual) did away with the cleaner and allowed the hired help (people) to be replaced by the resident in the house to clean for him or herself far faster.

Four years later, in 1993, Normann and Ramírez suggested that the offering design could also involve a change of what each person does. Thus, the offering design would change who does what — a given offering that "relieves" someone from doing something himself can be replaced with another offering with a design that instead "enables" him to do it better. For example, eBookers has replaced what travel agents used to do — one can shop for the best flights oneself.

Normann and Ramírez matched this "work sharing" dimension of offering design with a "risk sharing" one: a new offering may pass the risk

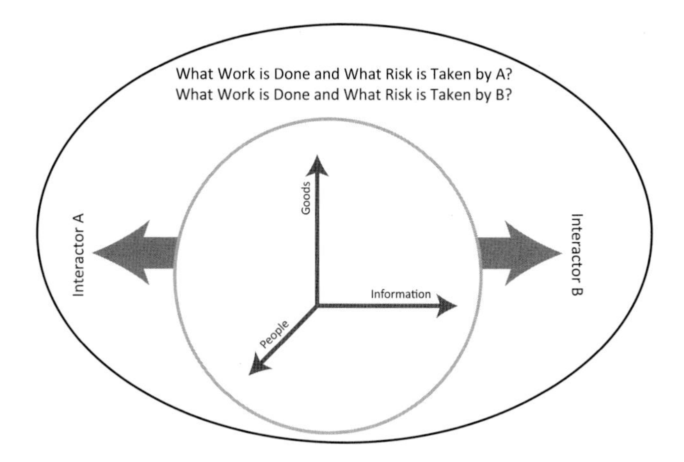

Figure 5.4: The Offering as a 5D Space of Potential Designs

one took to someone else (travel insurance) or instead allow one to take on risks more effectively (bonus or no malus pricing of insurance).

The enhanced opportunity spaces for offering design that resulted from adding these elements are depicted graphically in Figure 5.4.

From our more recent experience in consulting engagements with large firms in offering development, we have found it of help to expand that 1993 framework by adding the element "process". In the illustration here, "process" depicts the various standardised and repeatable formats that have been developed for interacting, and which can benefit from learning curve effects to render them more efficient, such as playing instruments together competently, doing soundchecks, marketing the event, welcoming people and filling and emptying the music theatre. This view of the "process" element is similar to how Blois and Ramírez (2006) described capabilities, which were taken to be "repeatable patterns of actions in the use of assets to create, produce and deliver offerings" (*ibid.*). As the term "process" thus depicts a repeatable pattern of action utilising resources to create or co-create value, its addition helps to consider offerings as consisting of both capabilities and resources.[5] We have in some of these engagements also found it of help to reinterpret the 1989–1993

[5]In this light, process is not something external to the offering, but is an intrinsic part of it, and thus one of its elements.

offering element "physical goods" as "technology" (see Chapter 6 for an ANT view as well as Appendix B, where "technology" is more precisely defined). Technology includes both hardware and software.

These more numerous elements can still be made to substitute for each other with a new offering design. Thus, if processes of recording and uploading are added to a music listening offering, as well as the required technology to do these interactions and to support transmission and listening, one can enjoy the "same" concert, but now it is streamed, in one's home. This novel offering requires another set of interactions by oneself and many suppliers, plus audio devices, along with one's living room, but not the original musical instruments, players or concert hall. Of course, the concert is not experienced in quite the same way in the two cases. Each can involve the same piece and the same performers with the same conductor in the same music venue, but the offerings, while obviously related, are different.

So a way to think about this that our clients have found of help is to consider the particular combination and integration of the four other elements — the combination and integration in the offering design that allocates different work tasks and risks to different actors and their interactions — as itself being a fifth element in the offering. We refer to this fifth element in several parts of this book as the "work and risk sharing" involved in an interaction or as it appears across the whole VCS. This fifth element seeks to reconcile and to balance the four other elements with each other. Its role is thus the very allocation of interaction roles, and of which risks each interaction should carry and — as compensation — what value creation it enables. As such, the offering designer pays specific attention to this fifth offering element. We thus consider an offering to consist of five elements that are mobilised though interactions in the VCS that the offering brings forth: (1) people who have different roles and skill sets and interact with each other, (2) processes that enable the conducting of given interactions, (3) technology both in terms of the enabling hardware and software, (4) information, or structured data that are codified references to interaction patterns that can be brought to use, and (5) the work sharing and risk sharing formula integrating the other four elements within a system of interactions. A given offering thus includes the elements in a specific combination to enable value to be co-created — this is graphically depicted in Figure 5.5.

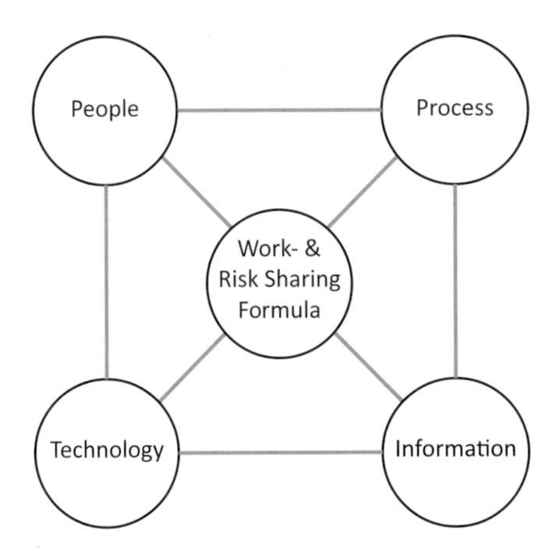

Figure 5.5: Five Elements in the Offering

We illustrate how this set of offering elements informs the transition by the medical technology company General Electric (GE) Healthcare from a product offering focused business to an offering focused on outcomes and the bringing together of a collaborative system of stakeholders (see Herhausen *et al.*, 2011).

In 2005, GE Healthcare identified two contextual factor developments that were believed to have considerable impact on healthcare, and thus on their business. These were the increasing shortage of public resources available to pay for care, and the effects of ageing populations for increasing demand for healthcare. Together, both factors implied cost pressures on medical technology products, including those offered by GE Healthcare, such as their imaging technology MRI scanners. This analysis led to GE Healthcare's embarking on the "ecomagination" initiative in 2006, and in 2009 the wider global strategic initiative "healthymagination".

Assessments of the care systems in which GE's technologies were used, including mapping of the stakeholders involved in MRI scanning care procedures and in wider and relevant parts of care, showed that what was valued was not so much the technical performance of the products, but instead the quality of care, the access to care, and also reduced care costs. They found that these values were not the result only of the product characteristics, but instead concerned a system-level set of outcomes in which different actors are interlinked and collaborate. Thus, GE Healthcare

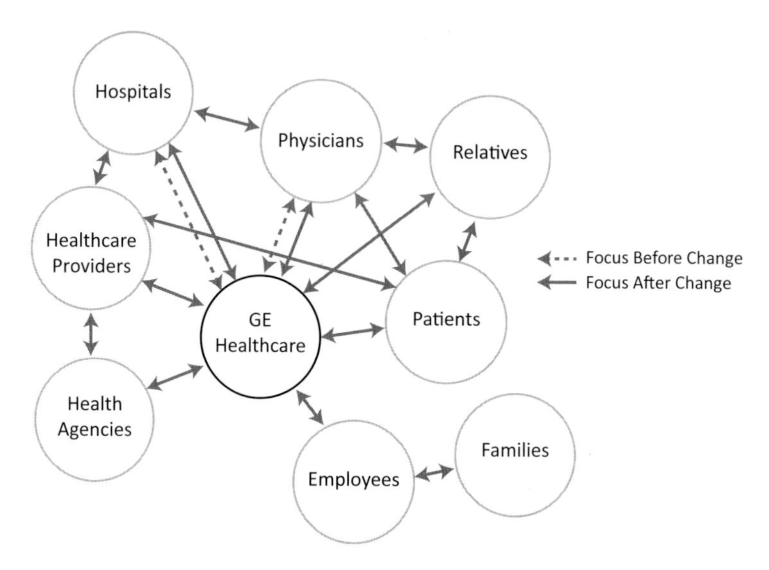

Figure 5.6: A Care VCS of GE Healthcare (illustration based on Herhausen *et al.*, 2011)

realised, what they could design was what in the language of this book can be described as a compelling configuring offering. This configuring offering sought to enable the provision of better care to more people at lower cost. To justify the cost of the scanners, it was important to be able to better enable what was valued by other actors in the system, so GE Healthcare took a big step forward into redefining its configuring offering from a technology-based, product-focused offering into instead a solutions and outcomes-based offering. This novel business design in our terms brought forth a novel VCS, see Figure 5.6.

An important element in this strategic shift was to develop measurable system outcome targets relating to the three main system values aimed for — lower cost, higher quality of care and better access to care. This involved a call for innovation projects both internally and externally, including open innovation sourcing to achieve the three objectives.

Given that the shift involved offering system solutions, and not a products-centred offering, GE Healthcare had to change its interactions and roles. From primarily a B2B company with a limited focus on direct clients and users such as hospitals and physicians — it now had to also consider broader system actors such as the patients being treated; their relatives and their concerns, opinions and views of the care for their loved ones; the healthcare related government organisations; other care providers; and relevant cooperation partners for other parts of care in the systems where GE Healthcare medical technologies were used.

Improving the system outcomes that GE Healthcare aimed for was not something they could achieve on their own. Instead, again in the language of this book, they created a configuring offering in which they enrolled various new actors and their interactions into a myriad of support offers (see Chapter 6 and Appendix B for more detail on enrolling). This they undertook as a global initiative, and the specifics of the configuring offering did of course differ in different parts of the world. To enable the configuring offering they developed a set of support offerings, enrolling people such as process experts from other parts of GE, who could work together with GE healthcare's medical technology technicians, mapping and improving processes in the care systems, and increasing utilisation rates of existing care infrastructure. GE Healthcare also acquired IT companies to develop software for healthcare providers. Partnerships enabled access to other technologies and processes, such as their partnering with clinics and health agencies to conduct analysis to gain better information of people's health habits and to enable improvements on how people communicate with their physicians.

The initiative went beyond the enabling of actual care, to also include communication with wider audiences to promote healthier lifestyles, and relevant values, and improved outcomes in the larger system. This promotion of better health also included their own employees and their families, which were seen as part of the wider health system. To support this a new IT firm was created in a JV with Microsoft, combining Microsoft's capability of building platforms and "information ecosystems" with GE's healthcare capabilities to jointly enable the clinical creation of value to enhance the health of whole populations (Millard, 2012). These internal new roles and relations and the co-creation with external stakeholders implied new allocations of work and risk across the VCS.

GE Healthcare's experience illustrates how replacing a traditionally product centric offering into a VCS can get a whole company to broaden its scope. A new configuring offering that includes and orchestrates value co-creation in the care system gets many actors to help each other to co-create many values.

7. Offering Evolution

To further analyse and describe offering design and risk sharing choices work we use the example of the development of offerings by what is now known to be the Shell Global Solutions (SGSI) company.[6]

The Royal Dutch Shell Group, with origins going back to 1907, was formed through the merger of Royal Dutch Petroleum Company of the Netherlands and the Shell Transport and Trading Company of the UK. This merger was done largely to be more competitive against the big American petroleum companies. For decades the responsibilities had roughly been divided so that the commercial side was driven from London and the technical side from The Hague. Up until early 1970s and the oil crises, world energy demand went up by 10% each year, keeping technical people in The Hague very busy with increasing global Shell refinery capacity.

The technology unit within what in Shell was called "Manufacturing" (and in other companies "refining" and/or "petro-chemicals") employed many young engineers and people with practical experience as well as top-notch scientists. It was a very technically oriented outfit. The contacts with refineries were managed through a small group of liaison people. The unit in that early period appeared to always be short of professionals, as the growth in energy consumption that started after World War II continued. But growth started to slow in the 1970s and reached a plateau during the first oil crisis in 1973. After that the high growth did not return.

[6]This case study description was produced for a client who wishes to remain anonymous but has granted us permission to use it here. It is based on publicly available information and half a dozen interviewees (current and former Shell executives), documents on SGSI which are publicly available, and on our own experiences. We excluded any normative opinion on what Shell should have done. To the best of our knowledge the opinions of the executives whom we interviewed reflect a credible overview of the history of SGSI: we strived to cross-check inconsistencies amongst our interviewees (some of whom had been colleagues, and some clients, of NormannPartners professionals at different points in the past) as much as possible; and we are reasonably confident that the story we report in this document is accurate. Specific reliable numbers, describing the size and profitability of the activity, at various points in time, have not been available outside Shell.

It is important to underline that the Manufacturing organisation had been designed in, and for, high growth. When growth slowed down, the technical staff in The Hague kept busy with maintenance activities and enhancements, while still working to provide technical expertise, despite global refinery overcapacity. The Centre staff in Manufacturing worked like this: "*Someone in a refinery had a problem, they rang the Centre and (the) response was (almost) always "here is a new technology""*.[7] This was possible for two reasons — First, central costs incurred by staff units, such as those in The Hague on behalf of the corporation, were allocated to decentralised Shell operating companies (such as those that operated refineries) through a service fee mechanism, which was not based on service rendered but on static company-wide parameters such as revenue, size and throughput (i.e. the offering design worked more like a "tax on operating companies" than as a "fee-for-service" offering). Second, following a huge reduction in oil demand, Shell's technical unit saw much more demand for enhancements where they had unique, specialised expertise like hydrocracking and distillation engineering or heat integration.

A commissioned "customer study" into the views of about 100 internal clients (in the operating companies) of the technology centre showed that many of the clients thought that they "got very little value out of the manufacturing central organisation" — partly, we feel, because the most demanding and most sophisticated clients had their own staffs anyway; and partly because the poorer clients could be helped by the most sophisticated ones (particularly if they were located closer to each other than to the experts in the The Hague offices). Thus, expectations from some of the more sophisticated refineries regarding risk-bearing and work-sharing were not met.

The two oil price shocks in the 1970s made it necessary to rethink many parts of the energy businesses. In what had been the Upstream (exploring, finding, and "producing" the oil crude) business, the necessity to reconsider how things were done was smaller (as prices were high), but in the downstream (refining the crude into different products, transport, trading, distribution, and retailing — sometimes also including the petrochemicals associated businesses) business, refinery margins were getting squeezed. It soon became evident that as refining had been considered a

[7]Interview with a former Shell Manufacturing Board of Management member.

"critical" national interest strategic factor by many governments, who encouraged locating a refinery in their own country, a lot of refinery overcapacity had been built up over the years in ways that the low margins underlined as unviable. Refineries all over the world — and within Shell too — had to learn to operate more commercially and to a larger extent than before, to compete with each other.

This change in the context meant that the extant approach in Shell's Manufacturing Technology Centre started to be seen as no longer "fit for purpose".

Also, the ethos of promoting "technical excellence at any cost" at the core of the Technology Centre's offering had to be reconsidered: as refineries had to compete harder and needed to act more commercially, they no longer had the human and professional resources and the money needed to continue investing in the latest technologies every time the Centre suggested it.

In addition, a number of external, competent, and agile consulting engineering firms had seen this change and they were proposing offerings to refineries far better suited to their new needs than the "latest good and information-centric offering" that the "the Hague centre" had been offering them.

The engineering contractors were not only offering solutions at less cost, they had also started to develop more complete services in process engineering and construction. With Shell's highly decentralised organisation at the time (a 3D matrix consisting of operating companies, geographies, and functions accounted for some 200 CEO's with profit and loss operating responsibilities[8]), these companies approached individual Shell refineries sending proposals directly to them. The refineries were accustomed to paying huge service fees for the not bespoke, standardised offerings the Manufacturing unit in the Hague had provided for them out of what for them was seen as general corporate taxation. This old, "defined from the centre", offering design was seen to be increasingly uncommercial and outdated.

As growth slowed down, value for money became a priority in offering design, replacing technical excellence as the core of the offering.

[8] See http://www.shell.com/global/aboutshell/who-we-are/our-history/the-beginnings.html (Accessed June 2015).

These external changes and the new offerings by external providers made it evident that Manufacturing had to reconsider its offering — that is, its role and ways of working in relation to the refineries.

In the first half of the 1980s Manufacturing's leadership started to change the organisation's business culture to ensure its offerings could become more "service oriented". With this new aspiration, the unit would start its work by thinking about customers and their requirements, not about the latest goods or information offering elements — be they pumps, catalytic converters, chemical processes, or crackers. The organisation, its offerings, role, contract, and economics were all to be changed, as were the reward systems. The transition took time, but by the end of the 1980s it was solid on the ground (Checkland & Scholes, 1999).[9]

This "reorientation", as the change came to be known, resulted in a newly constituted central Manufacturing Function (MF) organisation with three main departments, each centred on one distinct configuring offering: MF Services, MF Technology and MF Strategy. Each configuring offering manifested a distinct relationship with the co-creating counterparts — although in the case of two other co-creating departments, the co-creator was located in the same unit but the roles changed.

Thus, the offerings of the new MF Services organisation were paid-for services on an offering-by-offering basis with refineries, which no longer had to pay a standardised service fee taxed from operating company revenues, regardless of use and value. MF Services thus got its own bottom line or profit and loss (P&L) statement — it was no longer a cost centre, and whilst it was not meant to make a profit, it was meant to cover its costs. MF Services was given three main groups of people and their information to work with: Operational, Civil, and ICT. MF Services had to justify its existence in relation to the Shell operational companies, who could compare some of what they would offer to that which was offered by external suppliers. In the language of this book, this means that MF Services unbundled some of the elements it had previously offered in bundles to better reflect value for money for each offering (taking away the previously existing more or less opaque cross-subsidies that the

[9]See Chapter 9 — Part of the intervention team in the Manufacturing reorientation included Richard Normann and Rafael Ramírez, later co-founders of NormannPartners.

taxation model had brought with it) and this allowed it to concentrate on higher value niche offerings that external suppliers found hard to match.

The second department that was created in this change was MF Technology. It kept focusing on Research and Development (R&D), and was paid from a (smaller) tax on operating company profits, along the other "central" (Corporate) functional staff teams. MF Technology served both the high end of the Shell refinery needs (a "high tech R&D offering") as well as the Board of the company, which counted upon this team to remain world-class in technology and research (a "keep us in the lead of R&D and technology" offering). In the language of this book MF Technology thus had two offerings: an R&D (more D than R) one for the operating companies and an R&D (more R than D) leadership offering for the Board of the Corporation. A continuous flow of staff rotating through the Service and Technology parts and — crucially also through operating companies — would ensure up-to-date knowledge, knowledge sharing, and awareness of what was going on in the operating companies. So the people element in the offering remained high for both interactors, but without taxation cross-subsidies it had to have much clearer accountabilities and responsibilities to distinguish the role in technology from the role in services. One of us (Ramírez) was extensively involved in the hard work to make these clarifications of configuring offerings and supporting offerings stick in terms of roles, relations, and interactions to be well understood and to work across functions, departments, and levels, using responsibility charting (Gilmore & Kazanjian, 1989). We found that breaking up the interactions in each offering among all key units into some 30 specific deliverables was needed to be able to allocate clear accountabilities and responsibilities across functions, companies, and units as well as across hierarchical boundaries.

While as we saw above that following the oil crises of the 1970s Shell management had become more concerned about the company's cost structure, during the 1980s Shell's cost structure, compared to competitors, started to deteriorate. Shell benchmarked the cost "from source to sink" with competitors, especially with Exxon, and the comparisons were not favourable for Shell. Exxon had developed a very hard-nosed attitude towards costs. They looked at profits in whatever they were doing. Shell on the other hand invested considerably in relations with host governments in major resource holding countries to make sure that they got and kept access to these countries' oil and gas reserves, and cost had been less of a concern in their offering designs.

In part to redress its cost disadvantage, in the mid-1990s Shell reorganised its group structure, creating five globally operating businesses: Petro-chemicals, Exploration and Production, Oil Products, Gas and Power, and Renewables, to replace the country-by-country organisation operating model. Service functions such as research, shipping, trading, and manufacturing were organised into service companies operating in London or the Hague or Houston — the so-called "corporate centres". The R&D activities, previously all managed by the Research Function, were now placed under the responsibility of each global business, which needed to prioritise, fund and steer its own R&D directly. This led to the creation of the EP-R&TS (Exploration and Production research and technical services) and OP-R&TS (ditto for downstream) units. The most important consequence of this realignment was that R&D now had to create demonstrable value offerings to its respective businesses. An unintended but unsurprising consequence was that emphasis on fundamental research (which by definition does not initially have a pre-defined user) was reduced.[10]

Shell's established offering design approach also started to come under pressure not only from cost efficacy requirements, but also as governments to a growing extent started to take more control over the assets they owned. More self-confident people in governments with better training (often having learned things in companies such as Shell before being hired by national oil companies) questioned the old relations (in our language, offerings). This started to be felt in the organisation and also contributed to having Shell management become more attentive to cost issues. With Cornelius Herkströter becoming Chairman of the Committee of Managing Directors in 1993, the focus for offerings moved further away from technological excellence and more towards meeting more competitive "return on average capital employed (ROACE)" ratios. In the language of this book, the financial VCS started to have a bigger configuring offering design role and the technical VCS a less important role in designing the

[10] J.G. Wissema (2009). Towards the Third Generation University. Edward Elgar Publishing.

configuring offering. To some extent, finance moved from a support offering to take on a bigger role in the configuring one and the technology offering became more of a support offering.

Unsurprisingly, the company underwent what many inside considered to be radical changes — for good reasons. Analysing all possibilities for cutting costs to get the cost per barrel down involved a restructuring where a third of the jobs at Shell's headquarters were lost.[11] To some extent these changes were successful, as they helped Shell to have lower costs per barrel than Exxon. But it was in this overall context that Shell determined to also cut back on R&D and technology expenditures. One candidate for radical cost reductions was the technology part in the MF. There were two different reactions to this development. One reaction was that from EP, which followed the cost cutting logic of the new CEO; and another from the MF, which in a way was better prepared, as we describe below.

The MF felt that through the reorientation from a technology to a service focus, which they had undertaken in the 1980s, they had proven a capability to operate differently. They argued that the technical service unit could form a stand-alone operation, which could earn its right to exist by designing and making available competitive offerings in a way that was commercially viable. Their proposition was not framed as cost cutting, but as an opportunity to monetise existing information and people capabilities (manifested as offerings that were services, R&D, and technology) and to mobilise the technology knowledge in manufacturing to support the competitiveness of Shell's own core businesses. Their proposition was taken on and implemented.

The service organisation was thus separated from head office and started operating as a unit with its own profit and loss responsibility; first as "MF Services", then as OP-R&TS, and in 1998 reorganised to become SGSI (Shell Global Solutions), which is still in operation at the time of this writing (mid-2015).

Although the original argumentation to make this viable was centred on making money from technology investments by pricing offerings that

---

[11] See http://www.shell.com/global/aboutshell/who-we-are/our-history/the-beginnings.html accessed June 2015.

could be bought, it seems that the main reason for the Shell leadership to approve the structural change that was implemented was to save money on technology. That argument, as one of our interviewees paraphrased it, viewed technology as a commodity that no longer contributes to making offerings distinctive — a view expressed as "*technology can always be bought in the market, when needed*". As a result of taking action with that view in mind, not only were many technologists let go, but also project managers. The newly articulated need was also emphasised as times of "easy oil" were history.[12] For project managers, this turned out to be a costly decision: when the market changed and Shell needed to bring on board many project managers again, the company had to develop from scratch a whole project academy (opened in 2004) to train people back to acceptable levels of proficiency.

As per our assessment of successful offering designs, the success of MF Services, then of OP-R&TS and (in 1998) Shell Global Solutions had been built on:

1. Very talented people in both interactors (centre and operating companies of Shell) who operated in a world where world-class engineering resource was a scarcity;
2. Unique information and knowledge with extensive operating experience with Shell's manufacturing assets that nobody could match. In their archives they had collected everything (drawings etc.) even from times before World War II;
3. A strong offering design that went from a technical to a commercial configuring core and brought forth a strong customer-centric service culture.

In the beginning, SGSI was focused on the downstream business, given it was a legacy part of the MF (refining). In 1998 some upstream activities, mainly surface-based ones, also came into SGSI. Yet the more strategic elements of upstream R&D (mainly sub-surface activities) stayed with the upstream (E&P) unit.

---

[12] See http://viewswire.eiu.com/report_dl.asp?mode=fi&fi=1865031771.PDF&rf=0 (Accessed June 2015).

It is important to note in this chapter on offering design that from the beginning, the business logic (and thus design philosophy of its offerings) of SGSI was totally different from the dominant business logic of Shell. In Shell, money was made by having secured and built unique access to oil and gas reservoirs — the bulk of revenue and profits were made from shared production arrangements with governments. Instead, to earn a living SGSI designed offerings where it charged for services, based on a per hour unit of value for their work or on a per dollar gained efficacy for their customers (improved risk sharing). For a while, SGSI could also offer their services to competitors of Shell. This created friction early on as some people did not like that Shell's knowledge could be sold to competitors. Shell professionals would ask questions such as *"Why should we help Statoil with their refinery problems?"* One rationale to defend having such offerings within the Shell group was expressed as *"Well, if you do that, firstly you can charge them a large fee, a part of the millions they will be saving (anyway); and secondly, we learn a lot from our competitors and re-apply this knowledge to our own operations. Helping others well means we can help our own (Shell) people even better."* Initially, about 10% of total revenue came from non-Shell companies. This grew to a larger percentage over the next years.[13]

Other concerns with the SGSI offering within Shell also arose. As an example, very senior finance executives in the Group raised questions concerning possible fiscal consequences: Service Companies had traditionally been tax neutral, as they charged all their costs to the operating companies as service fees, so made no profit. They were cost centres for taxation purposes. Profits were always made in Operating Companies. So when MF Services was created and income started to come in from non-Shell entities, they were asked to "debit" the service fees with these revenues, to remain tax neutral. So in the language of this book, the commercial VCS that SGSI had designed with its fee-for-service configuring offering had to be redesigned to as to not impair the fiscal VCS that governments had designed for multinationals such as Shell. As the SGSI offering had to become a support offering for Shell, Shell's overall

[13] It has not been possible to get these figures — they are not in the public domain.

configuring offering configured limitations on what SGSI could do with its offerings.

Another concern about the SGSI business model related to what the Board might wish to keep tightly inside any company. There are always different types of "secrets" in any business. In the downstream operations of oil majors there are considerable R&D and technology assets that are worth protecting to keep commercial advantage. But in the upstream operations of necessity many innovations are shared with partners as many projects have to be joint ventures to share the major risks involved; or because the National Oil company that a "Major" international company like Shell has to collaborate with to exploit nationally held oil or gas reserves wants to grow or keep part of the activity.[14] The sensitivities about what to protect as intellectual property (IP) is thus different between each community, though exceptions exist in each. In the language of this book, the design of the SGSI configuring offering also had to take into account the IP offering designs of the Shell Company as a whole.

Given the different risks of losing distinctive IP between the downstream and upstream businesses, unsurprisingly a different approach for commercialisation of technology offering design was followed for the upstream part of the business: Shell Technology Ventures was created as a vehicle (and as a fund) for investing in spun-out technologies from Shell, and for investing in technologies from third parties Shell was interested in. Shell retained a smallish investment in the fund, which was for a time managed by Kenda Capital in the Netherlands and by some ex-Shell employees.

In 2006, following a massive reorganisation triggered by the reserve misreporting incident[15] Shell re-organised its five divisions, and what had been Shell Chemicals Technology also joined SGSI.

The commercial success that SGSI offerings had managed to achieve can be gauged by the fact that the CEO of Schlumberger got nervous when SGSI started to move into upstream, competing head-to-head with

[14]Though sharing goes some way, often subsurface (seismic, geology etc.) information is protected as a state secret.

[15]See http://royaldutchshellplc.com/2004/08/26/the-misreporting-scandal-shell-penalties-bolster-billion-dollar-class-action-lawsuits/ (Accessed June 2015).

Schlumberger.[16] Another indication of success was their ability to increase headcount. From an initial phase of downsizing from 2,500 to 2,000 people, by 2008 SGSI was again employing some 5,000 people (Wissema, 2009).

Some observers, such as Wissema, have suggested that SGSI could have become a Schlumberger or Halliburton as their technical expertise and level of customer service, enhanced by open competition, improved the quality of technology development. With its competitive offerings SGSI could have entered many markets where the parent company logic of getting access to oil and gas reservoirs would not have been sufficient. For example, operating in Mexico at that time could only be done if one could charge by the day. But the reality was that the limits of the offerings SGSI could design were limits imposed by the fact that it is owned by Shell, and Shell's configuring offerings constrain what SGSI can offer, and might have developed into. In the language of this book, SGSI offering designs would never be allowed to impinge on the offerings designed by Shell as the mother company for the company as a whole. This prevented SGSI from designing offerings that could compete with major so-called "services" companies such as Schlumberger or Halliburton.

In 2009, SGSI as a separate business was subsumed into the newly created Projects and Technology division.[17] Once again SGSI morphed, this time to become an in-house consulting unit of sorts.

In the special supplement "Winning in the downturn"[18] from 2008, two Executive Vice Presidents of Shell Global Solutions wrote the following:

> "Shell Global Solutions has become part of a new, group-wide business called Projects and Technology, which will manage the design of all major

---

[16]Reflection from a senior engineer with experience of both Shell and Schlumberger.

[17]The rationales for creating the new Projects and Technology division included cost control and reduction, organisational effectiveness, better learning, knowledge management and technology deployment (Thuriaux-Alemán & Rogers, 2012). The reason why the name "Shell Global Solutions" continued to exist was because there was a legal entity called SGSI BV, and because of the brand value that was created.

[18]http://www-static.shell.com/static/globalsolutions/downloads/aboutshell/special_supplements/hcp_supplement_foreword.pdf (Accessed June 2015).

new projects, upstream and downstream, and which will consolidate technology R&D and technical services on a truly global scale.

"We have entered a new set of world circumstances. It is clear that our immediate future lies in a downturn with low margins. Within the industry, this could mean that less capital is available to maintain investments in operating facilities and future supplies, which may lead to price volatility. Moreover, oil demand has fallen and prices are less than half of their historical peak in July 2008. Yet industry costs, though softening, remain nearly twice what they were in 2004. ... Studies have ranked improving cost discipline as one of the most important business imperatives of 2009."

One of the interviewees we consulted to prepare this case expressed the change as

"it is about business models, and about how the business is organised. The big thing Shell achieved is the total integration between upstream and downstream technology and the service approach. There is tremendous synergy between the various families of technology: downstream, upstream, chemicals."

All in all, this example shows how it is possible to change an offering from one centred on technical excellence to one centred on enabling customer value, while also demonstrating the limitations of being constrained by an over-arching configuring offering — that of the mother company, Shell.

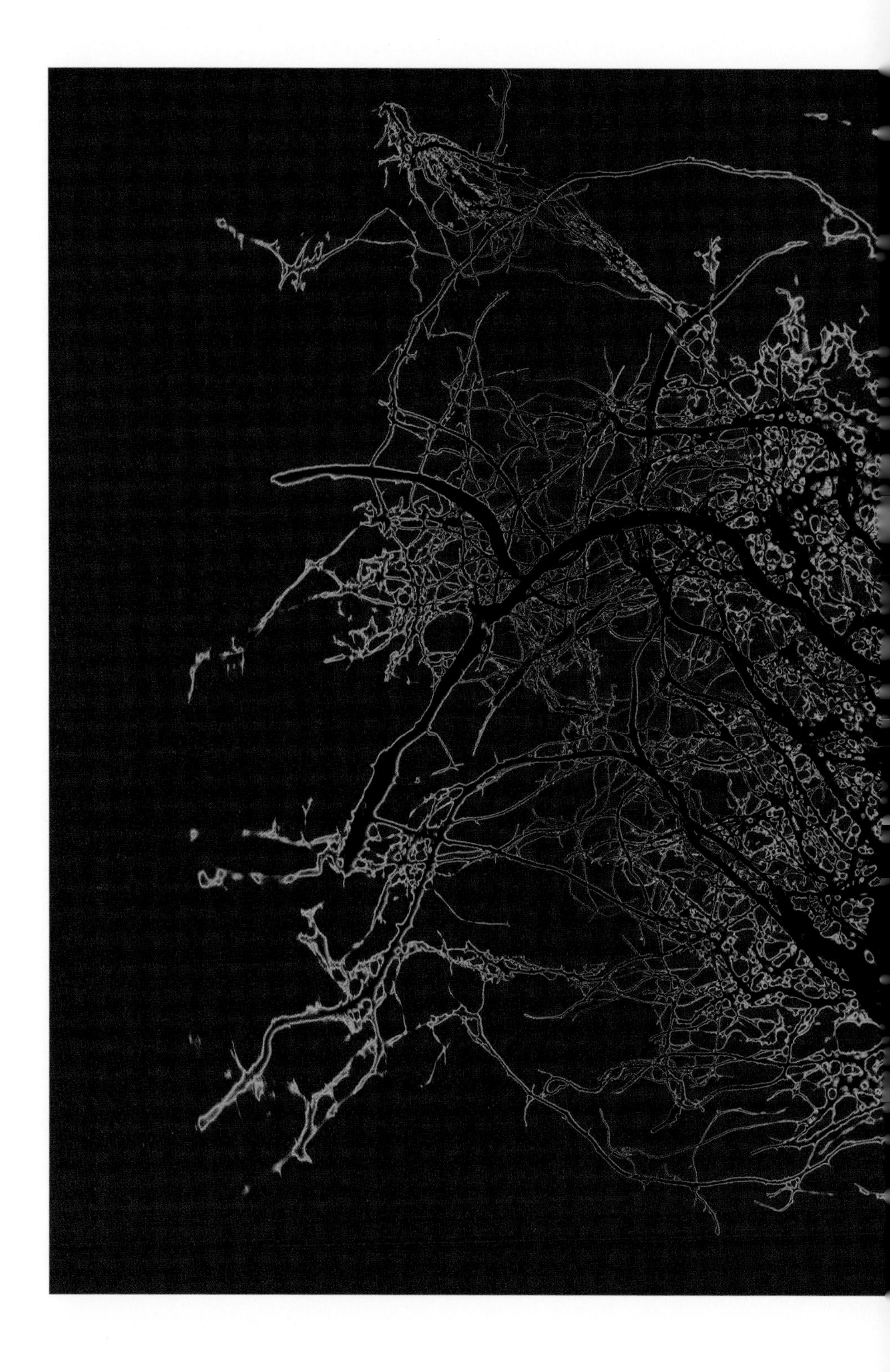

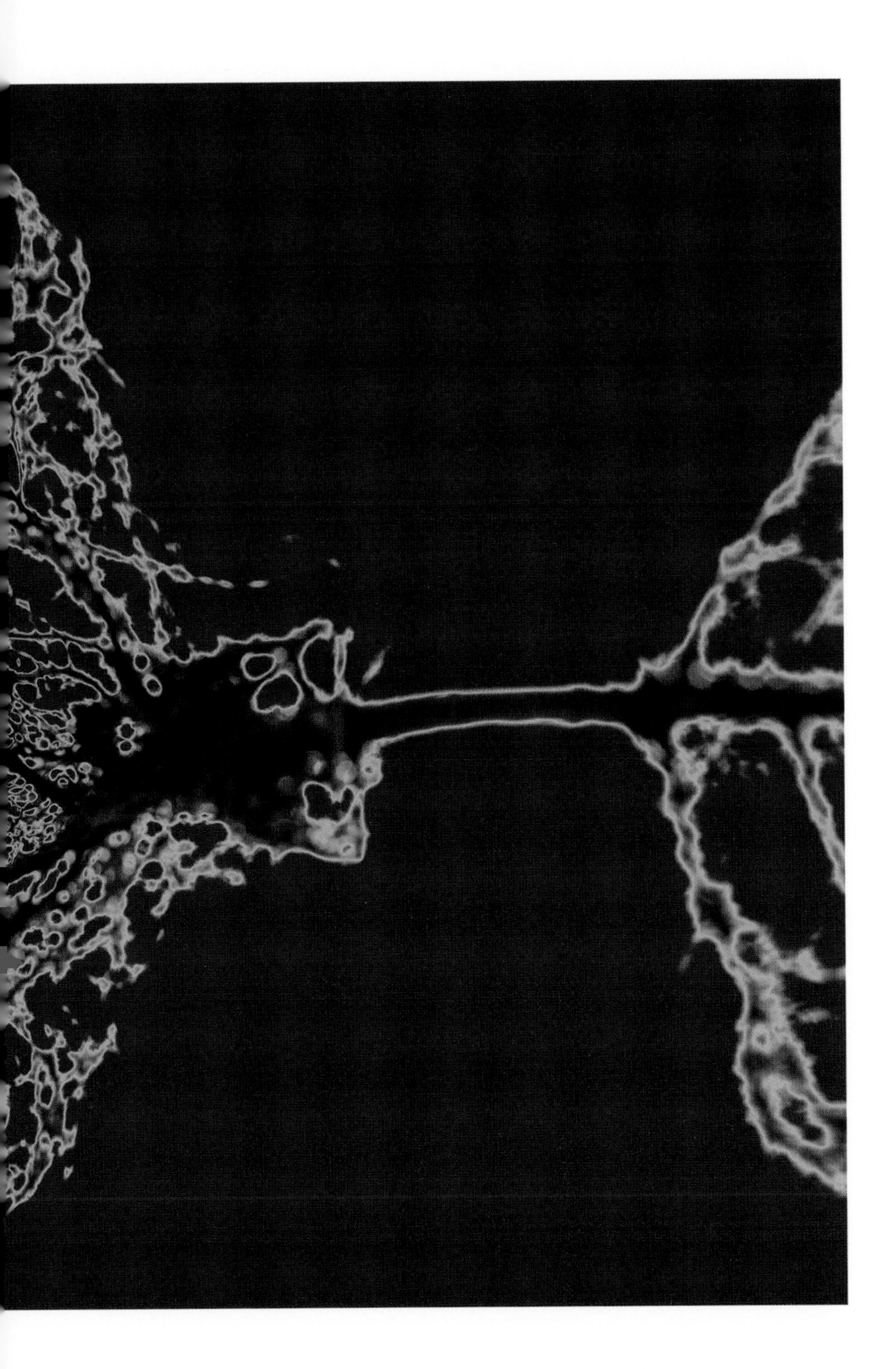

Chapter 6

Analysing the Designs of Existing Value Creating Systems[1]

Box 6.1: Chapter 6 at a Glance

This chapter articulates our thinking on how to use Actor-Network Theory (ANT) — actually, more a methodology than a theory — to "reverse engineer" an existing Value Creating System (VCS) to determine its design, so that it may become capable to redesign it and transform it. We show how the use of the ANT methodology helped the French energy utility EDF to distil common elements in many different ("pluralistic setting") situations it had experimented in, to be able to develop a coherent strategy for electrifying the billion inhabitants of the planet not connected to the electricity grid in the late part of the 20th and early part of the 21st centuries. The complex web of interrelations that were brought together to design and create different alternative electric VCSs by EDF professionals across the globe were analysed with ANT. These designs were compared using the same VCS configuring and support offering design patterns we discuss in this book; and conclusions were drawn from this experience. ANT, its history and development, and its use as a methodological approach to understand the original designs of VCSs and their development is described in detail in Appendix B.[2]

---

[1]This chapter was co-authored with our NormannPartners colleagues Fredrik Lavén and Shirin Elahi and with EDF Executives Claude Nahon and Assaad Saab.

[2]Readers unfamiliar with ANT would be well advised to look at Appendix B before reading this chapter.

1. Using ANT to Explore VCS of Energy Provision to the Bottom Billion

The issue of access to energy has become increasingly important, and also more politicised. Electricity is considered to be essential to many aspects of human development, and as the gap between the haves and have-nots becomes increasingly visible,[3] societal tensions become increasingly marked, discussed by the media, and thus a priority for political representatives.

These tensions express themselves as debates around fairness and equitable sharing of resources. They are a challenge not only for governments everywhere, but also for those involved in the provision of energy, which enables so many aspects of human development that we value. Navigating this turbulence offers new opportunities and risks for EDF.

EDF is a global electricity player as well as the world's leading nuclear energy operator. It is a publicly listed state-controlled company. As the French State owns approximately 85% of the company, the firm is not only a major energy player, but also an important part of French policy.[4] At the time we worked with them they employed 160,000 people across the world.

EDF approached NormannPartners in 2011, the year of the UN-orchestrated "Access to Energy for All" campaign, to explore how its multiple historic experiments across many different operating environments could be analysed as a coherent overarching strategic initiative that fit the "Sustainable Energy For All" (SEFA) conceptual framework. This SEFA framework sought to better understand and respond to the diverse needs of EDF's then 37 million customers worldwide. Through the process we set out below, we were able to create a shared conceptual framework and a shared language that allowed EDF to link the business opportunities and challenges of meeting fuel poverty in Europe with (1) the provision of

[3]Oxfam in March 2014 reported that the top five families in the UK have more wealth than the bottom 12 million families (or 20% of the population), and their wealth has increased by four times as much in the last two decades — http://www.oxfam.org.uk/blogs/2014/03/a-tale-of-two-britains also see Piketty's work on Capital in the 21st century.

[4]Refer to http://shareholders-and-investors.edf.com/fichiers/fckeditor/Commun/Finance/Publications/Annee/2013/F&F_2013_VAdef_v2.pdf.

energy to the inhabitants of Favelas and other peri-urban settlements in Brazil and Argentina, (2) with electrifying remote villages in the developing world, and (3) with helping local partners in emerging economies such as Morocco to electrify large regions of their countries.

The provision of energy is a complex and capital-intensive business. It involves VCSs that typically include: customers, a relevant statutory framework and legal system, power generation, transformation, control, metering, and utilisation technologies, power transmission and distribution networks, ways to price and account for and trade energy and to enable subscribers to pay; support functions such as repair and maintenance; customer education, support and retention — including systems to handle complaints quickly. The resulting VCSs interconnect technologies, subsystems, institutional frameworks, people and social processes such as norms.

Establishing a sustainable energy VCS typically requires securing substantial upfront resources and investment — not only financial, but also technological, institutional, human, and organisational. Over the years, the skills required to undertake this in large-scale projects have become embedded within EDF's culture. The dominant part of EDF's culture assumes that once the scale required to break even or become profitable is reached, the VCS will be sustained for a very long time, if not forever. However, the examples of electrification initiatives EDF had been involved in that we were given to review called this assumption into question: some initiatives struggled to reach that critical point, others to maintain it. We concluded that some of the underlying principles necessary for successful large-scale electrification over the long run have become so implicit that they have been almost taken for granted in that dominant culture; while many of the smaller-scale electrification VCSs we were asked to review, on the other hand, required local examples of innovation — political, institutional, social, organisational, technical, and financial, to reach and keep a critical scale. Many important aspects of these innovations appeared to have remained tacit knowledge kept among those that invented and enacted them, remaining largely invisible within the dominant culture. We found only limited evidence of the different, very ingenious, small-scale alternative VCS designs that EDF had harboured because they were appreciated as inherently and explicitly replicable. They had rarely been recognised as important, repeatable innovations worth integrating into the mainstream of the organisation as "distinct" competences.

At the core of the vast majority of successful (typically large-scale) energy VCSs is what we called "the law of large numbers". This involves gathering a large and diversified enough pool of consumers to offset risks and costs; and to enable cross-subsidisation between different groups of consumers and users, across different places and times, so that the cost of the energy provision system per consumer per year becomes acceptable. If the group is sufficiently large, not only will more and more of the overall risks become calculable and insurable, but the costs per user to cover the upfront investment will be sufficiently small as to be accepted. In such a case, the energy provision VCS builds an increasingly virtuous cycle, increasing solidarity across the group and lowering costs for each member of the group. Here, the business model becomes both profitable and sustainable. However, building the size up to when the virtuous cycle "kicks in" takes time and costs money — as does keeping it at that size or helping it become bigger. This is illustrated in Figure 6.1, where initial "small

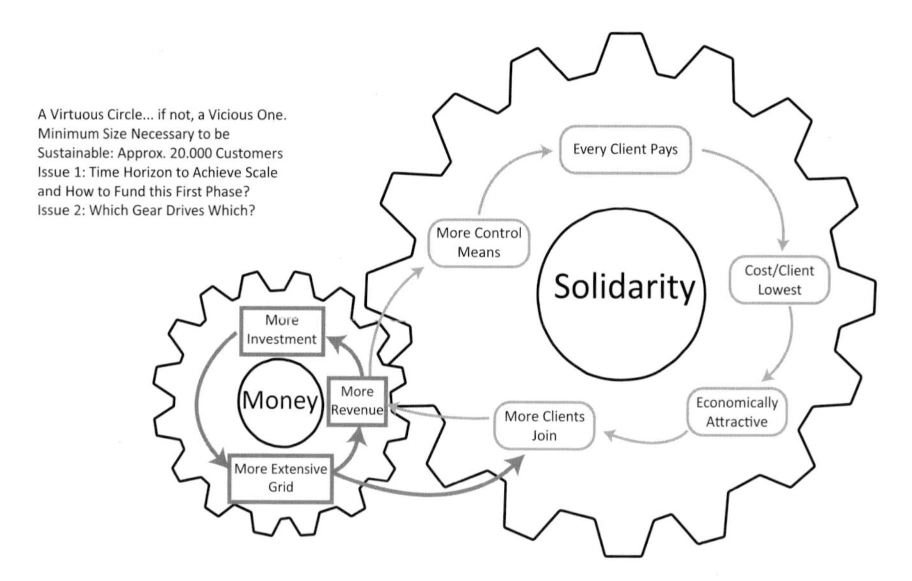

Figure 6.1: A "Gear" View of the Electricity VCS Design[5]

[5]This figure was produced by NormannPartners for EDF. Reproduced with permission.

wheel" investments get the "big wheel" going until it reaches or surpasses scale, and its resulting momentum and size keeps the big wheel turning — and then drives the small wheel's profitability.

In effect, building an energy system requires upfront infrastructure costs before it can become economically viable. These (often significant) infrastructural costs need to be recouped, and this takes time; and requires building up a large number of clients, each paying a little bit towards the shared infrastructure. Our research indicated that the designed infrastructure required a minimum of 20,000 clients in order to break even. When there are fewer clients, the cost of the system per client increases, so making it less financially attractive to the individual client, thereby creating a vicious cycle with less incentives for each client to participate and diminishing social solidarity. When there are more than 20,000 clients, the cycle becomes increasingly "virtuous" and attractive to all parties — to the clients who each pay less for the advantages of the service, thereby attracting more clients and greater social solidarity; and thus to the investors and those who tax revenues. The great attraction for the infrastructure owner and/or operator is that they obtain sufficient revenues to be able to recoup investments and can invest further in the energy system. Once the "virtuous" cycle has been created, the system becomes financially sustainable.

EDF presented us with a series of case studies of efforts they had undertaken across the globe to make electricity available to populations that had either not had access to it or for whom the access had been curtailed. In our analysis, we found ten well documented but disparate case studies that fitted four very different operating environments, namely:

1. **Development in emerging/developing countries:**
   These were large-scale electric infrastructure joint ventures with national or regional electricity providers.
   (The two studied examples were Nam Theun 2 in Laos; and BPC Lesedi in Botswana).

2. **Access to energy in rural areas of emerging/developing or poor countries:**
   These were small-scale Société de Services Décentralisés (SSD)/Rural Electricity Supply Companies (RESCO) for decentralised rural electrification projects, sometimes only developed as pilot projects.

(The three studied examples were Temasol in Morocco; Koraye Kurumba and Yeelen Kura in Mali; and KwaZulu Energy Services (KES) in South Africa).

3. **Urban poverty in emerging/developing countries:**
   These were the electrification of favelas and so-called "peri-urban" (low income, possibly illegally occupied) city suburbs.
   (The three studied examples were Light in Brazil; Edenor in Argentina; and Khayelitsha in South Africa).

4. **Fuel poverty in developed countries:**
   This category involves situations dealing with fuel poverty in "developed" countries, both urban and non-urban.
   (The two studied examples were in France and in the United Kingdom).

Once we categorised these case studies, we developed a three-stage methodological approach, iterating our draft case studies with interviews with EDF professionals who had been involved in developing them. The three stages of the approach we developed are set out below:

Stage 1: Understanding the resulting VCS: The static picture

Our first task was to make sense of the VCS, describing it as a system of interconnected relations. At this stage, we focused on the value(s) that the actors generated with and for each other. We connected actors to each other according to various "values" that linked them to each other in the VCS: financial values, as well as commercial, political, social values. For each case, we drew a VCS diagram depicting these relations, coloured to clarify these different value co-creations.

A VCS can be described as a static representation or "photo" of the system at a given time and situation. It is this static picture of a VCS that can be represented diagrammatically as a system, with the nodes connected by arrow links in the direction of which the main benefit of co-productive relationship occurred. Once we had produced these "static" VCS diagrams and understood the interconnected relationships and how they were configured to produce value, we then moved on to Stage 2, to investigate the dynamic process or "film" that had created the VCS.

Stage 2: The dynamics that create the VCS: using ANT as a dynamic representation over time

While a VCS can be seen as a static snapshot in time, usually taken at a late stage of the value creating process, every VCS is generated as a result of a myriad of actions and interactions over time — and across space — among many parties who come together to co-create value for and with each other, for themselves, and for and with third parties.

For strategists, it is not only important that the key attention in VCS is the configuring offering (as it sets out the relations or interactions), not the actors; but also that these are designed and enacted over time — or if they just arose (or no one remembers how it was designed), that all such offerings and their corresponding VCS arrangements have a "design" within it.

So in this second stage we looked at how the dynamics of the networked relations had developed over time to constitute each VCS. We used Harrison and Laberge's (2002) ANT approach to "reverse engineer" the actual reported stories of how the intended design of each case study of electrification had come about, exploring four moments of the emergence of an actor network: Problematisation, Intéressement, Enrolment, and Mobilisation (more extensively described in Appendix B):

1. Problematisation involves identifying and/or discovering, then formulating and defining some situation into one that can be called a "problem", implying a solution — in our terms, a vision of a relevant VCS.
2. Intéressement includes the actions a designer of the configuring offering that constitutes an actor-network (the "focal" individual actor who tries to enrol others) takes to interest other actors as stakeholders in an innovation initiative (Callon, 1986a; Normann & Ramírez, 1993).
3. Enrolment is the process whereby the proposed role to be played by any given actor that will form a part of a VCS is defined, negotiated, and accepted. Enrolment typically results from successful intéressement.
4. Mobilisation involves having the allied co-creating actors in the actor-network that is being formed, which the network designer orchestrates with the configuring offering, to begin to actually work together as a coherent new structure, where the innovation project they co-constitute becomes reality.

Once we had described and drawn our various models, they were then tested with those that had brought them forth through interviews. We found that the four moments were not entirely distinct from one another, but were often overlapping and intertwined. These moments also did not always take place in a linear fashion as stages, but quite often involved a number of tries where those enrolled did not mobilise, others were potentially interested, the problem had to be reformulated, and so on.

Stage 3: Comparisons and analysis:

With all 10 cases set out in common — and thus comparable — static VCS and dynamic ANT formats, which were approved by the interviewees, we then compared the cases with each other and identified similarities, common criteria for success in designing and creating a new VCS, and steps that had been taken in some of the cases but missed or neglected in others. Based on these analyses we made tentative conclusions for further action in creating electrification VCSs.

Here, we lay out what we learnt from comparing the cases, following Harrison and Laberge's (2002) methodology for "reverse engineering" VCSs.

(a) Problematisation

The solution to any problem depends on how that problem is defined. What became apparent from the ten case studies is that different definitions of "problem" (and indeed, of purposes) existed from the start.[6] We found that different actors, including those within EDF itself, perceive a given problem differently. This meant the issue of electrification could be framed in a range of ways, such as being primarily a humanitarian, economic, political, French foreign policy, environmental, or corporate social responsibility (CSR) endeavour. In addition to this initial ambiguity, or the holding of multiple purposes at the same time, problematisation also changed over time within several of the projects to create the new energy

[6]This has indeed been acknowledged in previous ANT studies — see for example, Callon, 1986 and Kjellberg, 2001 for a more recent example — but they generally tend to focus on what becomes the dominant problematisation, resulting in a so-called "obligatory passage point", along with the networks which are constructed.

Table 6.1: Tensions Affecting EDF's VCS at the Time of Our Study[7]

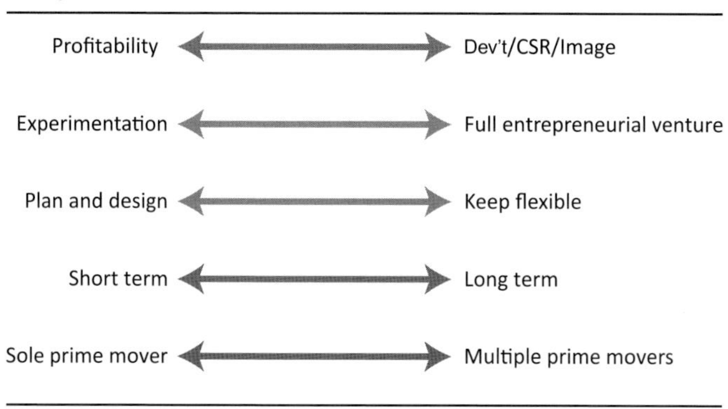

VCSs that we studied. In this way, our approach has become richer for strategists than the original ANT framework.

Indeed, whilst the dominant logic of EDF — and therefore its approach to problematisation — has traditionally been more technical-economic, its positioning over time in its access to energy electrification efforts appeared to have evolved depending on the political climate of the time to include other purposes in many of the initiatives we reviewed. We noted that in many of the cases we reviewed intended users (subscribers, households) were not directly engaged at this problematisation stage. In fact, one could say that already within problematisation EDF was balancing a series of unresolved (some possibly irreconcilable) tensions, including those described in Table 6.1.

Barbara Czarniawska, co-editor of *ANT and Organising* (2005) identified two mindsets that result in two disparate approaches to problematisation: diffusion and translation (these are summarised in Table 6.2 below).

The case studies we researched indicated that while EDF appeared to officially — but implicitly so — prefer the Diffusion/Reform model, it had in fact used the Translation/Project model in many instances of creating successful new energy VCSs to connect new populations to electricity. Yet, this Translation/Project approach was not always immediately politically

[7]This figure was produced by NormannPartners for EDF. Reproduced with permission.

Table 6.2: Two Mindsets Related to EDF's VCS at the Time of Our Study[8]

Diffusion/Reform model	Translation/Project model
• Changes in the original idea must be prevented (as they mean distortions)	• Changes in the original idea are inevitable
• Outcomes are difficult to operationalize (in terms of time, money, quality)	• Outcomes are easily visible (in time, money, quality)
• Planning clashes with improvisation and tinkering	• Planning, improvisation and tinkering aid one another
• Political supervision; little supervision from the clients	• Little political supervision; client supervision
• "Muddling through" is a norm but must be hidden from view	• "Muddling through" is a norm
• Agents are in the hands of the tools/plans	• Plans are tools in the hands of agents

acceptable within EDF, so it tended to be pushed to the margins of company's core activity and paradigm. This meant that this different way of working for the successful creation of a new VCS within the culture of the firm tended to remain unacknowledged. It constituted different competences that could be used in other settings, but these had not been recognised and were not used as well as they could have been. In at least one case, those operating in the Translation/Project model even pretended to work in the Diffusion/Reform model.[9]

(b) Interéssement

The interéssement element involves enticing other actors to come together to co-create value, based on their accepting the definition of "the

[8]This figure was produced by NormanPartners for EDF. Reproduced with permission.

[9]A possible explanation for this can be found in institutional theory, suggesting that norms and rational beliefs influence actors to do certain things in order to gain legitimacy (Meyer & Rowan, 1977; Powell & DiMaggio, 1991; Scott, 2008). It may indeed be more legitimate to represent oneself as operating in a Diffusion/Reform model, with its emphasis on rational planning, as opposed to a Translation/Project model. Czarniawska (2001) developed this point, arguing that actors may enact different logics of representation, practice or theory, depending on what they want to achieve. They may experience a need to represent things rationally (as in the diffusion model), while it may be more pragmatic to act according to a translation model.

problem" given by the configuring offering designer who is calling them together. We found that interéssement was often based on economic and/or socio-political interests, such as concession investments, testing technical-economic alternatives, taking up roles in "energy for all" politics, or seeing opportunities for development or grid consultancy.

However, the lengthy timescales and extensive resources often involved in creating an electrification VCS complicate the ordering of this phase. In several of the cases, the contextual environment (see Chapter 7 for a definition) of the emerging VCS we analysed had seen radical change during this phase, such as having new political agendas or economic crises. Other examples were shifting stakeholder interests, radically changed input prices, or seeing initial objectives becoming subverted or renegotiated for other reasons. In many cases the perspectives of the intended beneficiaries (e.g. subscribers, customers, users) were not taken up in this phase, resulting in unanticipated complications and a need to rethink the building of community relationships when problems arose that could have been foreseen if they had been involved in co-design.

Unlike many commercial organisations, EDF as a state-controlled firm, did not appear to have built in any exit strategies — at any stage — in its different electrification VCS initiatives. There are several possible reasons for this. The most obvious one is that the technical-economic focus in the "main business" is one of staying the course, with no possibility of exiting — or even considering failure upfront. Another reason is image or reputation, which entailed little upfront thinking about under what conditions EDF might be persuaded to leave; and how to do so honourably without compromising its image. A third reason might be that many of the ventures to create the new energy VCS resulted from French foreign policy initiatives determined at the State's highest levels, and could not be seen to fail as part of the larger diplomatic issues involved.

(c) Enrolment

Enrolment is the element where the configuring offering designer enrols other interactors into a shared model of value creation, and into a shared structure or network, with associated interaction processes.

Building electrification VCSs in rural or less developed areas, which are often impoverished and have a low population density, is characterised by high upfront investments with non-obvious investment returns. So enrolment here appeared to have often depended on foreign aid (or sometimes commercial) investment and subsidisation structures. These structures included improved concession terms, state and intergovernmental subsidies, and development aid. Very often — and this was stated as a success factor in some of the cases — electrification VCS were integrated into broader development initiatives. These entailed complex contractual arrangements with organisations such as the World Bank or other funders, and while respective contributions did not always materialise as planned, once agreed, contracts appeared to be nearly impossible to change, as they had no built-in flexibility or slack. So — paradoxically — a "successful" enrolment in electrification VCSs may have entailed huge opportunity costs in mobilisation, as well as risks due to unanticipated events. In some of the cases, details became so overspecified that they included the type of grass to be used in a construction project, which could not be changed later. When adapting the planned vegetation by replanting to a more suitable local species, very difficult contractual changes were required. This meant the worst of all possible worlds: restrictions and limitations upfront and little to no possibility to change these when changing conditions or unexpected results were found later on.

In some of the EDF VCS cases, expected revenues failed to materialise due to reasons such as subsidies having been withdrawn, non-payment, or a limited or deteriorating customer base. We found that such changes were often caused by failing to enrol local actors such as municipalities, local operators or franchisees, and/or beneficiaries and their representatives in the VCS. This "enrolment deficit" then led to changing rules of the VCS, often requiring that intéressement and even problematisation be revisited. Clearly, the creation and maintaining of such co-productive relationships through appropriate support offerings is a crucial factor in achieving sustainable success in electrification VCS.

(d) Mobilisation

The mobilisation element is where the designs and decisions of the other three moments become enacted as a reality in terms of interactions and actions on the ground. In our review, it became clear that mobilisation had been unplanned in several of the electrification VCS cases, so that the resultant VCS configurations were often not best suited to harness the reality on the ground. In those cases, the VCSs did not seem to be able to come to belong naturally, nor contribute effectively, to their context.

However, other electrification VCS cases exhibited a significant capacity for social innovation, in addition to manifesting versions of the technical and financial innovations more aligned to the dominant EDF paradigm. "Learning by doing" seemed to have been one way in which EDF professionals managed to achieve the "translation" of these technical and financial innovations into the field during mobilisation, often as a response to uncertainties in the environment and/or a changing actor configuration. This type of innovative mobilisation capacity led to EDF being recognised as a utility that countries and communities seeking to extend access to energy could count upon. It included the creation of new organisational forms (RESCOs), innovations in payment systems (e.g. pre-payments with codes), learning to involve local representatives in all moments and phases of designing and creating a VCS, and education and competence transfers. However, at the time of the engagement we are reporting here, although multiple assessments had been made and workshops to review work had been held, EDF had not built up an internal mechanism to capitalise on these multiple VCS design experiences and to institutionalise learning across the wider organisation.

The long timeframes, numerous stakeholders, multiple environmental uncertainties and extensive resources required for creating energy VCSs mean that constant adjustments and readjustments are key to achieve success. Yet, from the cases we reviewed in all four settings, there appeared to be a consistent underestimation of the time required to realise the electrification VCS business model in the field. There was also underestimation regarding the need to minimise critical contractual constraints, allow for flexible, collaborative responses and to keep options open. Successful electrification VCSs appeared to require thinking through and designing how to "give back the work" (Heifetz *et al.*, 2009) to the local stakeholders to make the VCS both acceptable to start with and sustainable over time.

The contextual changes affecting an electrification VCS we reviewed could take many forms — technology breakthroughs and discontinuities, increases in materials costs, transformed political agendas, provision of heating or cooling requiring more energy than had been planned for, or newly arisen social movements following economic crises. There were signs that such issues are increasingly recognised within EDF. Whilst in one electrification VCS case EDF became locked in for reasons of reputation (and possibly French State interests), in some of the more recent SSD/RESCO projects we reviewed EDF appeared to have supported a local operator, so that for example when subsidies were suddenly removed by the national government, this had no impact on its reputation. In another case, negotiations changed when EDF was no longer involved, and the authority negotiated very differently with local stakeholders who did not have access to EDF's "deep pockets".

In some cases, mobilisation was followed by a new problematisation effort, where changes in the contextual environment transformed a previously virtuous cycle to a vicious one and the VCS had to be radically redefined. An example here would be the case of fuel poverty in Belgium, where new legislation limited EDF's license to operate.

2. The Complex Web of Collaborative Relationships in Designing New VCSs

The intellectual underpinnings of both the Normann–Ramírez VCS research with its focus on value creation and the Akrich–Callon–Latour ANT research (see Appendix B) with its focus on the dynamics between actors have synergies that we found worth exploring.

We discovered that by looking at the two we were able to better focus on interactions that have the potential to create value and also translate into roles. As stated above, in VCSs the focal attention is the "configuring" offering that defines the design of the system with its interactive dynamics (manifested as support offerings rather than the actors themselves) which encourages creative thinking and helps organisations to avoid focusing simply on the "usual suspects" when they are exploring new ways to create value.

We found that this focus of attention on interactions as offerings — not as actors — is important for an understanding of how to design VCSs, and at least as important to keep building and operating them under the inevitable conditions of uncertainty. Indeed, actors become actors with given roles only when they get to interact — or are acted upon, not by being assigned a given position in a network (Latour, 2005; see Lavén, 2008 for an empirical example of this). Actors' roles and relationships thus change in interacting; and it is the configuring offering that encapsulates this interacting.

Exploring the EDF case studies with this lens has produced helpful VCS design insights. We identified five important interactions[10] that combined to constitute the new energy VCSs that EDF designed and developed in its electrification efforts, namely:

A) **Commercial**
These interactions involve offerings such as the selling of generated/distributed electricity; contracts for the operation/maintenance of equipment; technical advice and project management, and the design of effective payment systems; as well as the less traditional adaptations of micropayment systems and market creation and stimulation in order to create adequate return on investment. These relations were generally within EDF's core competences, primarily with shareholders, partners, customers, suppliers and contractors.

B) **Political**
EDF could not escape its unique position as a (rich) state-owned organisation, which conferred both advantages and disadvantages on it in its global operations. At times, it appeared that its relationships were impacted by French government policy. These political relationships were often critical to the success of EDF and its ventures, and existed at every level — global to national to local. Interactions were not only with politicians, but also with NGOs and the media — which impacted upon public perceptions and therefore politics in general.

[10] We do not see this list as exhaustive, nor necessarily as always being the most important types.

C) Statutory

Energy is a lifeline that underpins economic development, reduces inequality, and can enhance environmental or climate protection. As such, many actors are involved and those who define the legal frameworks within which provision of an essential public services is delivered are primarily regulators and statutory authorities. Whilst these are often initially equal relationships, they can become asymmetric over time as interests diverge and social pressures become political pressures, then translated into statutory action and changing subsidisation. For example, in the cases of fuel poverty in Belgium, France, and the UK, relations may start as a humanitarian issue where EDF is an interested bystander. Over time, the issue is taken up by NGOs and becomes media-intensive and politicised; and then demonising the electricity provider (particularly if it is a foreign one) becomes expedient. A result may be statutory changes that impact the energy provider's bottom line, as was the case in Belgium.

D) Investment/Upfront Financing

The history of electrification in the developed world is dominated by lobbying for funding and subsidies of various sorts, correlating between obtaining such funds and the timescales over which virtuous cycle were created — or even recreated. Clearly, once this has happened relations with investors are no longer the primary ones. However, in many developing markets, relationships with donors and intergovernmental or non-governmental organisations remain critical over long time periods and impact directly upon success.

E) Humanitarian Roles/Corporate Social Responsibility

In a global transparent world where multinational corporations are highly visible, tested, and contested, it is important to be seen as a force for good. Many members of the public and civil society argue that large incumbents should put back some of the profits they derive from serving the public. These services can include activities for local people, educational opportunities, employment and empowerment projects, gender- and race-based mechanisms to enhance fairness, capacity building and other development initiatives. Here, important relations are with grassroots authorities and international, well connected, media-savvy civil society groups; and success will depend on the organisation's ability to adapt to local contexts and cultures to contribute to create a sustainable local economy. Of course, the contribution to local economic development is a means to enhance sustainability of access to energy through the impact on customers' capacity to pay.

These Interactions and How Their Relative Importance Evolved Over Time

In all the 10 cases we reviewed we found instances where the relative importance of the type of interaction to ensure the success of EDF's electrification VCS with respect to terms of the Sustainable Energy shifted at least once over the VCS history. As a result, we found it is necessary to be very attentive not only to the nature of the interaction or relationship, but also to its salience relative to other types at any given point in time in the history of the VCS development. For example, no VCS electrification project moved past problematisation without a strong input of the "investment" and statutory interactions that also made the VCS initiative viable, and more or less concurrently set the rules of the game internally (within the VCS) and externally (between the VCS and its context). However, once mobilisation was underway, these interactions became less central in the functioning and development of the VCS (they gave away their role as "configuring" offerings and became "support" ones); unless external shocks (such as an unusually hot summer in Rio, which made air conditioning demand peak beyond the norm) brought those relationships back to the fore. It was by focusing on relations among interactions and their relative importance that EDF's electrification VCS designs succeeded — or got into trouble.

An instance of how such problems occurred was when a central relationship that was not political became political, and political relationships suddenly became the configuring offering. We observed that in cases of growing fuel poverty, humanitarian issues become politicised over time. At this point, governments revisit the statutory interactions or legislation. In fact, sometimes a government used statutory interactions to meet its political needs, leaving EDF to foot the bill. This course of action may become more widespread as government coffers empty just as energy prices rise. It is prudent for those seeking to maintain a central role in energy VCSs to attend to such possibilities, imagining their happening prior to their doing so, and preparing options to deal with them.

We also observed blurred boundaries between the humanitarian and commercial relations in several cases where this sort of ambiguity could become troublesome. For example, should a manager decide to fund payments to an NGO that will help certain customers better manage their finances and become sound payers? If the reply is positive, is this a commercial relationship with the prime objective of doing business, or a CSR/humanitarian gesture? In other words, in strategic design terms, which schemes should be undertaken as part of EDF's desire to be a socially responsible global player; which to keep its commercial license to operate; which to do "the right thing;" which to do well? Some interviewees from the company suggested that the EDF group might wish to become more explicit (at least internally) about its policy on humanitarian relations, and set aside a percentage of its revenue for good causes. Their proposal could eventually result in a set financial limit for humanitarian spending at a time when there are increasing demands for this due to the growing number of people requiring affordable access to energy — both in the developed and developing worlds.

We thus learned that in any real situation a variety of VCSs will co-exist within a given set of actors, and there will be interrelationships among the VCSs. For example, there could be a tension between the desire of the French State to engage in countertrade, using EDF expertise and French financing on the one hand; and the local government's priorities in relation to their own citizens. The roles any one actor plays will correspond not only to what the members of the "coalition" that has been enrolled and mobilised expect and give back in any one VCS; but also to what those in another co-exiting VCS seek. Thus, I may hold the role of being an aid recipient in one VCS and hold the role of being a taxpayer in another. The tensions that multiple roles within a given VCS (as well as with multiple different VCSs) entail are now more open and public than previously — one can go online and start an open sourced blog on issues, such as — when is one a consumer and when a citizen? When is something a commodity one buys and when is it a human right?

The testing and contesting of roles and interactions and trust and reputation that information ubiquity and social media bring on is one reason: At an organisational level this affects entities such as EDF — a highly visible player, with "social" objectives that also involve "externalities" whose costs and consequences are now being brought back to bear on institutions (such as governments facing fuel poverty in Europe) that are ill-prepared to cope with them. It could be that the experiences of EDF are stimulating the development of an enriched need to design, better articulate, and strategically enact more flexible, adaptable, and sustainable VCSs.

What Defines Success?

Success for each of the various energy VCSs we explored was defined in several different ways, in no small part depending on the purpose(s) for the electrification VCS in question. Ultimately, however, a key factor appeared to be (sometimes implicitly, sometimes explicitly) the achievement of a (socially and economically) sustainable virtuous cycle. Having reviewed literally hundreds of pages of in-house and external documentation and with the help of our interviewees, we narrowed down a long list of criteria — all underpinned by collaborative or co-creative relationships — into four critical criteria for success in strategically designing and enacting successful electrification VCSs. These criteria may well extend to all electrification or energy VCSs — not just the ones we reviewed. These criteria are:

A) Sustainable Profitability

Without sufficient profit (enough for the VCS to break-even at least), there is no way to create an energy VCS of any size that will be sustainable over time. So attention needs to be given to the following links to design viable energy VCSs.

- Financing: Ability to attract financing for the VCS being designed, including the upfront, one-off subsidies required for initial investments, as well as the financial support over time to fund the scaling of operations of the VCS in the process of building the virtuous cycle.
- Critical mass of those holding the role of customers achieved and sustained: Whilst the VCS size will vary, there appears to always be a

critical minimum size, which was estimated to be 20,000 users for the SSD/RESCO model, as set out in Figure 6.1. Without this critical mass the cost per user escalates so as to be unsustainable, resulting in growing user defections and often theft until the point that the VCS collapses.

- Diversity: In the VCS client base, in services and products and across geographies. Diversity supports the necessary cross subsidies to occur across groups, products, geographies, and time-scales that support a VCS. Diversity could be extended to also include technologies and business models to make the VCS less vulnerable to single entity faults.
- Payment systems: Ability to create a workable payment (or micropayment) system, if necessary with diverse forms of cross subsidies and built-in limitations (pre-payment), that create (more or less visible) solidarity and willingness to pay by all users to sustain the VCS. Good payment systems reduce theft and thus decrease costs per user.
- Realistic timescales: Explicit awareness of the timescales to reach critical mass involved in designing, testing, and building the VCS — and their impact upon profitability, thereby ensuring adaptability to delays and local modifications.

B) Collaborative Relationships

Every VCS EDF had convened or allowed itself to be convened into that we studied and almost every interview indicated that a (and arguably "the") key to success was co-creating and maintaining collaborative relationships at every level: with global donors/funders, national authorities, local political structures, local partners, social services, technology suppliers, installers, users and households. Something to be attentive to: as stated above, the nature of some of these relationships changed over time as well. Of these relationships, often the most important appear to be those that embedd EDF in the local communities that each VCS serves.

- Strong local relationships: Whatever the context, in a globalised world of high visibility, EDF requires good relationships with its local partners, stakeholders, and customers in order to provide a sustainable energy for economic development.

- Links to local economic development: In the cases we reviewed, ranging from the villages of Africa to the local authorities of France, the links between economic development and energy provision in every VCS are strong. Secured access to energy gives people choices that impact their lives not only economically, but in every way, and energy VCSs must be designed to accommodate and promote these links.
- Links to other stakeholders, development initiatives, experts: Our research underlined the power of being a configuring offering designer in developing a new VCS. Remaining a configuring offering designer required extending that role in relation to a broader set of stakeholders further afield — by proactively developing new and extending old strategic frameworks with a broader set of actors, including local authorities, NGOs, social services, other utilities to understand and address what they perceive as the critical issues.

C) Resilience and Adaptability

The turbulent contexts within which EDF operated were becoming increasingly complex and unpredictable.

- Resilience included the ability to imagine how these future conditions might unfold, and the ability to invent options that allow one's VCS to reframe its constitutive interactions and possibly even purposes. Where that was possible, there was an ability built into the VCS to adapt and respond to unplanned changes, helping the VCS to learn from experience. All this means that in designing a VCS, instead of privileging cost efficiency (where only one element has one role) one would also privilege functional redundancy, where the failure of one element would be compensated by the re-allocation of the roles held by other moments to fulfil the role played by that element.[11] This involves allocating "hard" resources to cover contingencies that are generalised, soft and uncertain. For that, as for all considerations of quality, top-level commitment is necessary.

---

[11] J. Selsky and R. Ramírez and O. Baburoglu "Collaborative capability design: Redundancy of potentialities", Systemic Practice and Action Research. Online on 11 November 2012. See longer explanation in Chapter 7 of this book.

- Adaptability: In "learning by doing", each of the various actors in the VCS has to have flexible approaches to operational constraints and local conditions, and be ready to adapt and reconfigure moments of the VCS as contexts change. Strong institutional learning feedback loops, where the successes and failures of each initiative can become valuable lessons for individual actors such as the EDF Group, help to build both guiding principles and a repertoire of mix and match approaches that can be deployed to develop new electricity VCS. Adaptability also involves designing a VCS to accommodate emergence (Alexander *et al.*, 1977) rather than going for all-inclusive, comprehensive, locked-in designs that prespecify everything in advance. This need for VCS flexibility extends to the ways in which contracts with other actors are built. Finally, adaptability includes the capacity for the VCS actors and the managers of its component organisations to understand and adapt to local cultures for sustainable mobilisation. Indeed, as the ANT literature suggests, any control initiative must be adapted to the situation at hand, and it may be more relevant for strategists to seek out and to understand differences between situations rather than attempting to find general recipes for success (Akrich *et al.*, 2002).

D) Leveraging Reputation with Proven VCS Design Capabilities

EDF has a reputation which precedes it and eases its capacity to operate in the long term. At the time of our research with EDF, only two other companies in the world had a similar reputation in electrifying those that had been disconnected from the grid — Nuon and Eskom.

EDF is and will continue to be highly visible, simultaneously making it vulnerable and providing it with unique opportunities to strategically design and develop new energy VCS. Our research suggests that in its role as a configuring offering designer in creating a new VCS, it is well advised to continue attending to:

- Trust and fairness: Trust has three components — fairness, consistency of approach, and competence (Elahi 2008). Of these three, fairness appeared to be critical to electricity VCS, due to its inherent cross subsidisation. There are different conceptions of fairness: equity, equality, and Rawl's theory of needs. As different actors push for the conception that best matches their interests, the answer to the question of what is fair is likely to become increasingly contested. Hence, the acceptance of the fairness of an action depends on prior trust in the actor; the relationship is reciprocal and complex.

- Environment: Environmental preservation and climate change mitigation.
- Humanitarian/Social: Integration with other development/solidarity initiatives.

We next survey some of the cases in detail, before offering some concluding comments.

3. Some of EDF Electrification VCS Cases

3.1 The First Case: Nam Theun 2 Electrification VCS

The Nam Theun 2 hydropower dam in Laos was at the time of our research one of EDF's flagship projects (Figure 6.2). It was the largest cross-border structure in South Asia. The Nam Theun 2 Power Company (NTPC),

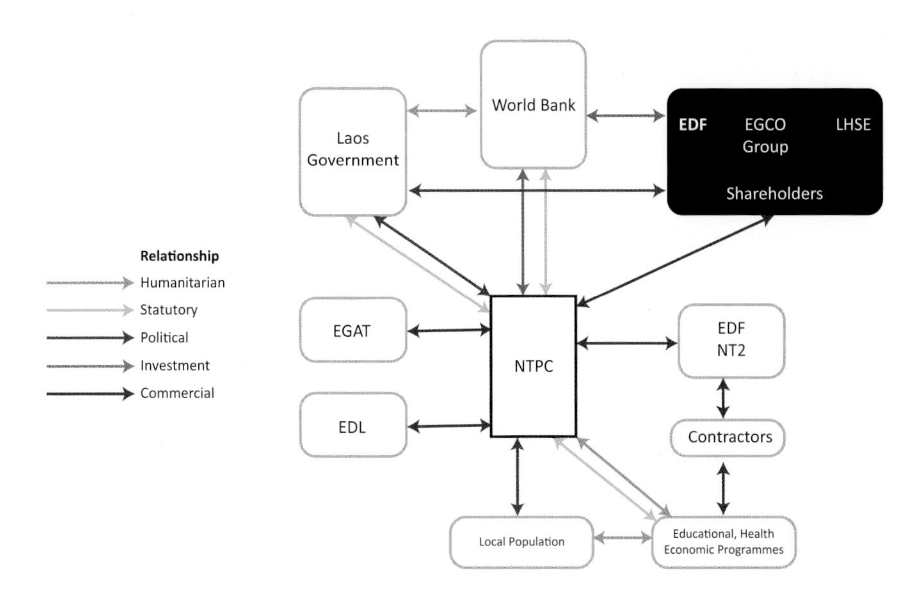

Figure 6.2: The Nam Theun 2 Electrification VCS

established in 2002 in Laos for the development, construction, and 25 years of operation of the 1070 MW capacity Nam Theun 2 hydroelectric power plant, was 40% owned by EDF. The remaining 35% was held by EGCO (the Thai electricity generation company) and 25% by the Laotian government.

The VCS was groundbreaking and highly complex in part due to its scale, which necessitated the involvement of many multilateral and bilateral agencies, as well as many financial investors and commercial banks — each with their own interests and environmental and social standards that had to be reconciled. EDF played a key role, almost since the inception of the VCS, which has evolved as indicated below:

Problematisation

In 1993, the Laos government invited the World Bank to develop a project outline. The government and various private investors set up the Nam Theun 2 Electricity Consortium (NTEC) to research and develop the scheme. The partners developed a shared vision for a scheme to divert the Nam Theun River into a reservoir and then channel it downstream to the Xe Ban Fai and Mekong Rivers. The hydroelectricity from this dam in Laos would be able to produce 95% of its energy for Laos' neighbour Thailand, which was more developed and able to pay a higher price for energy, thereby creating a cash revenue stream for the Laos government.

EDF's role in problematisation was that in 1994 it joined the nascent VCS, together with Italian–Thai Development Company of Thailand (ITD), and became a key shareholder as well as the VCS architect.

Intéressement

In 2002 and 2003, the Nam Theun 2 Power Company (NTPC) was formed between NTEC and partners. A Build, Operate, Transfer (BOT) concession agreement was signed with the Thai Power Generation Company and Laos Government with a 25-year time frame. At the time, initial approaches were made to various banks to involve them financially. Public consultation began with a series of meetings with villagers from the areas likely to be affected. The chiefs of these villages played an important role in this intéressement process. In addition, various non-governmental organisations expressed interest to come on board.

Then in 2003, the Asian financial crisis almost put an end to the nascent VCS. President Chirac concluded that conditions were not positive to invest and officially announced EDF's withdrawal from the nascent VCS and said it should refocus its priorities on the European electricity market. A French parliamentary commission had come to the conclusion that EDF's international plans were putting taxpayers' money at risk. When it seemed likely that the VCS might come to an end in 2003, EDF held discussions regarding the French government position, and decided to pursue its role nevertheless. So the announced exit was reduced to an item in a parenthesis and a few months later EDF returned to the VCS and signed a Power Purchase Agreement.

EDF's role as Intéressement at that time was that of VCS designer and constructor.

Enrolment

In 2004 and 2005, a wider consultation process was undertaken with all types of stakeholders and NGOs, including possible donors and investors in Washington, Bangkok, and Japan. A public participation project got underway. However, increasingly strong opposition from NGOs arose, culminating in 2005, when the social and environmental programmes were being designed. The World Bank then committed to join the VCS, and in doing so, this enrolment ensured the project's financing.

EDF's role in enrolment is a textbook case of a configuring offering designer, where it was capable of setting the stage and undertaking detail design and bringing on board through effective interactions the stakeholders it needed to make the VCS viable. All technical choices were fixed and contractually bound, although sometimes in too much detail, leaving no room to adapt the VCS to change and to respond to different contextual conditions.

Mobilisation

In 2005, building construction commenced under very public scrutiny. The socio-economic programmes got underway, including construction of resettlement villages and relocation of flooded villagers to new homes. In 2009, the dam was completed and electricity supply commenced. The power plant went into commercial service on 30 April 2010, although the social and environmental programmes continued from 2010 to 2015. The penalties for missing targets for social, economic and environmental performances were put in place to monitor performance over 5, 10, 15, 20 year time frames.

EDF's role in mobilisation was that of constructor, principal investor, coordinator and manager of NTPC.

3.2 The Second Case: KES Electrification VCS

This South African case study was one of EDF's many RESCO initiatives. It illustrates that for poor communities renewable energy can work, but the issue of profitability is very complex. In addition, it underlines the imperative of gaining political support for access to energy as all too often politicians use grid electricity as a bargaining tool to induce communities to do other things in return for their being electrified.

This electrification VCS also had major issues with regard to non-payment (Figure 6.3). KES proved that with concerted management effort, non-payment is an issue that can be controlled, with levels of payment increasing from 77% in January 2005 to 90% in January 2006. This led us to the conclusion that non-payment is a management issue that needs to be designed as such to make the VCS viable. However, non-payment was and probably always will be significantly affected by the introduction and later removal of operating subsidies. In this instance, initial targets were undermined due to budget cuts that had major impacts on business models. For this type of VCS business, government support must remain constant.

Problematisation

In 2000, the South African government announced its policy to provide energy (electricity) basic services to the poor. It also launched a call for access to energy initiatives. EDF submitted a VCS design initiative to the Department of Minerals and Energy (DME) in the Northern Province of South Africa for a Renewable Energy Service Company (RESCO) approach utilising both solar heating systems and mini-grids. Tenesol and TransEnergie, which shared the French oil company Total and EDF as shareholders, also applied to do VCSs in KwaZulu-Natal.

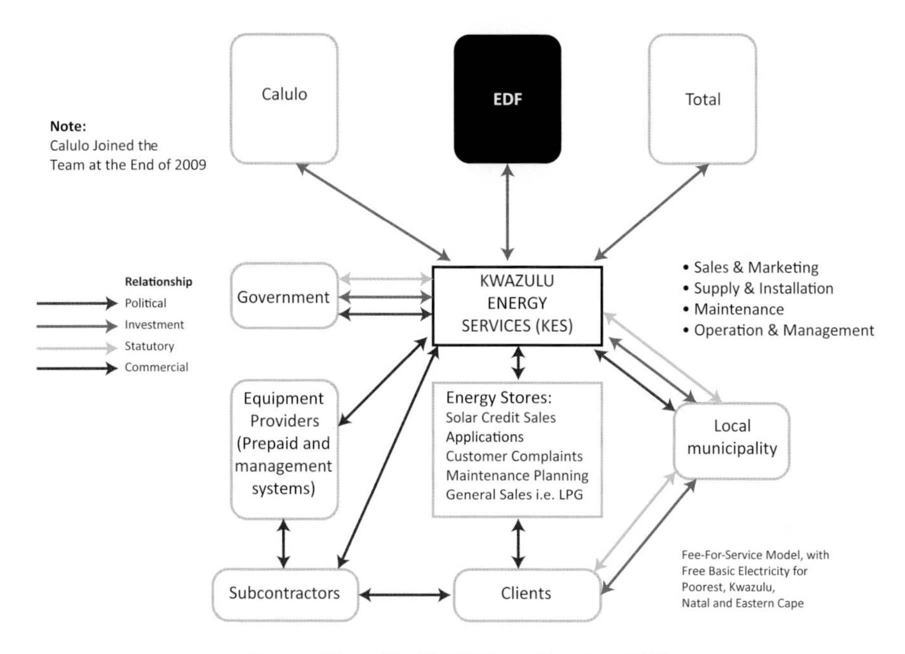

Figure 6.3: The KES Electrification VCS

EDF's role in problematisation: EDF decided to develop the RESCO approach in South Africa, where it has had a presence since the launch of Khayelitsha in Cape Town and its support to the nuclear power plant of Koeberg. It was thus aware of the continuing "problem" that South Africans had with finding solutions to produce and deliver more electricity.

Intéressement

The Department of Minerals and Energy instructed EDF and Tenesol and TransEnergie and Total to combine their efforts to create new electrification VCSs and tried to involve ESKOM, the national utility of South Africa. ESKOM refused to get involved as there were no guarantees regarding subsidies.

EDF's role in this part of Intéressement was that of being one of those actors who were "interested into" joining the VCS by the Department of Minerals and Energy.

Enrolment

In 2002, EDF and TOTAL jointly established KES. KES was awarded an interim contract for one year for central Zululand for 15,000 customers. In 2004, a longterm 20-year contract was signed with KES for solar home systems and gas. The chosen solution was solar home systems, as the population is scattered and cannot be reached by the grid, with a 69% subsidy for investment. By 2005, KES had connected 10,000 customers.

The EDF role in enrolment was that as a joint owner of KES with TOTAL it was again in the configuring offering designer position of enrolling others in the KES electrification VCS.

Mobilisation

Less than one year after the launch of KES activities, in 2003, the South African Government released its Free Basic Electricity Policy, to provide a limited amount of free electricity for the rural households, compared to the 50 kWh/household/month to (poor) households connected to the grid. This meant that instead of customers paying R58 per month, they paid R18 per month and R40 was given directly to KES via the municipalities. Each municipality had different criteria for payment.

This model lasted for several years, and when the government changed, the subsidies were withdrawn and customers were obliged to pay the full fee for service of R58. KES was branded a "thief" and as "enemy number 1". Non-payment was drastically affected by this changed regulatory and economic context. However, as prepaid meters had been installed from the beginning, attrition in the number of customers of the electricity VCS was very low. At that point, two other operators, Shell Solar and ESKOM, withdrew from their Eastern Cape electrification VCS (started one or two years earlier) stating that the scheme was unworkable.

This prompted the Department of Minerals and Energy to question the RESCO model and to put a brake on its payments until it had undertaken its own research. Since 2003 unfortunately the relevant rules have changed year after year.

Also, the Department of Minerals and Energy with its international donor, KfW, approached local operators and launched a tender in 2005 for a similar electrification VCS in the Eastern Cape (25,000 customers and 80 schools and clinics). The tender was for solar home systems and KES won as the lowest bidder, but due to international political interests, contracts were only signed in 2007. However, the rules here too have changed (withdrawal of clinics and schools) and ESKOM was also considering extending the grid to these villages, which would mean a loss of business. Yet, in 2010 the Department of Energy awarded KES approval to extend its customer base in KwaZulu-Natal with 10,000 more customers.

EDF's role in mobilisation: EDF was, through KES, involved in this. Indeed throughout the changes to subsidies that would impact customers, yet KES was recognised at the local level as a South African company, not as EDF. In 2009, EDF took this further and sold 15% of its share to Calulo, a South African company.

3.3 The Third Case: Fuel Poverty UK Electrification VCS

Since market liberalisation brought about in utilities by the Thatcher and Major governments, the UK Government has undertaken a series of different initiatives to improve access to energy and reduce fuel poverty. Although initially liberalisation appeared to solve the issue of fuel poverty, when global energy prices have risen, so too has the problem (Figure 6.4).

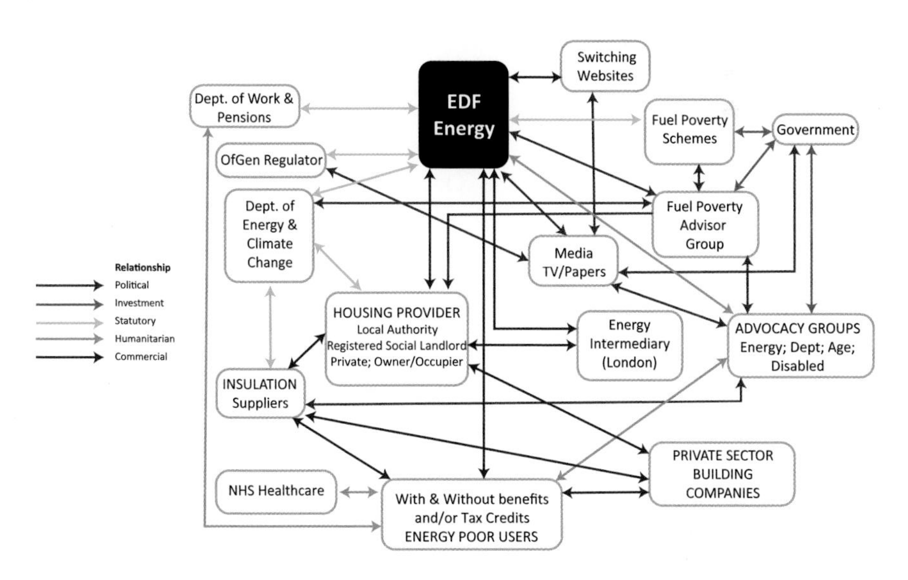

Figure 6.4: The Fuel Poverty UK Electrification VCS

Problematisation

In 1990, the UK Government privatised the UK Electricity Supply Industry in England and Wales. This led to a fully deregulated market in 1998, supported by the regulator office of gas and electricity markets (OFGEM). Soon afterwards, in 1991, the Home Energy Efficiency Scheme (subsequently Warm Front) established a fuel poverty programme.

In 2000, the Government enacted the Warm Homes and Energy Conservation Act, setting a maximum target for the elimination of fuel poverty as 2016 (2018 in Wales). The UK Fuel Poverty Strategy became a policy tool the following year.

EDF's Role in Problematisation: EDF bought London Electricity, and then South West and South East Electricity and created EDF Energy, becoming one of the "big" utilities in the UK — and thus part of the problem/solution.

Intéressement

In 2000, the Government introduced the Utilities Act 2000, which contained an Energy Efficiency Commitment (EEC) that enabled energy saving targets to be set by and enforced through OFGEM, funded by a levy on domestic annual energy bills. Several different charges were set through an array of policies. In 2002, the Government established the Fuel Poverty Advisory Group (FPAG) as an advisory Non-Departmental Public Body (NDPB) sponsored by the Department of Energy and Climate Change (DECC).

Between 2000 and 2004, global energy prices were low, and this was reflected in UK domestic energy bills. The number of English households affected by fuel poverty fell by three-quarters from 5.1 million households in 1996 to 1.2 million in 2004. By 2005, the 2003 English House Condition Survey (EHCS) concluded that the number of homes that were not up to official standards had fallen by 13% since 2001. In 2010, the Government announced that the fuel poverty Warm Front scheme had assisted over 2 million households (separate to EDF/government supplier initiatives).

EDF's role in Intéressement: EDF Energy took the formal position that fuel poverty is a poverty issue and should be addressed by Government through wider social programmes. However, it was also the first energy supplier in the UK to create a social tariff to help customers at risk of fuel poverty from 2006. In 2003, EDF Energy also established the industry's first Trust Fund for customers with household debt problems.

Enrolment

In 2008, the Climate Change Act 2008 imposed a legally binding obligation on the UK Government to reduce greenhouse gas (GHG) emissions by 34% by 2020 and by 80% by 2050. The 2008–2012 Carbon Emissions Reduction Target (CERT) programme was created. This CERT programme was a supplier obligation to deliver an energy efficiency programme. This programme, together with the Community Energy Saving Programme (CESP), an energy/carbon saving programme, required energy suppliers and generators to deliver a £350 million programme of energy-saving interventions to around 90,000 low-income households across the UK, coming at an additional cost of approximately £1.3 billion annually. Both programmes were to be delivered as part of suppliers' mandatory obligations, a condition of their licence agreements.

Between 2004 and 2009, the number of households in fuel poverty rose more than threefold, reaching 4.0 million in 2009. In 2008, OFGEM carried out a probe into the electricity and gas supply costs across all suppliers, generating widespread media interest.

EDF role in Enrolment: EDF Energy and the other five main energy suppliers agreed to increase spend on social programmes voluntarily through a formal Supplier Voluntary Commitment from April 2008 to March 2011. The suppliers undertook to spend a total of £375 million on programmes of support to those customers most likely to be living in fuel poverty.

Mobilisation

In 2010, the Government changed and the so-called Green Deal was introduced in the Energy Act 2011 to reduce household carbon emissions by means of a finance mechanism. This financing was designed to allow households to benefit from energy efficiency measures at no upfront cost, by attaching a charge to the property and making repayments through the electricity bill. There was also a new yearly £1.3 billion Energy Company Obligation (ECO) established (2013–2015) to replace previous programmes such as CERT, with 25% of the scheme designated for subsidised energy efficiency measures for low-income and vulnerable households. In 2011 the Warm Home Discount was introduced by the Government, with the aim of offering additional support to people at risk of being fuel poor by offering support, including rebates, through the electricity suppliers.

EDF's role in mobilisation was that of a proactive participant, establishing an Energy Toolkit, offering free insulation, and building partnerships.

4. Concluding Comments

The three-stage process we developed enabled EDF to compare "apples and oranges" — VCS projects previously considered so different from each other that there were no overlapping lessons that could be learned. By involving key professionals who had initiated the various EDF projects across the world, we were able to capture their insights for the first time for the organisation. Many of these key individuals were close to retirement, and had this reflective project that EDF initiated and invited us to collaborate in not been undertaken, the tacit knowledge they had acquired would have walked out of the door with them. In addition, the project enabled EDF to consider some of the implicit assumptions it holds about its role in the provision of energy.

This project taught us that the combination of the VCS and ANT approaches is greater than the sum of the parts. By drawing on the VCS work of Normann–Ramírez and the ANT work of Akrich–Callon–Latour, we were able to understand the critical moments required to create value and provide sustainable energy systems. Value is created within and by a system by the interactive dynamics of the actors rather than by the actors themselves; and by diagrammatically illustrating how these work (see examples), an organisation is able to explore novel and innovative ways to reconfigure value, and outsiders are able to quickly and effectively grasp the complex dynamics of involvement required to achieve this.

One additional outcome of the project was that EDF was able to better articulate the roles of the various parties, thereby putting it in a unique position to leverage its competences in this area and be a configuring offering designer in creating new VCS configurations. Another is that it helped us to better ascertain what it takes to design and bring forth an effective VCS.

Chapter 7

Assessing the Future Contexts a VCS Design Might Inhabit[1]

Box 7.1: Chapter 7 at a Glance

In this chapter, we assess two of the key roles scenario planning can hold when assessing the viability of existing value creating system (VCS) designs and as a support in the designing of new VCSs. We very succinctly review the thinking and practice of scenario planning, and we relate it to the business idea and to the design of offerings. Scenario planning redirects attention to contexts — which is particularly useful when these might become uncertain. We articulate our reasoning as to why collaborative strategy becomes at least as important as competitive strategy, in uncertain contexts where scenario planning is of help. We review two applications of scenario planning. The first is the design of new, collaborative, inter-organisational forms with the express purpose of decreasing the turbulence (particularly, the aspects pertaining to

(*Continued*)

[1] This chapter is partly derived and adapted from R. Ramírez and K. van der Heijden (2007), Scenarios to Develop Strategic Options: A New Interactive Role for Scenarios in Strategy; Chapter 4 in Sharpe and K. van der Heijden (eds.), *Scenarios for Success: Turning Insights into Action*. John Wiley and Sons, and also from R. Ramírez and A. Wilkinson (2016) "*Strategic Reframing: The Oxford Scenario Planning Approach*", Oxford University Press.

Box 7.1: (*Continued*)

unforecastable uncertainty and complexity) that would buffet the organisations if they did not come together. The second application is the use of scenario planning to support the design of technology and competence roadmaps and the new VCSs that these investments allow.

1. Scenario Planning in the VCS Approach to Strategy

Scenario planning is a powerful and effective way to explore future conditions that a VCS might find itself in when it is exposed to uncertainties in complex environments within a given time horizon.

So scenario planning can be used for testing an existing or intended strategy for a current VCS — its configuring and supporting offering designs — as well as to explore plausible future contextual conditions and relevant design criteria to inform the designing of a new VCS.

Put simply, scenario planning involves the manufacture of a set of plausible, challenging, useful, and relevant future contexts that an intended strategy or VCS design might inhabit: produced for someone, for a given purpose, and for a specific use (for an up to date assessment of the field, see Ramírez & Wilkinson, 2016).

Scenario planning has been used in companies since the 1960s (Lesourne & Stoffaes, 2001; Grant, 2003; van der Heijden, 2005) and even longer by military planners and policy-makers. It serves a wide variety of purposes, which may include efforts to reframe the understanding of a situation, to help to reperceive strategic opportunities, to improve the quality of strategic conversations, to correct judgement biases, to enhance organisational learning, to influence stakeholders, to help different parties identify and agree upon common ground, to create new relationships, to reach out to new co-creators, to surface and question assumptions in models or strategy; to make sense of ambiguous settings; to have a common language to join up disjointed organisational divisions; or to research and clarify complex issues.

As Figure 7.1 illustrates, in scenario planning we distinguish between the more immediate business (or "transactional") environment that a strategist (CEO or team in a firm) influences through their interactions with counterparts (who, from their point of view, are "actors" or "interactors") from the "factors" around these interactors, which remain beyond the

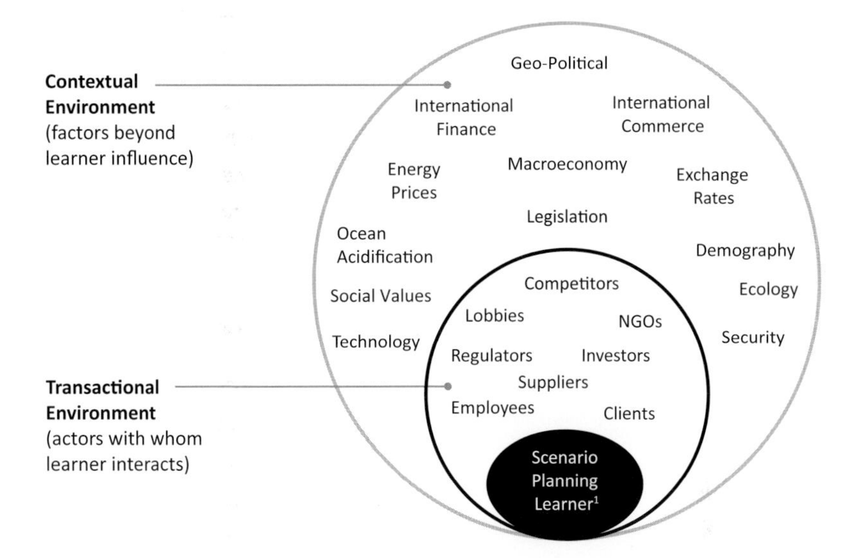

Figure 7.1: The Transactional and the Contextual Environments[2]

strategist's influence — and which constitute and are situated in the broader "contextual" environment.

Scenarios are constructed by analysing the factors and how these might relate to each other in the future; and once a plausible contrasting set of such scenarios are constructed, then the inquiry moves into what transactional or business environment might arise in each of those scenarios.

While there are very many "methods" to develop a set of scenarios in scenario planning, with different authors proposing different numbers of steps (for an overview see Ramírez & Wilkinson, 2016), all involve the aspects, which were summarised by Wilkinson, Selin and Ramírez in the Oxford Scenarios Programme (see Figure 7.2).

Research has established that scenario planning is an approach well suited to support strategy in conditions where forecasting is either unreliable or less applicable. These conditions are turbulent environments (van der Heijden, 1996; Ramírez *et al.*, 2010); and situations that in addition to turbulence exhibit unpredictable uncertainty, complexity, novelty, and/or ambiguity — TUNA conditions (Ramírez & Wilkinson, 2016). As we

---

[2]In this figure the central scenario planning learner is assumed to be top management. If it is a division head, then other division management teams, and HQs, would be in the transactional environment; if it is a government ministry (e.g. Natural Resources), then other ministries (Finance, etc.) would be in the transactional environment.

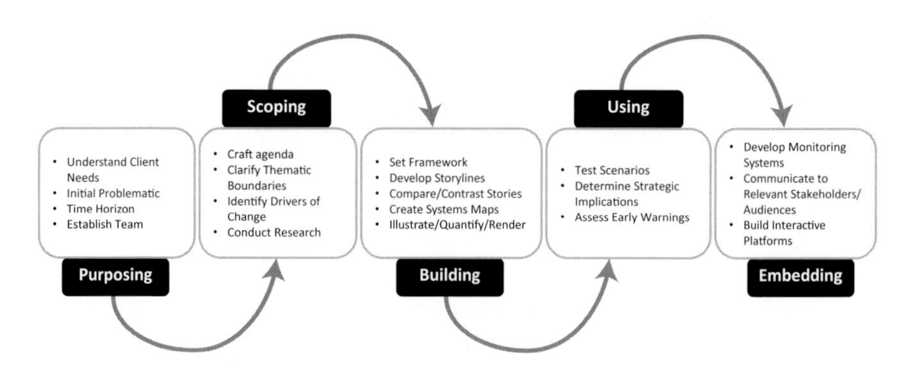

Figure 7.2: A Generic Framework for Scenarios Planning[3]

have argued in previous chapters, these are also the conditions where VCS thinking and strategy approaches are useful.

2. Scenario Planning as Structured but Flexible Inquiry

As we see elsewhere in this book, the designing of new VCSs is not straightforward. As we further describe in Chapter 8, this designing includes complex analyses of possible interactions (and relations among interactors in constellations of roles); and the design of viable configuring and support offerings that enrol people and their organisations into the roles that the design requires to become operative and remain sustainable. This can be structured into a design process of exploring user contexts and other actor contexts (Normann, 2001). This process should also allow for iterative inquiry (Churchman, 1972) in various loops of framing and reperception (Ramírez & Wilkinson, 2016), where conceptual and intersubjective processes link the individual and collective minds of managers. When done well, the process of inquiry — done with the help of scenario planning — helps groups move away from groupthink while avoiding becoming too fragmented (Ramírez & Wilkinson, 2016).

Both testing of existing strategies for VCSs, and designing new offerings and the VCSs they engender, might involve courageous conversations where professionals working in incumbent firms have the courage not to

[3] *Source*: Wilkinson, Selin, and Ramírez, Oxford Scenarios Programme. Used with permission.

reject promising possibilities, which they could perhaps perceive as making the continuation of their roles or jobs unviable (Christensen, 1997). Van der Heijden (1996, 2005) demonstrated how scenario planning can help to improve the quality of strategic conversations and help people to be more courageous in productively contesting the established views.

We consider scenario planning to be a good approach to support search and research approaches that can be adopted by managers seeking to either test existing VCSs or innovate new VCSs. Existing practices — particularly if they have encountered success for some time — can conceal tacit assumptions about existing and future roles. These assumptions may have made sense in the past but with changed conditions may now appear to be arbitrary demarcations between "what is (or can be) ours" and "what cannot be". Obsolete assumptions that remain unsurfaced and unquestioned may render potentially valuable strategic configurations difficult to explore.

Fortunately it is possible to safely surface, question, and even challenge what might otherwise remain as a tacit assumption — and scenario planning can be of very valuable help with this. This surfacing, questioning, and constructive challenging requires tailored "safe spaces" that help people to together rehearse and feel a possible transition from that which exists now to possible futures — which change management calls the "transitional approach" to change, based on ideas of Winnicott (1965) and Bridger (see Amado & Ambrose, 2001). In such bespoke spaces, exploratory VCS designs can be prototyped and tested under different plausible future conditions with the help of scenario planning before (and without) committing to them. Scenario planning is an excellent way to design such transitional spaces and to test strategies under plausible future conditions (Ramírez *et al.*, 2008).

3. Support in Testing or Developing VCS Designs

How does scenario planning work in helping to see the implications for existing VCS designs or new opportunities for new VCS developments? It works by exploring contextual trends and uncertainties, informed by research, and by attending to the aspects of the present that are already shaped by the future (hopes, fears, expectations); that is, by attending to the future in the present. It does so by looking at the present and its context from a small set of manufactured and specified points of view located in the conceptual future (Normann, 2001). From those future standpoints, scenario planning helps someone (the VCS designers in this case) to look at something; and it does so in a way that helps the VCS designers to surface the assumptions that have been used (typically tacitly) to model the existing VCS designs. This makes it possible to constructively and productively question established assumptions and, with the alternatives, come up with more a resilient VCS design. In Chapter 8, we overview the (iterative) process steps involved.

This surfacing and questioning of assumptions matters, as an analysis of 80 failed strategies (Finkelstein *et al.*, 2009) attributed 82% of these to "misleading prejudgments", 64% to "misleading experiences" and 43% to "inappropriate attachments". Thus scenario planning can play a role in questioning whether prejudgments and prior experiences (and the attachments one may have made to these emotionally) are relevant or unhelpful for the next strategic situation at hand.

Scenarios are always inquiries about what possible future contexts a VCS might inhabit. Using scenario planning can help strategists to redirect their attention to how plausible contextual changes could alter the effectiveness of their intended design. Scenario planning can play an important role to help them to surface assumptions (which had often remained tacit) of the existing design and with these create alternative VCS designs.

3.1 Scenario Planning and the "Business Idea"

It was our colleague Kees van der Heijden (1996, 2005) who introduced the concept of "the business idea (BI)" in the context of scenario planning after collaborating with Normann and Ramírez.[4] Below, we show how our systems- and interactions-based view of the business idea differs from that of van der Heijden, and suggest when to use our more recently developed

[4]Normann (1977) defined the concept of "the business idea", and in 1996, van der Heijden adapted it as the grounding reality of scenario planning engagements. Following Normann, van der Heijden considered that any VCS entails a business idea — whether it is a "business" or not. For him, wherever there is a management team, there is a business idea. With VCS analyses such as those we describe in Chapter 6, it is possible to unearth and clarify the design for value creation underpinning any business idea.

view of the business idea, building on the reasoning on the offering we covered in Chapter 5.

A business idea according to van der Heijden involves the initial conditions of scarcity for something in a society that gave rise to a business (e.g. the wish by many to go to sunny beaches in winter at affordable prices); the entrepreneurial idea that arose as a result (e.g. package holidays); the activities that make that possible and how they contribute to the sustainability of the business (e.g. tour operators; massive hotel development; charter airlines) and the distinctive competences (Selsznick, 1957) firms like TUI or Thompson have developed to make the whole business viable season after season. For van der Heijden, it is the package of distinctive competences and their manifestations (brands, locations, processes, etc.) that make a given business sellable and allows it to be bought, for it is these distinctive competences that make the design of the VCS, which the BI marshals viable over time.

4. The Interactions-Based View of the "Business Idea"

For van der Heijden — importantly — any business idea "depicts what is fundamental for success in specific terms in one holistic representation" (van der Heijden, 2005: 63) — and it integrates both the organisation as well as its context in terms of the "scarcities in [the] society" it serves.

As "business ideas" are relevant for anyone creating value, whether it is financial or not, a business idea is at the core of a design for a VCS. However, in a VCS the business idea is centrally manifested in the configuring offering and its supporting offerings. Given that in this book offerings are inherently highly interactive, we differ from van der Heijden in our thinking that the business idea is much more manifested in these interactions (embodied in offerings) than in the distinctive competencies that van der Heijden focused on.

So, as opposed to van der Heijden, who invited strategists to rethink the distinctive competence of their organisation in different scenarios, we instead invite them to rethink and (if required) redesign the configuring offering in each, and thus the VCS. An effective configuring offering design defining the VCS in one scenario may be far less effective in another scenario. We describe a design methodology for this in Chapter 8.

5. Using Scenario Planning to Transform the Boundaries between the VCS and its Context

Strategy is considered "contingent" in the sense that its success depends upon obtaining fit between an organisation and its environment. It is thus not surprising that notions of the "environment" have a long history in both strategy and scenario work. Successful strategy involves the discovery or generation of new and effective ways for the organisation to relate to its environment.

We saw in Figure 7.1 that in scenario planning a distinction is made between the more immediate "transactional" (or "business") environment and the broader "contextual" one in which both the organisation for which the strategist works and the organisation's transactional environment are found. So by definition, the "contextual environment" is that part of the environment of every organisation that it cannot influence; whereas the organisation has offerings in relations to all parts of its transactional environment, and therefore can influence it to a smaller or larger degree.

A new design of a VCS by any one firm (typically carried out with others) can challenge the existing distinction between that individual firm's transactional and contextual environments (Emery and Trist, 1965; van der Heijden, 1996; Ramírez, Selsky & van der Heidjen, 2008). In that established distinction, the more remote part of the environment, which (*by definition*) a given firm cannot control or influence, is the "contextual environment". Within the transactional environment, managers can interact and to the extent they interact with others, influence them. That is not possible for them to do in the contextual environments, which as we saw above is made up of factors[5] beyond their influence.

So in the transactional environment, every one actor has an influence on the others in this environment, but not total control. In this immediate environment, the reciprocal actions by any one actor will elicit actions by

[5] Illustrative examples of contextual factors in business (which may involve many different time scales) include larger developments in politics and society such as the Arab Spring or the invasion of Crimea; economic breakdowns as witnessed in the 2008 financial crises; social phenomena such as the rise or fall of the middle class and ageing societies; and novel technological developments such as fracking and nanomedicine.

other actors, which in turn stimulate further rounds of interaction. For this reason, the transactional environment is sometimes referred to as the "playing field". Scenario planning can be used to role-play the actions and interactions that might logically arise in the contextual conditions given by one scenario. We have over the years designed and run detailed "simulations" of collaborative and competitive interactions with new VCSs in place with the help of scenario planning.

Such simulations can be run as so-called "war games", which help strategists to explore how different actors in their transactional environment might react to each other's strategies and actions within different contextual conditions (made up of systems of factors) manifested in a small set of plausible scenarios. Conducting these scenarios-based simulations, the game is played in different scenarios. Each scenario implies a distinct path into a separate future, with playing actions and reactions for each player as the scenario unfolds. This allows strategists to combine the exploring of the implications of contextual change by understanding which future structural market dynamics might unfold. These include assessing the opportunities and challenges that each scenario poses, and the strengths and weaknesses their organisation has to face. In a recent engagement for a client in the global energy field, such analyses enabled their strategic team to assess potential decisions before these were taken. When a situation that was similar to one described in the scenarios actually unfolded, they were better informed on the possible courses of action to take, and on what actions those they interacted with might take.

In the context of the strategic design and redesign of potentially new configuring offerings and the new VCSs they would bring forth, the boundary between the two environments is to a marked degree subjective, with assumptions about roles to a surprising extent determining how far one senior manager believes their company can exercise influence compared to another senior colleague, who believes that less is actually possible to influence. More adventurous management teams might be more prepared to consider a wider playing field than their more conservative colleagues — and will bring this consideration to life by interacting with a broader set of counterparts.

Ramírez and van der Heiden suggested that probing the boundary between contextual and transactional environments not only helps to surface tacit assumptions about roles and relationships, and to challenge established beliefs about constraints that may no longer be valid, but can also be undertaken specifically to assess how to reduce turbulence. It is in this role that scenario planning can help new VCSs to come about.

This redrawing of the transactional/contextual environment boundary by coming together with actors that remained outside the existing VCS with a new offering that configures a new VCS is depicted graphically in Figure 7.3 below.

Our experience suggests that this shift — which helps to (at least in part) convert contextual uncertainties into transactional environment standards and thus keeps turbulence away — can, however, also bring about other important changes that one is well advised to consider before enacting them. For example, those interactors whom in one scenario one thought of as customers may actually become competitors in another scenario; competitors might become partners; partner may become investors, etc.

A good example of how this has been achieved is what VISA (Ramírez & Wallin, 2000, analysed the French part of the business as a case study)

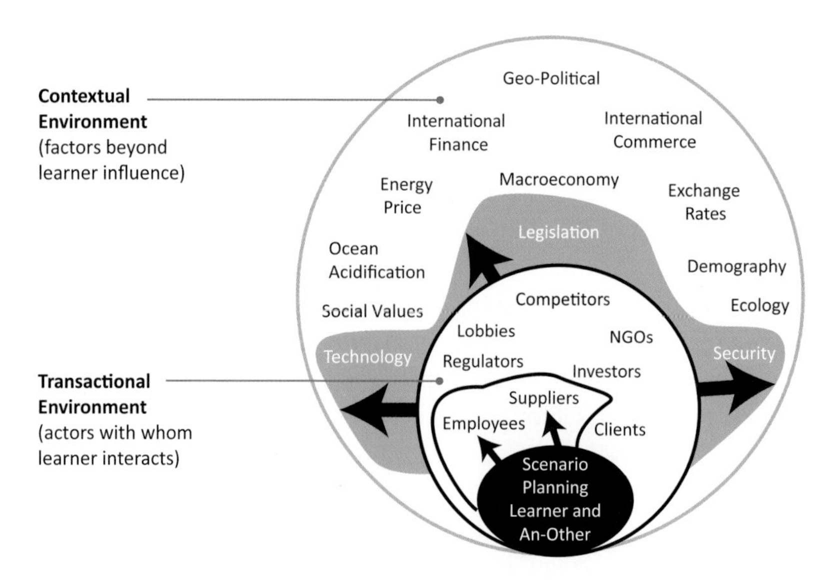

Figure 7.3: Collaborative Strategy to Shift the Transactional/Contextual Environment Boundary

or MasterCard did for retail banks. By bringing together the banks with major retailers, with telecommunications and network providers, with terminal makers, and with consumers, VISA and MasterCard enabled the banks to take forces beyond their control or influence that had been converging on them from the contextual environment (such as those brought forth by new technologies, globalised trade, security concerns, and legal payment standards) and instead made it possible for these factors to become influenced. The joint venture, cross-sectoral (Selsky & Parker, 2005) VCS architectures that were spawned by VISA and MasterCard allowed the banks and their enrolled colleagues in the VCS they designed and brought together to convert and combine these forces into effective processes as agreed upon standards and protocols.

In this view, VISA and MasterCard's distinctive design competence was essentially to transform uncertain and turbulent contextual environment domains into transactional environment ones. In the language of this book, this competence was a design competence that read a future scenario where contextual forces might become turbulent and acted to design a configuring offering (payment cards) and then support offerings (payment contracts, technical standards, branding, etc.) so that they and their member banks and other co-creators could influence factors which would otherwise have remained unpredictable uncertainties in the contextual environment, thereby decreasing uncertainty, complexity, and ambiguity.

Scenario planning, with the open and inclusive visions it affords, with the ability to dramatise and test new possibilities quickly and vividly, and with the power to weave together previously unconsidered connections, offers an effective way to redraw the map, to reframe possibilities, to reperceive the landscape, to even assess the boundary between the transactional and contextual environment, and to draw together different actors in a constructive collaborative endeavour.

This novel way of thinking about scenario planning in strategy extends the traditional uses of scenario planning. For the reasons we surveyed above, scenarios used for strategy development have tended to treat the contextual environment as a given; perhaps because the contextual environment is by definition beyond one's control or influence — all one can do is to identify and analyse the driving forces emanating from it that might change one's transactional environment. So the uses of scenarios have in this manner entailed a more limited set of possibilities of what might plausibly occur as the possibilities have tended to be limited to that which could happen within the transactional environment — at best, a different transactional environment is to be expected in each scenario. In any case, in that view the existing transactional environment has been seen as the main domain for strategy, as it is thus only within this narrower environment that strategic options can change relationships. Ramírez & Selsky (2014) contrasted that traditional ("neoclassical") approach with what they called a "social-ecological" approach to strategy — where firms might come together to stabilise the environment for and with each other. The 2006 assessment by Ramírez and van der Heijden, upon which we build here, proposed a use of scenarios in a process of designing new VCSs (see Chapter 8) with precisely that intent as its central strategic proposition.

6. Using Scenario Planning in Technology and Business Roadmaps

The transport company Scania, known for its premium trucks, buses, and engines is an example of a global firm that is using scenario planning in several parts of its organisation, including in cross-organisational initiatives to inform the assessment and design of different parts of its VCS.

Each application area is informed by a common set of scenarios which is adapted and enriched as required, each time. The company also has a common way of working on the creation and progress review of its roadmaps. Scania is interesting in the way it uses scenarios to explore future business conditions to explore and to develop new systems-based businesses (see Chapter 8). It uses scenario-based roadmaps to build competences over the long term, consistently focusing on methods, an approach that is also reflected in how they work with these roadmaps. In what follows here, we describe Scania's use of scenarios-based roadmaps to secure access to competences, and how it uses its methodology skills to manifest the roadmaps as processes.

The group has a global VCS, consisting of interactors that include transport company customers, transport buyers, cities, other large transport users or stakeholders, workshop networks, distributors, production units, logistics partners, research and development (R&D) partners, and supplier networks — on various markets throughout the world. Access to competences includes but is not limited to skilled engineers. Such access is seen as a question of strategic importance in Scania. Unsurprisingly, a key factor behind Scania's success — as the leading company in its field, with a profitability far above that of its peers — has been the co-location of key functions such as marketing, R&D and production of strategic components in Sweden. This has enabled strategic cross-organisational co-ordination and the leveraging of its methodology skills to make continuous improvement possible.

The group has located many strategic functions in Sweden, which is fairly remote from several of Scania's large markets. Yet its main hub in Sweden, which has in turn both benefited from and contributed to the development of an advanced regional supplier network, in particular concerning heavy powertrains. In the terms of this book, Scania's VCS has a high density of interactions in this geographic region, where several of its support offerings can be found (suppliers, current as well as future employees, academics who conduct relevant research, etc.). One of the most important questions for maintaining this interactivity density for Scania as well as for its suppliers and partners is future access to skilled employees — including research networks in academia — who maintain world-class competence in their relevant areas.

Engineering and research competences take a long time to build, so a key strategic question for Scania is determining what competences it will be needing in the mid- to long-term, to be able to maintain, develop and further leverage one of the corner stones of its historical success of effective interactivity. One of the main applications of scenario planning at Scania has concerned how it develops scenarios-based technology roadmaps to explore how customer contexts might change, who their future customers and other interactors might be, what might be in demand, and what all of this implies for Scania's R&D so it can contribute to develop the right offerings. This of course extends to also comprise assessing what future competences its R&D and production and logistics will require.

Upon focusing their global transport scenarios on the concerns of Scania's own production and logistics, they explored how their current production and logistics model might need to develop within the next 20 years. The possibilities depend on several factors, such as how their larger context and the world of production and logistics might unfold. Informed by extensive external and internal research and iterative scenario planning enquiries, Scania developed a novel technology roadmap that stretches beyond the more traditional and conventional technology roadmap it had at the start of the initiative. This included their analysing not only how global high impact factors might develop, assessing how they could affect factors and interactors such as supplier networks, production and logistics technologies, vehicle-related materials, workforce demographics, and energy efficiency-related technologies. They also considered how such changes might affect more "close to home" production and logistics technologies. With this use of scenario planning, they have assessed a company-wide research portfolio and competence structure, "wind tunnelling" it in different plausible future scenario contexts to define future target portfolios, to carry out gap-analyses between what might be needed "there and then" compared to what is available "here and now", and to develop research and competence pathways to reach these targets.

This way of utilising scenario planning to explore the VCS in each scenario has thus been helpful for Scania in defining roadmaps which are scenario-independent. That is, the agreed roadmap includes a set of technological and competence pathways that are robust in all scenarios, and they also include contingency elements required only for one or two scenarios, but not for all. This enables the company to have bought itself flexibility, with well-prepared alternatives for more than one possible future development of its business context.

In designing the roadmaps as cross-silo, multilayered, organisation-wide initiatives, the scenario planning has enabled Scania professionals not only to surface assumptions upon which the business and its VCSs depend today and may need to depend upon in the future, but also to identify what competences, technologies, and businesses they ought to develop to remain successful in each future scenario. Scania has been doing this in ways that allow for the flexible inquiry that we have described above. Their process of inquiry allows different parts of the organisation — and in some parts, also dialogue with external partners — to have more courageous strategic conversations, conversations that otherwise can be more difficult to hold.

6.1 Scenario Planning as a Process

After describing how Scania uses scenarios to see what competences they need to build, we turn to how it uses its methodology skills to manifest scenarios-based roadmaps as processes.

One of the things that has made Scania different from its peers is its philosophy of focusing on methods rather than on results. At Scania, they believe good results follow from clear principles, manifested as effective methods when these are combined with fostering employee commitment to enable customer profitability. This formula has served them well, and as mentioned above, for many years it has been by far the most profitable company among its peers.

Their focus on methods is reflected in several ways, including their highly modularised design of trucks and components. This provides them with a cost effective way to offer many premium quality variants of their products and services at competitive cost. In the VCS terms of this book, their offerings are customised for specific interactions between many types of specific transport companies and their own clients. This approach also simplifies supplier networks and production, and reduces the cost of warehousing, logistics, etc., which supports their field leading profitability.

Consistent with its focus on methods, Scania does not consider roadmaps to be plans, but processes. These are processes with which people across concerned units can review progress, attend to deviations, do cause analyses, and follow-up on actions — a principle that Scania is very used to and skilled at in its organisation at large.

Thus, they have translated their methods skills into their roadmap work in ways that allow them to attend to both the immediate concerns of the business and its current VCS, as well as also being able to redesign competence and technology development for VCS changes that they have been exploring with scenario planning. This helps them to set robust contingency plans and to define ambitions over the mid- and long term. This approach of method as process supports the development of the Scania group both in terms of being able to build competences that allows them to be more prepared to meet different plausible futures, and in terms of institutionalising scenarios and scenario-based roadmap work as a way of working, allowing, and enabling flexible inquiry.

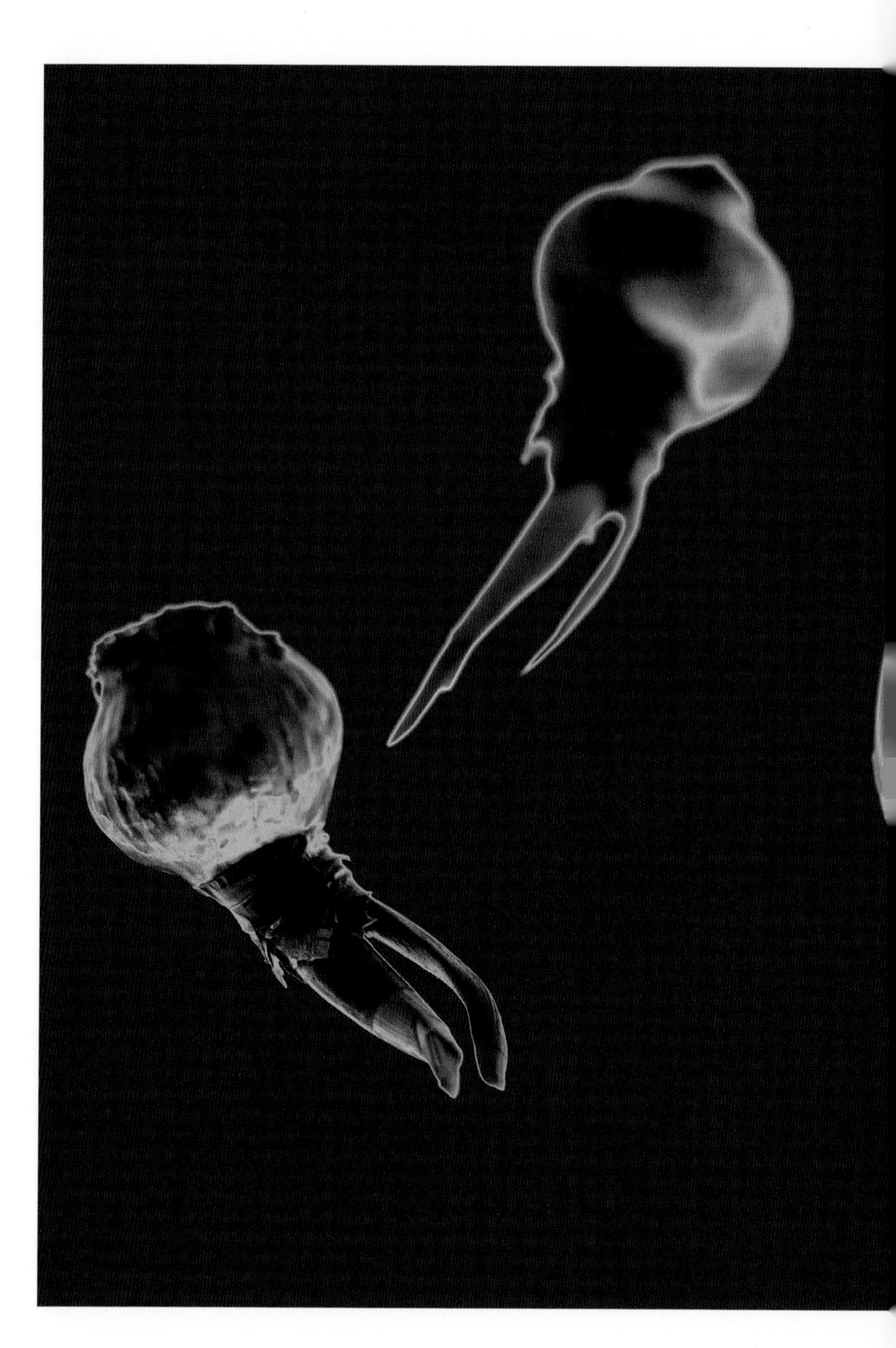

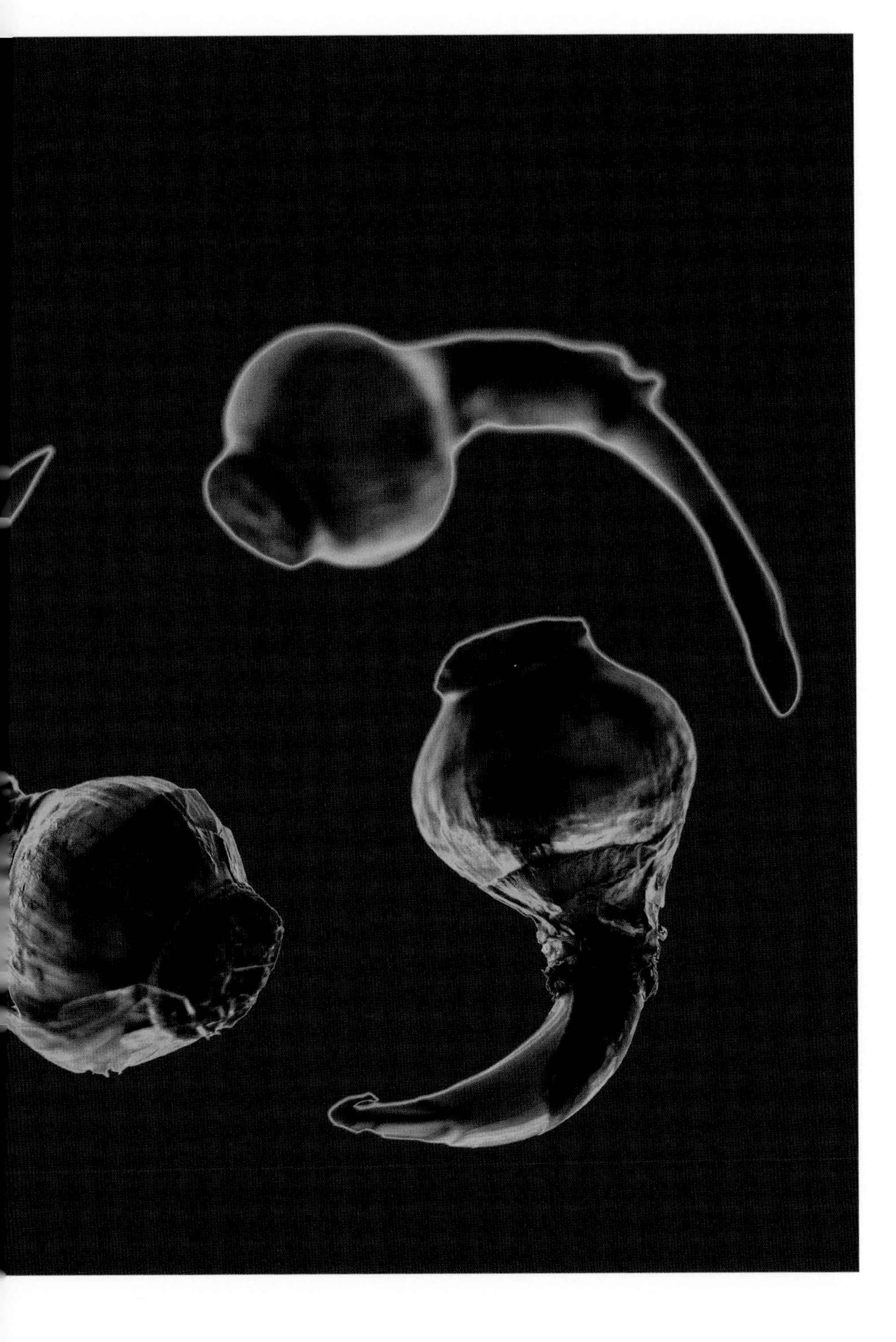

Chapter 8

Designing a New Value Creating System

Box 8.1: Chapter 8 at a Glance

This chapter outlines methodological guidelines for designing new value creating systems (VCSs). The design process and its approach can include ANT analyses and scenario planning and also other iterative steps. Sometimes the VCS that a strategic team designs is entirely new (such as the one that put a human being on the moon, and returned him home safely), but often a new VCS is set up to capture newly understood opportunities, or to address threats or shortcomings that an existing VCS cannot engage, but which can include aspects of an existing VCS design. The argument in this chapter follows and develops the business design approach described by Normann in his 2001 book *Reframing Business*. After overviewing this background, five main components are described. The first is a historical overview of the shaping factors of the VCS context and distinct competences of the organisation that aims at designing the new VCS. This is followed by analyses of VCSs, including all co-creators, whether they are denominated customers or hold other roles, and assessing what potential invaders (typically from other fields or "industries") might enter that space. The next stage involves exploring opportunities as well as challenges for the VCS design to define the strategic intents and

(*Continued*)

Box 8.1: (*Continued*)

the first version of the configuring and support offerings manifesting these. Chapter 9 describes the fifth stage — building strategic pathways and preparing for governance. The chapter uses several references to the global companies SCA[1] and Scania,[2] who are leaders in their fields, and users of VCS approaches to continue pioneering these fields.

How can a strategic team systemically explore the bigger value creating field it is in, the context of use for its current and intended co-creators, so as to design new VCSs — or further develop existing ones?

As we showed in Chapter 1, Facebook's success can be attributed to its having considered the system of users' value creation — what values they can achieve, enabled by Facebook — better than Myspace. The latter had a more conventional strategy approach where it concentrated its focus on adding new features to the existing "product". Facebook had a far more effective idea of what "bigger value creation" it was in, in terms of enabling people to build communities, networking, and staying in touch with friends and families. The development of its configuring offerings (organised system as a set of interactions) and supporting offerings (individual interactions, within the organised system) enabled value creating interactions for those who were part of the system.

Based on research in the fields of innovation, strategy and design, and emergence and self-organisation (e.g. Dorst & Cross, 2001; Normann, 2001; Schön, 1983; Varela & Maturana, 1987, 1998), and our consulting experience of VCS innovation and strategic change, we propose methodological guidelines that our clients have found helpful for designing new VCSs. The approach builds on the methodology proposed by Normann (2001), and has since been further developed by us (see Ramírez & Mannervik, 2006; Ramírez & Wilkinson, 2016) and deployed in consulting

[1]Björn Ålsnäs, Global Brand Innovation Manager, Service, SCA Hygiene Products, co-authored that part of this chapter.

[2]Sigvard Orre, Business Development Director at Scania, and Board Member of LOTS Group AB, co-authored the LOTS case description.

engagements, including with some of the companies mentioned as illustrative cases in this book.

1. Normann's Crane as a Design Process for VCSs

Normann's process can be thought of as a "scaffold" for designing a new VCS or redesigning an existing VCS. One way to depict the process is in three stages, as is found in Figure 8.1. First there is an "opening phase" — in which one maps and develops knowledge about what an existing VCS does today and of the larger system of which it is a part. Then there is a middle "exploration phase" to consider how value creating in this space might change, what opportunities the strategic team can envision and which offerings might be designed to realise these. Finally there is a "closing phase" to define and refine the configuring and support offerings, to evaluate, prioritise and further develop these offerings; and to enact strategic intents as new interactions.

To enable a creative approach that would also be actionable, Normann suggested that strategists would be well advised to build themselves a "crane", which he saw as a conceptual and experimental process for VCS design that followed the logics of innovative processes. As he put it, doing so would allow one to:

> "take stock of what (one has), yet distance (oneself) from it and explore new territory. The crane must be able to bend minds. It must open up a

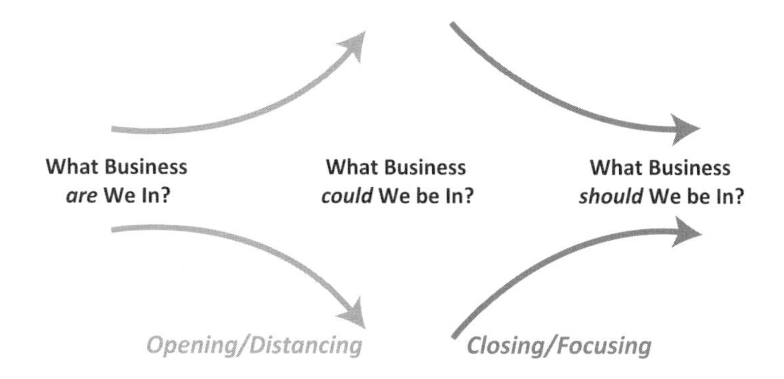

Figure 8.1: The Three Stages of the VCS Design Process (based on Normann, 2001)

conceptual space beyond what is known and can be imagined today, and it must then allow (one) to fill that conceptual space with new design. It must start from where (one is) — here and now, take (one) into unchartered territory, yet allow (one) to come back with new insights and start concrete construction work on a reframed business strategy." (Normann, 2001: 201)

The metaphor of the crane reflects that the design and experimentation process involves a structure — in Normann's words a scaffold — that operates both in terms of height and time. As is shown in Figure 8.2, the crane inquiry is designed to allow strategic planners' views to be lifted "vertically" to a higher system level view of their business in ways that "sweeps in" the business context, as well as to a lower system level where the ideas can be tested "on the ground". The other dimension is temporal and allows the strategic mind to be moved horizontally; "backward" to consider the past and "forward" to imagine future possibilities. Normann borrowed the crane metaphor from Dennett (1995), who used it to contrast the teleological explanation of evolution as something where "skyhooks"

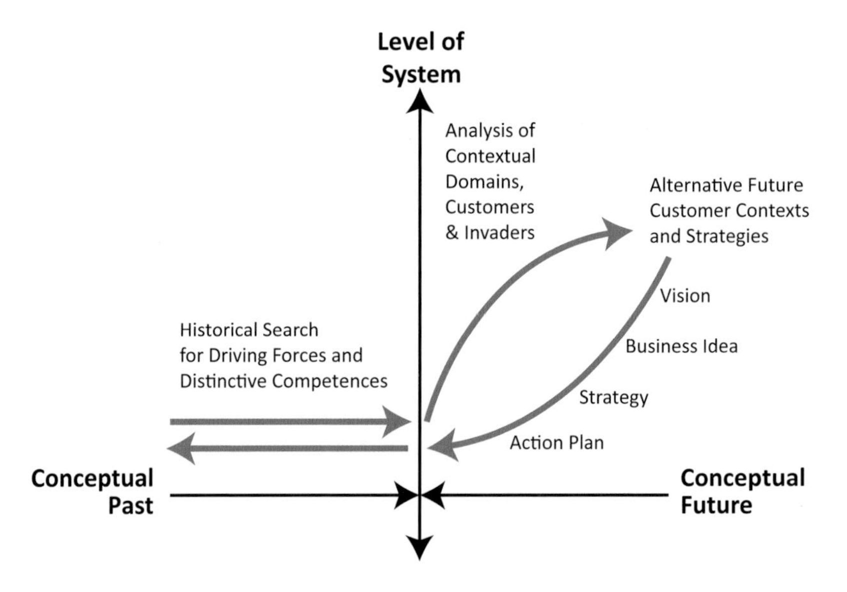

Figure 8.2: Richard Normann's Crane (from Normann 2001, used with permission)

lift the mind up to higher states of understanding with creative ideas coming at the thinker. It involves a view of evolution as something that is both conditioned by what history imposes, what the future might bring, and by agency on the part that strategists can affect.

So, the crane helps strategists redirect their attention along two dimensions, each with two directions. "First there is a North–South" dimension along which they can upframe their attention, to include more of the context and get a "bigger picture" view than that which is held "every day" by the senior managers they work with. On that dimension they can also downframe it, to get a more grounded and detailed view of implications when the strategy is put into place. In addition there is an East–West dimension with the past on the West and Conceptual Futures on the East.

A strategic team using Normann's crane might first build an understanding of the historical roots and drivers of the offering and VCS and its context. Secondly, they would upframe the offering to attend to how it works within the larger system of interactors and value co-creation it is part of. This upframed system would simultaneously be considered within a small set of conceptual futures to assess how it might look from these future perspectives. The inquiry would then move and begin exploring how it might change, as well as threats and opportunities for value creation, including a firm's own role. Then there is downframing the offering back to the here and now.

In Normann's view, the upframed system for exploring strategic innovation involves assessing how one could redesign and change the system one is part of, with the learning this affords being brought into designing and realising interactions to transform one's company's role and its VCSs.

Ramírez and Wilkinson (2016) extended the Normann view to manifest the downframing as a reperception loop where new options are rehearsed below the "usual" level of top management or strategic attention, looking at how the detail of the insights afforded in the upframing are seen in the downframing. This is graphically depicted in Figure 8.3.

Ramírez and Wilkinson's development of Normann's crane reflects the grounded work that can be undertaken to properly provide scrutiny and testing of specific options in designing new VCSs.

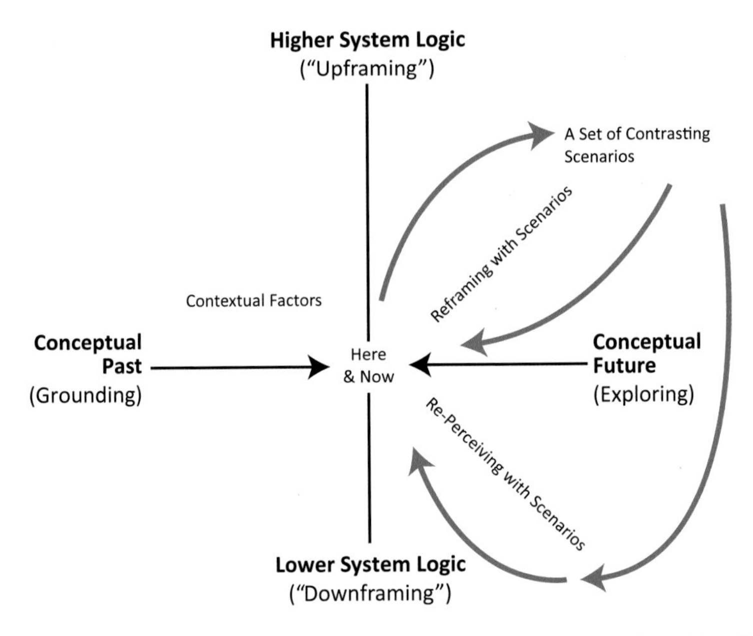

Figure 8.3: The Crane as a Re-framing and Re-perception Loop (from Ramírez & Wilkinson 2016, used with permission)

To make the use of the crane explicit in designing new VCSs, we have built on Ramírez and Wilkinson's version of the crane, as seen in Figure 8.4 below. Firstly, the ANT methodology described in Chapter 6 can be used to assess historical factors and their impact on the emergence of a given VCS design (say, an energy provision VCS design in Figure 8.4). Secondly, scenario planning can be used to explore plausible contexts the VCS might inhabit in the future. One part of this is to explore overall implications by reframing configuring offering designs (e.g. one of the novel VCSs that EDF pioneered is surveyed in Chapter 6). Another part, in the downframed part of the diagram, involves reperceiving what this means in practice with specific actor–actor interactions. Thirdly, the design methodology, which we discuss below in this chapter, can be used to design new configuring and support offerings.

We have found Normann's crane and its development to be a useful design process for VCSs. Although we describe the stages of the process

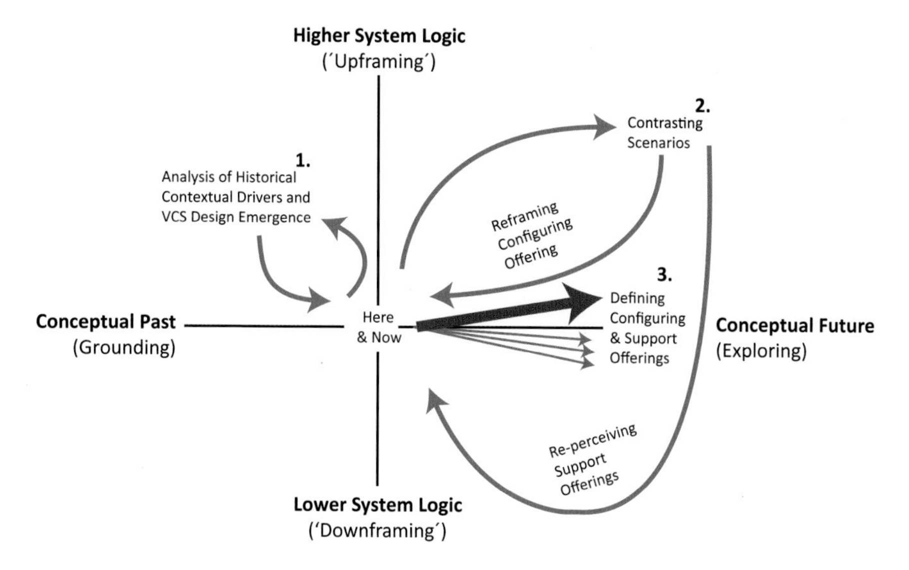

Figure 8.4: The Crane as Used in Designing a New VCS

as sequential, as did Normann, they can be looped back iteratively as needed (see Ramírez & Wilkinson, 2016), in order to reformulate both problems and ideas for solutions. Design research has found this to characterise creative design (see for example Dorst & Cross, *Ibid.*).

In practice, rather than first defining possible opportunity spaces, and then designing the offering, both inquiries feed from each other and co-evolve, forming spirals over time. This is similar to what Schön (1983) described when studying how creative practitioners such as architects think when engaging problems. Here too we see the VCS designer as having a conversation with the evolving drawings of the intended VCS design. Each stage in this iterative design process — in more detail than as manifested in Figure 8.4, is graphically shown in the example in Figure 8.5. Each stage is further described in the rest of this chapter. Again, while the stages are suggested here as a design process in sequence, in reality the process typically iterates among stages; and in some circumstances the strategic design process might involve some specific stages but not others.

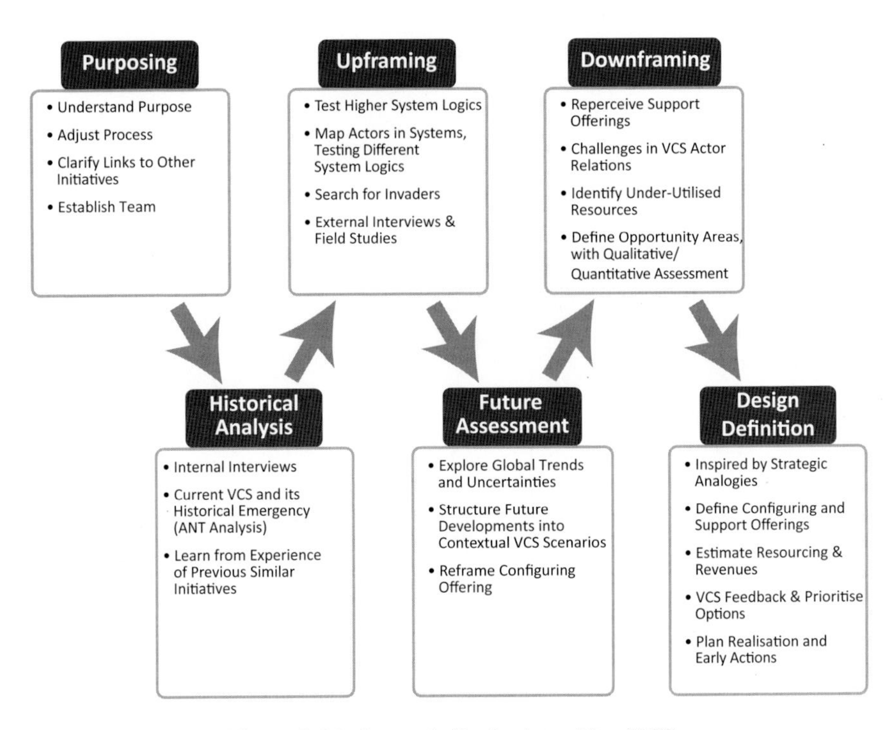

Figure 8.5: Stages in Designing a New VCS

2. Purposing the VCS Design Initiative and Grounding an Existing VCS

A first step involves establishing the user and purpose, situating these in relation to other initiatives. All the usual engagement and project management aspects need to be put into place, such as resourcing, scheduling, accountability, and responsibility, charting.

The design process then starts with building an understanding of the historical forces that played a part in shaping the existing VCS and its context. This may be done as an evolving picture more than as a snapshot ascertaining how the offerings, distinct competencies, and comparative strengths have developed — as we did with Facebook and the World Economic Forum in Chapter 1.

> "Understanding of our current predilection involves taking a systemic view much in accordance with Selznick's "distinctive competence" idea, with special emphasis on the "business idea" concept." [...] It means interpreting

> the success — and failures — of the organisation both in structural terms [...] and process terms [...]. It means identifying the possible "hubs of reframing" (assets, capabilities, customer relationships and customer bases) [...]. It means understanding the competitive structure — not least the invaders who nibble or make indents into our territory and therefore help us understand our weaknesses — as well as mapping the stronger values that may be emerging in our business context." (Normann, 2001: 219–220)

This analysis can be done through internal interviews, interviews with retired executives and former co-creators, and by reviewing documented previous offering and business development initiatives. The focus is on understanding the origin and basis for the value co-creation upon which the business (or possible new business) rests (or could rest); the values that have played a role; and which factors that have shaped the current offerings may persist going forward. This helps to appreciate how money has been made in the past, and how it is still today earned and how and which other values are co-created and reconciled. In assessing how the VCS has evolved, it is particularly helpful to surface and render explicit the existing assumptions it uses and how these might evolve moving forward.

The analysis includes mapping the interactions the company has with its customers and other interactors today, and how offering designs have evolved and why.

Figure 8.6 depicts a high-level overview of how the offerings of the global hygiene company SCA[3] works in some of its market segments today. There are of course local market variations to this, but the figure depicts the main interactions and relations. The figure illustrates the VCS of SCA in some of its "home nursing" markets, where it provides offerings based on incontinence products and related hygiene system products and services that help people to be cared for in their homes.

[3]SCA is a leading global hygiene and forest products company. The SCA Group develops and produces sustainable personal care, tissue and forest products. Sales are conducted in about 100 countries under many strong brands. [...] The Group has about 44,000 employees. Sales in 2014 amounted to approximately EUR 11.4 billion. Source: www.sca.com (Accessed December 2015).

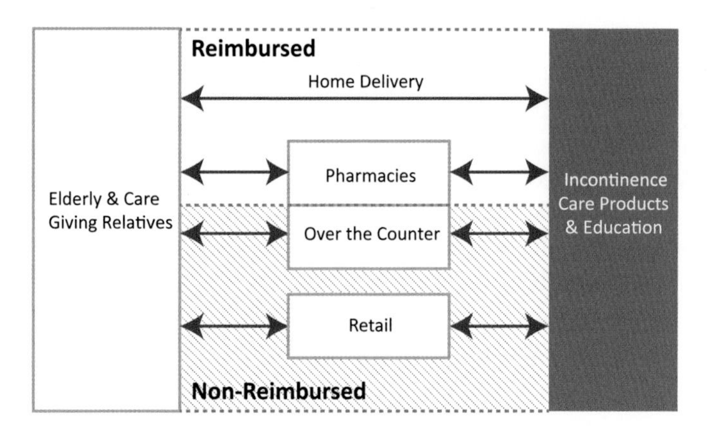

Figure 8.6: A SCA "Home Care" VCS

In Figure 8.6, the VCS is visualised as a simplified system of interactions. SCA provides incontinence products and related service offerings, reimbursed by the insurer (public or private) for the elderly or their care giving relatives (CGRs). The products and services can be accessible through home delivery or pharmacies. When not reimbursed, distributors provide them over the counter in pharmacies, or in other retail outlets. In the particular consulting engagement where this model was co-created to illustrate the initial offerings and the existing VCS, this graphic representation was perceived as helpful and effective for communicating the design with managers and decision makers outside of the VCS redesign initiative, as they were more accustomed to value chain depictions of value creation.

Another example of mapping an existing offering and system of actors creating value is shown in Figure 8.7. The example is from Scania, the global truck, bus, engine and a transport solutions company. As we wrote in Chapter 7, Scania outperforms its peers and has a very long track record of being the most profitable company among them. Scania has managed to balance a structured yet flexible mid- to long-term strategy and technology planning with a pragmatic, entrepreneurial, and action-oriented culture. Figure 8.7 offers a schematic view of the offering and actor system for one of their larger geographic markets and segments, as mapped in an explorative strategic innovation initiative. Again, this figure depicts the main interactions and resources, including non-Scania ones. So, this mapping explores a somewhat upframed system, beyond also the

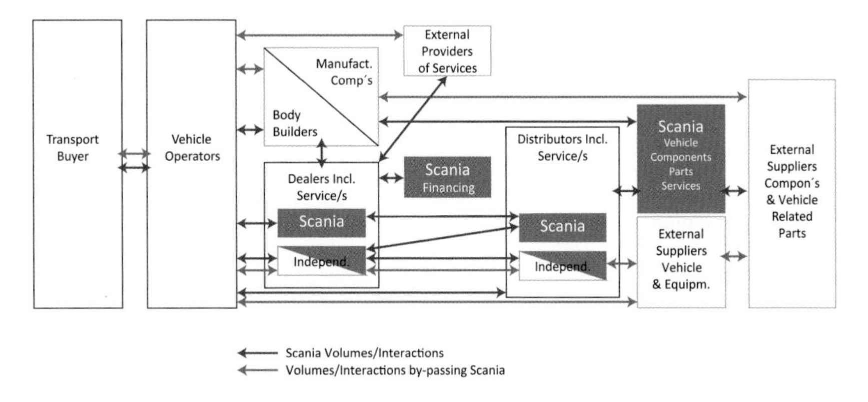

Figure 8.7: A Scania VCS

Scania specific interactions. We discuss upframing more in the next section of this chapter.

Mapping and illustrating the offering in this way enabled the development of a shared understanding of the existing offerings and of the larger VCSs in which these are inscribed — as well as making it possible to carry out qualitative assessments of how and why the VCS emerged and developed over time.

This depiction of specific relations then allowed their strategists to make further analyses in terms of future potential roles and required capabilities. It enabled the calculation of business volumes and margins for Scania — and to the assessment of how it was or might be bypassed as an actor in the VCS. This included quantification of the market as it exists today.

We mentioned above that understanding the existing VCS can be begun by an exploration of which historical factors and events helped to shape the business conditions in which an existing VCS operation works. These may include not only the business itself and the interacting actors involved in the offerings, but also various external factors such as societal developments, demographic characteristics, assessment of what has been and is now valued, economic development levels, political factors, legislation and regulations, technologies and logics of what and how value is created, developments of the natural environment including factors such as climate change and water scarcity, and attitudes influencing various behaviours.

In addition to what has been mentioned above, a historical ANT analysis of how the existing VCS has emerged can be an effective way to identify both constraints and enabling features of the larger VCS, as was shown with the case on EDF in Chapter 6. Such historical analyses can provide valuable guidance for exploring future innovations of a VCS, as well as linking to the business design and innovation methodology described in this chapter.

We have found that the initial analysis can also helpfully include building a view for why related previous innovation initiatives have failed or succeeded. This can help strategists to build on what has been effective for development before, and to avoid repeating historical mistakes. In Chapter 9, where we dwell on the realising of a new VCS design, we describe some of the challenges which we have encountered in our research and in organisations with whom we have worked as consultants.

Such analyses can also be useful to understand the managerial mindset, and sometimes organisational or professional biases that may have formed norms (socially approved practices and beliefs) in the company. Such norms might include the perception of what is included in the firm's proper role (and thus excluded from it), what contexts and field the company is in, how priorities are reflected in terms of what is rewarded, and how deviations from such spaces are looked upon.

This has been discussed in Chapter 3, and is also discussed in Chapter 10. Is the norm influenced by the old industrial era strategy focus on narrow product categories and industrial sectors? Or is the norm based on more open system approaches and perceptions of distinct competences, allowing for greater adaptability and system reconfiguring? How adaptable has the organisation proven itself to be over its history of experimenting outside whatever had been its current offering?

Additionally, organisational adaptability is important not only to enable experimenting on the existing offerings. In an extensive study of links between cultural behaviour and financial performance in US high tech firms, Chatman *et al.* (2014) found that companies with strong and widely shared adaptability norms also performed better financially.

After having mapped the existing VCS, including its offering and the involved interacting actors, the view can be upframed so that the boundaries of the current VCS can begin to be redefined.

3. Upframing the VCS

The customer and larger stakeholder interactive contexts, rather than just a given customer situation — are the focus for a VCS-based strategic upframing process.

Upframing with this focus involves continued mapping and tracing of interactors, the offerings relating and distinguishing and linking these actors, as well as the resulting roles the actors have in relation to each other (see Appendix B on ANT as well as the analyses we carried out with EDF in Chapter 6). It also sweeps in interactors beyond those with whom the company has interactions today.

The aim is building an understanding of current and possible interactions as a VCS, in terms of the main (VCS-defining) configuring offering and the interlinked relations (support offerings), which in turn interact with each other on a recurring basis.

In Reframing Business, Normann offered examples of procedures that can help in upframing one's business system:

1. Studies of invaders, who tend to disregard and redefine existing VCS boundaries.
2. Drawing a VCS of one's customers and of one's customers' customers, guided by the questions (a) of what larger system is one's main offering for the customer? (b) who are the other actors giving input to the customers' larger system? (c) what are one's clients' (and other stakeholders') key issues in their value creation? (d) what are strategic assets and roles of each interactor in relation to each other (including assets that might currently not be monetised nor utilised, e.g. time)? We have found that the inquiry can be used not only regarding customers, but also for those who in the current VCS hold other central roles such as "supplier", "partner", "distributor", "investor", and so on.

When VCSs are seen as upframed, it becomes easier for strategists to devote specific attention to areas where there are constraints for creating values, where there are opportunities for as of yet unrealised values and interactions, and where there are underutilised resources that can be better used. In a recent engagement, we looked anew at what the company had considered to be "ageing" assets — which sat on real estate that other actors would kill to get access to. These opportunity areas in the customer's and other interacting actors' contexts are an important focus for innovation efforts aimed at redefining how actors could interlink in the system, enabling more effective creation of values for different actors. This may lead to developing new offerings (commercially denominated as services or products, or combinations of these), creating new categories and shaping new markets, as we show below.

As described in Chapter 4, how a VCS and its larger actor context system is seen depends on how one chooses to define it. In some cases with different perspectives, one may expect to find a set of at least partly different — or even competing — VCSs. For instance, if one looks at healthcare, and in particular at care for the elderly as SCA has done, the VCS may differ depending on whether one looks at institutional care, or at home care, or even at institutional care across different parts of the world. If one focuses on one type of interacting actor involved in all of these systems, such as the care giving relative (CGR), one will see that their role in each specific system — and in particular their underattended needs — appears to be very different. The perception, and the resulting policies to address the relevant issue, will depend strongly on whether these CGRs are depicted as being a more passive actor, or if the CGR is taken to be the one who really has the most profound role in the care of the elderly relative.

The global hygiene company SCA wished to explore further growth opportunities in a field where it, at the time, offered tissues and incontinence care products and services. Together with SCA, we explored some undercharted parts of the healthcare sector: the elderly home care market in some specific geographic regions. Part of this work involved spending days in various care units, and together with the SCA team, mapping different VCS archetypes and their interacting actors, exploring underattended challenges in the relations between actors. For instance, ergonomics emerged as one of the underattended challenges in the relations between an elderly person and a CGR. Another finding was that lack of care and hygiene standards was an underattended challenge in the relation between care providing companies and care authorities which required regulatory compliance formats that did not clearly articulate what means or standards were required to be met. A culturally related challenge was centred on the relations between employing care providing organisations and their employees, some of whom were immigrants from other countries where care cultures were different from the one that the setting called for (e.g. in terms of length of sleeves, when hands are washed, etc.). Furthermore, when nurses cared for an elderly person in hygiene care situations, they often found it challenging to access the right products within that care situation. These were often not available at the site, or close enough to the bed. Also, some of the care products they needed were not brought by the nurses, who expected these to have been bought and brought in by the elderly patients or by their relatives. Not having access to the right products made hygiene compliance particularly challenging.

Such anthropological or ethnographic field visits helped to generate new and unforeseen insights, through observing actors interacting and using offerings in their own contexts. Through our experience, which corresponds with practices of companies like W. L. Gore, Xerox, HP, and Samsung, all recognised as excellent at observational field and user studies, we have found that using multidisciplinary teams in these field studies and then elaborating outcomes in explorative follow-up workshops is an effective way to identify and generate deep understanding of underattended challenges.

Figure 8.8 below shows a simplified view of a VCS in SCA's elderly home care market, where it offers its incontinence care products and

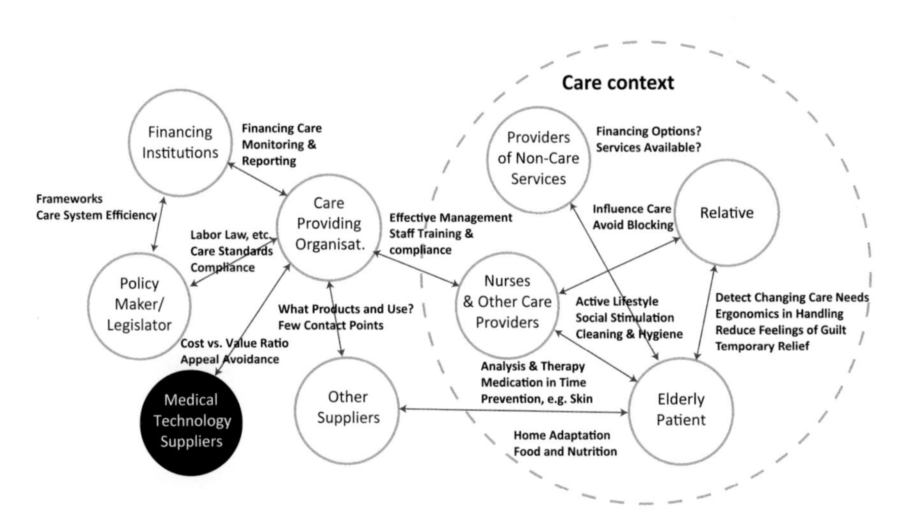

Figure 8.8: Larger SCA VCS, Regarding Care of the Elderly

supporting services. The figure shows key types of interacting actors and the typical values and challenges in the relations among these, beyond what was involved in the parts of the VCS that SCA was involved in.

As Figure 8.8 illustrates, depicting the context of use of the offering in social and healthcare VCSs in an upframed manner allows strategists to appreciate a space richly populated with opportunities.

While involving systems sciences, researching use contexts with VCS is also an art or craft. In our consulting, we have found that traditional market researchers, who may be excellent at research within confined and well-defined product categories, found themselves at a loss and sometimes genuinely frustrated when they were invited to observe without the need for haste in finding answers related to existing products, but to seek opportunities related to use. Once they learnt this inquiry process of observing and bringing the findings into disciplined analyses, they were amazed at the opportunity spaces that their research opened up, and the offerings that they then could design, leveraging their comparative advantage of understanding hygiene and care, to enhance their capacity to identify new growth opportunities.

As mentioned earlier, there are many possible definitions of the upframed VCS. Depending on how it is upframed, it might involve different interacting actors — and opportunities and threats. The transport business we saw above here is an example. The VCS and its actor context is different if one defines the system as a logistics system, as a trucking system, or as an urban retail system. While there will be trucks in all of these systems, they will be used for different purposes, valued in different ways, and they will provide different value and values (uptime of vehicle use, reduced warehousing costs, deliveries at night in cities to improve transport flow by day, etc.) in different offerings. Also, the conditions under which the trucks are operated will differ; the interacting actors involved in the user context will be different, etc. So, if one is a truck and transport company such as Scania, different opportunity spaces will open or close depending on which VCSs their strategists consider. At a first glance, this may seem obvious. But when one then starts to map the actors and the relations between them, a whole myriad of potential new interlinked values to be enabled opens up. Traditionally, a truck manufacturer may have held its focus on serving its distributors, or perhaps also vehicle operators and their drivers. It may have seen itself as competing against other truck manufacturers in doing so. But the VCS upframing offers an entirely different set of strategic possibilities, where the executives in charge would consider their company as part of the VCS of transport operations, or of industrial or retail logistics, or even of city mobility solutions. Such upframings thus also bring new sets of competitors and collaborators, and new threats, and — most importantly — new opportunities.

IKEA has also been used as a good example (see Normann & Ramírez, 1993, 1994). IKEA does not see itself as being in the furniture or furnishing business, but in the business of creating a better everyday life for as many people and homes as possible, with the business idea "to offer a wide range of well-designed, functional home furnishing products at prices so low that as many people as possible will be able to afford them". This upframed view of offering sofas and tables opens up new potential actors (and activities to take on) to engage with, based on understanding of the wider context of the "everyday" uses of its offerings at home. When we worked together with a key individual from IKEA on concept development, together with a client in the tourism and experience field, the IKEA executive even jokingly noted that the tourism company was a competitor to IKEA, since it wanted people to long to get away from home, whereas IKEA wants people to long to stay at home. This comment from the IKEA executive reminds one that VCSs will include different actors and offer different opportunities and threats depending on how one defines them.

The means for upframing systems involves interviews with various actors in the VCS, review of company and interactor information available in various sources. Explorative analysis in collaborative settings such as workshops with participants with several and complementary and potentially even contradictory and contesting perspectives can help upframe the system from the established understanding of the business and the company's offering, role and competences and business ideas.

4. Exploring Challenges and Opportunities for the Upframed VCS

Having upframed one's view of the VCS (helped in doing so by having studied data, interviews, imagining plausible moves by different actors in relation to each other or those who might attempt to enter the field, and the anthropological field studies), one can then collaboratively analyse the VCS in multidisciplinary teams.

As we saw in Chapter 7, in turbulent contexts this should involve scenario planning analyses. There we saw that Scania is using scenarios partly to explore future markets segments, for which their VCS map described in Figure 8.7 was defined. One of the scenario planning analysis outcomes in that case was that it became plausible that one important customer segment might change its character quite significantly within the concerned time horizon in two plausible scenarios. Were such a change to occur, it would imply that opportunities for significantly changed offerings had become available. That analysis guided their exploring the development of a new type of business, with a new configuring offering for a market segment that did not yet exist. We describe this further below.

An upframed view in any case affords the possibility to consider how factors in the wider fields in which the VCS is located might impact the existing VCS. For instance, for SCA, in European healthcare, this involved exploring factors such as how the viability of care financing in ageing societies and stalled growth might impact value creation. Furthermore, diseases such as dementia and Alzheimer's might bring forth increasingly difficult and burdensome care situations, both for professional care givers and for CGRs. More migration may entail having to deal with a greater variety of multicultural elderly populations and care cultures, which involves addressing challenges such as educating care professionals and finding new ways for securing consistent compliance with local care standards. Climate change, combined with excessive use of antibiotics, may lead to having to deal with more multiresistant bacteria, raising the priority for good hygiene as a critical way of containing unnecessary escalating care costs. The linking of these contextual conditions to each other may have big impacts on how the configuring offering and the VCS will be designed.

Considering opportunities and challenges with the help of an upframed VCS as seen from the future also includes assessing how other actors might shape the field under changed conditions. This includes disciplined imagination to consider who might be the main actor types, what roles they might take on (e.g. as suppliers and co-creators), what their strategies and intentions and ongoing technology developments might be, and how they might relate to the offering and its strategic development. Other questions to consider include: Will some areas and challenges in the upframed VCS be crowded with resource rich actors driving both innovation and commoditisation? As Cusumano (2010) observed, many firms today face such challenges as global companies with deep pockets (perhaps part of emerging market family-controlled conglomerates — see Dobbs *et al.*, 2015) disrupting the field that Western companies have dominated. Yet other questions to examine are: What areas might be underattended, perhaps because they do not match current service or product categories, or because as an emergent area, it has not yet been given attention by other organisations?

As we mentioned earlier already, the set of actors to include in such a review very much depends on how the VCS is upframed, and will quite likely differ from those included in a traditional sectorial or industry actor analysis. Structuring maps of future potential interacting actors is a cognitive process that is helped by developing a language that purposefully includes new terms to describe both existing as well as potential shapers of the landscape. Doing this helps one to conceptualise, perhaps even bring forth, a system not yet emerged, as Maturana and Varela studied in biology (1987/1998). Their work suggested that living is a process of cognition, and that cognition is the ability to adapt oneself to an unfolding environment. Adaptation in their research occurs as a consequence of continuous interacting with that environment, and in such interactions, one will also be influencing the cognition of others and thus the environment itself.

At first glance, considering a novel actor system with new interactions might be seen as mixing apples and oranges, at least when seen through lenses of traditional product categories. But with a more careful and considered second glance, the new combinations may help to open new understanding and creative insights of potential shapers of a system-to-be.

Returning to the healthcare case of SCA, Figure 8.9 maps actors in the social and healthcare management system in home care as they might work in relation to each other in a specific large regional market. The person receiving care and being enabled is depicted at the centre, and the actors with whom this individual interacts are situated in three fields where different but related forms of value — body, mind, and place — are

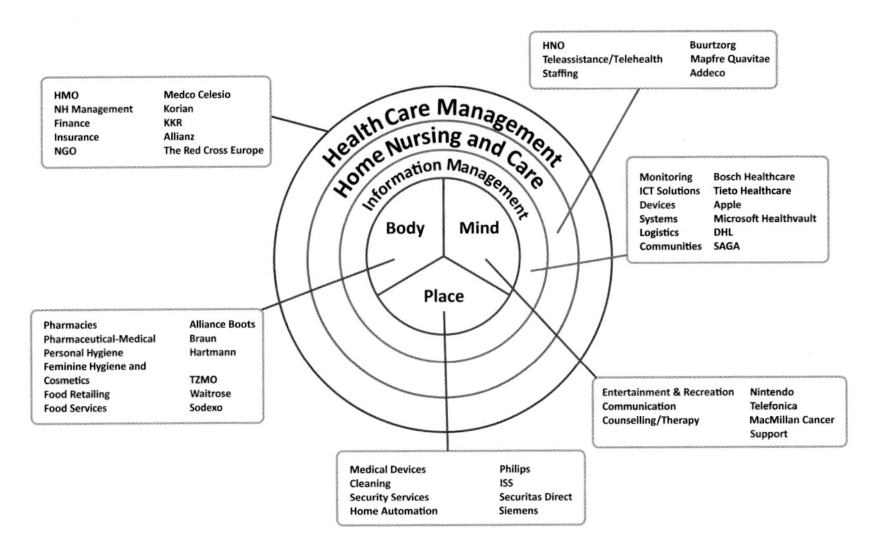

Figure 8.9: Key Actor Fields and Listings for an Upframed VCS in Home Care (by SCA)

manifested. In turn, these are surrounded by three fields with different actors supporting care — information management, home nursing and care, and healthcare management.

After having mapped the VCS, upframed it to explore the larger contexts it is part of, having considered this from the perspectives of future contexts, and having identified opportunities, challenges and underattended needs, one can explore what these possibilities mean in more detail, prior to redesigning the VCS.

5. Downframing to Explore the Challenges for the VCS Design

In downframing (see Figures 8.2–8.4), the individual relations and interactions in the actor system are studied in more detail. Here one considers related potential developments in the larger context, as well as plausible changes that might emerge from actions among existing or new actors. One also assesses specific challenges involving — or concerning — several actors, new possible uses of (underutilised) resources — and the opportunities and challenges for the new designed VCSs these might entail.

When one has explored the challenge areas, they can be described in terms of a small story. Such reperceived insights (Ramírez & Wilkinson,

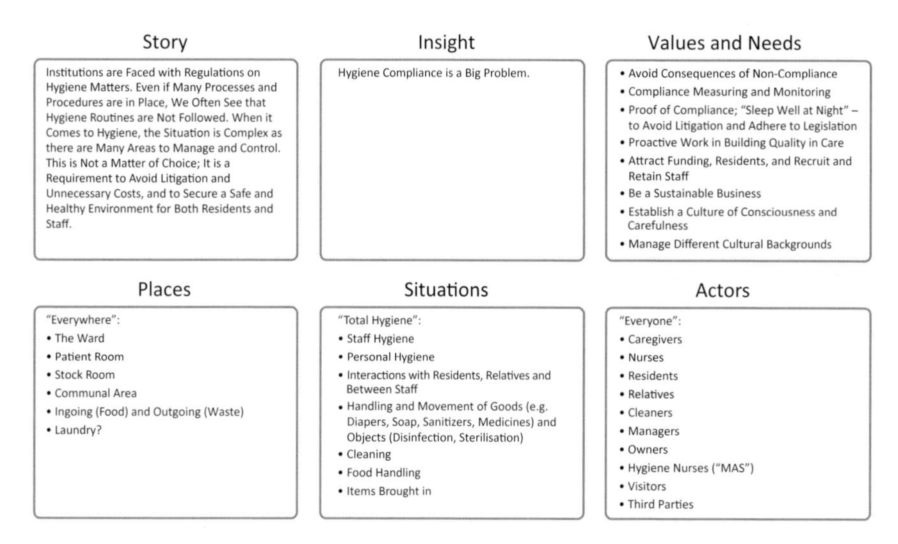

Figure 8.10: The Challenge "Hygiene Compliance" in Elderly Care Institutions (by SCA)

2016) are based on appreciating possible concrete time/place sweet spots where and when the interactions might occur. In such reperceptions, one considers how the different interacting actors concerned by the challenge might be related, and what their individual challenges or underattended values at play one needs to take into account. As is depicted in Figure 8.10, the underattended challenge of "hygiene compliance" within institutional elderly care was described as involving six different considerations.

With such descriptions of the challenges and opportunity areas, further analyses to estimate how well other actors today engage with the challenge help to make qualitative and quantitative assessments of the opportunity space. This is done iteratively, going back to the data and information that has been collected and generated in the earlier stages of the upframing process.

The stages up to, and including, the identification of challenges and opportunity areas is part of a divergent search phase of a business design process. Here the opportunity areas are explored, deepened, broadened, expanded; they are qualitatively and quantitatively assessed in terms of what kind of business volumes and size of prize they could contain. Questions considered include: Are there already other companies addressing the opportunity with existing offerings? Are these offerings effective, or can they be unbundled into separate offerings or rebundled with other offerings? The opportunity areas that represent intriguing business prospects qualify for offering design efforts, as we describe in the next section.

6. Defining (or Redesigning) a New VCS

The crane process is an iterative ideation methodology for imagining and testing offerings that up to now had remained unimagined. In defining strategic intents and designing offerings, the VCS designing strategist generates options (or brings to use dormant options) to address opportunity and challenge areas, guided by questions such as (but not limited to):

- What seem to be the critical aspects of the challenges, potentially overlooked by others?
- What can our firm (alone or with others) do to activate or better make use of underutilised resources?
- What can our firm (alone or with others) do to relieve actors from activities that others can do more effectively?
- What can our firm (alone or with others) do to enable others to more effectively create value?
- How does our firm utilise our own distinct competences, and what comparative advantages do these afford?
- Do our competences need to be complemented, or for some challenges possibly transformed or even abandoned?
- Are there sub optimisations between disconnected flows that matter to our intent?

It is important to note that a challenge does not necessarily equal an offering — different offerings could be envisioned to address one and the same challenge. Making people use safety belts is an offering design challenge. An offering to address that challenge might include education about the need to do so, or it might involve an automated reminder signal for safety belt use. These are two very different design solutions to the same challenge. So, one can allocate different offering elements to address a specific challenge, and try different alternatives, even determining how an offering could be designed to meet combinations of several challenges.

Effective offering designs orchestrate resources in ways that help several underattended challenges to be met. Good designs seek to leverage the comparative advantage of the organiser and convenor of the VCS. With VCS, the business idea transcends the convenor's configuring offering, as it also mobilises support offerings that make its value creation viable, involving other actors that are linked with these support offerings into the configuring offering. By addressing relevant challenges, the design engages both collaborative and competitive possibilities. A good design ideally makes it less easy to replicate the VCS, and prevents its being invaded by competing offerings or VCS designs.

Originating from the Scania actor system mapping and scenario planning-based analyses of how the business context might develop, as we described earlier in this chapter, Scania went further in its exploration of various other transport system solutions. They mapped various values that can be created in transport flows, and not only in the part of the systems where Scania normally has interactions.

Instead, this led them to find an uninhabited opportunity space. It is a space where interactions happen with existing customers, such as vehicle operators and large global companies with very specific transport needs (whose transport needs are similar to those of Scania itself as a global manufacturer of trucks, buses and engines, with global production structure and logistics flows). Building on its own expertise, distinctive methods, and competence, it deployed such maps to improve value.

To this effect in 2015, it launched a separate company under its own brand LOTS Group AB.[4] LOTS is now initiating change in what was traditionally strictly a transport business, where customers bought transport from transport companies, with the transport looked upon as an isolated flow. It instead has initiated a journey of transforming its offerings to fit a system-based business, connecting disconnected flows outside the traditional road transport. There are several factors they took into consideration to this effect, including the realisation that large international firms with large transport volumes increasingly were expected to provide more systemic solutions to meet combinations of values, challenges of cost,

[4] See www.lotsgroup.com.

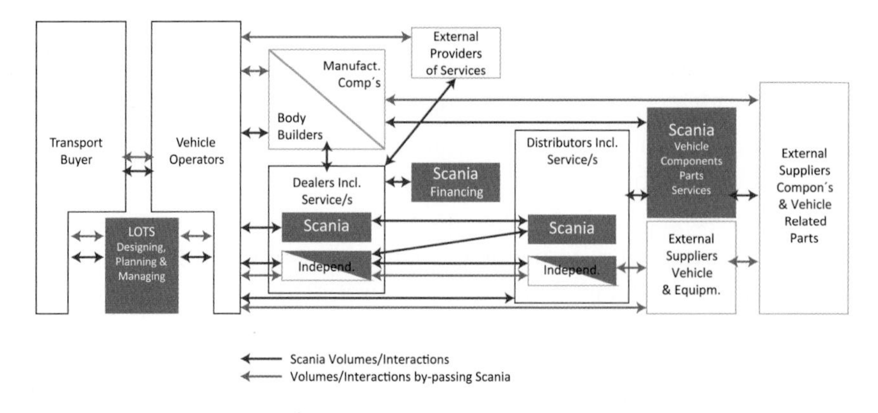

Figure 8.11: New Scania VCS, with LOTS Group AB Addition

sustainability and corporate social responsibility. Figure 8.11 shows the actor system, with the new actor type Scania created.

LOTS Group takes a systems approach to be able to reconfigure and optimise a transportation system. They analyse and provide solutions for global large firms' total transportation, including the design and optimisation that relate initial given supplier's internal processes with the in-house logistics of another firm's production. Their offering includes stock management, balancing transport capacities and means, physical layouts, visual management systems, transport and production concepts such as "pull planning", and avoiding the sub-optimisation of internal logistics.

LOTS can map the various forms of waste that could be reduced, for example reducing the use of environmentally damaging and costly chemicals a client might deploy to keep high quality outputs from raw material stored during long time periods. They also take into account the reduction of more obvious forms of waste, such as reducing waiting times or improving filling ratios.

With their focus on large industrial clients with stable operations, LOTS Group does not compete with traditional transport companies, but can insource transportation from such companies.

To succeed in creating this new market space, LOTS Group shares system efficiency gains with its customers. It seeks to improve value creation for all of the actors involved in its VCS. The scenario planning work also helps them identify another growing business potential that concerns the plausible paradigm shifts toward the adoption of autonomous vehicles.

The LOTS Group has been founded and is owned by Scania, but this company is not selling trucks. Its configuring offering is "good logistics", aiming to provide more cost effective, less wasteful, socially more responsible and more sustainable transportation solutions. Its support offerings enable large global transport intense firms in fields such as manufacturing, forestry and mining to better interact with truck manufacturers and other transport means providers.

With capabilities for consulting in transportation system waste identification and quantification, and with the operation of full logistics systems, LOTS Group is a part of Scania's exploring of future business ideas and VCSs.

LOTS Group illustrates how the design of a new VCS with a VCS approach to strategy that develops effective offering designs can orchestrate resources and interactions to engage underattended challenges. The example above shows how system opportunities and challenges — beyond conventional industry and value chains definitions — can be explored; and how new VCSs can be designed.

For the SCA incontinence care business mentioned earlier in this chapter, its offering strength depended not only from its being the global market leader in incontinence care products, but perhaps more importantly from its having developed a deep understanding of how nurses and other care givers help elderly patients to use these well; and how they in so doing create value together. The organisation employs numerous nurses to provide advisory services to care units. The profound understanding of care value creation developed by SCA strategists and innovation managers has helped the company to improve the quality of care and quality of life for numerous elderly people. SCA's comparative advantage lies in the understanding of care as value creating and of the VCSs involved — including financing care improvements through reimbursement systems for medical products.

The distinct competence of understanding hygiene-related value creating in care enabled SCA to open and broaden their opportunity spaces, and to become more attentive to more customer context challenges. It also helped SCA to design support offerings, moving its interactions and roles well beyond those defined by its previously existing products and categories.

The ideation of offerings can be further enabled and targeted through techniques such as strategic analogies. These bring in examples from other contexts — e.g. a company that has changed its offering from a product focus to an outcome and system focus can be inspiring a similar change for a company in another field but with a similar challenge. In the same way, an analogy from nature, such as an insect, may inspire an automotive concept development team to imagine a radical high potential concept for system solutions. The analogy is translated to the VCS context and its challenge to help imagining, exploring and formulating new or changed offering designs that effectively address challenges and improve value creation.

Once generated, novel offering concepts can be mapped against priority criteria or dimensions, such as fit with strategic intent, fit with comparative advantage and existing values, feasibility to realise, and flexibility for withdrawal if the offering idea eventually turns out to be less promising than first envisioned or even too harmful (e.g. in terms of uncontrolled cannibalising on the existing business).

From our experience, it is advisable to bring the definition of such criteria into the crane process itself, although setting criteria too early or in an inflexible manner can stalemate the exploration — the EDF cases in Chapter 6 provide good examples. One can include the search for such criteria in management and expert interviews and in initial desk research, as existing criteria may be overly dependent on historical reasons for success that are no longer pertinent.

It may not be meaningful or even possible to define the future business volumes that the offering will enable — particularly if the VCS it will bring forth (or the future "market") is in a very emergent stage. In such situations using the criteria for assessing today's business or even defined growth businesses might lead to missing of substantial new business opportunities, as was the case for IBM when in the late 1990s it concluded it had been doing that repeatedly for partly that reason. To prevent such errors, IBM launched a venture called Early Business Opportunities with criteria adjusted for exploring emergent offering areas. Over 10 years, the venture generated new offerings representing 26% of IBM's revenue (Harreld *et al.*, 2009).

The offerings that are given high priority in explorations described in this chapter can then be assessed in terms of their business models with description of their offering elements, as we described in Chapter 5 — people, process, technology, information, and work and risk sharing formula. The detailed and quantified business models might include expected volumes and resourcing requirements. This is followed by development, testing and prototyping in an iterative manner. In testing new offering ideas, it is advisable to be attentive to who may resist and who may welcome the changes involved. Such resistance or welcoming may be external or internal. Some heroes of existing product regimes — be it heads of divisions, functions or top sales people — may resist future offerings, however promising they may seem in their business potentials. This is addressed more in Chapter 9, which describes realisation of new — or redesigned — VCSs.

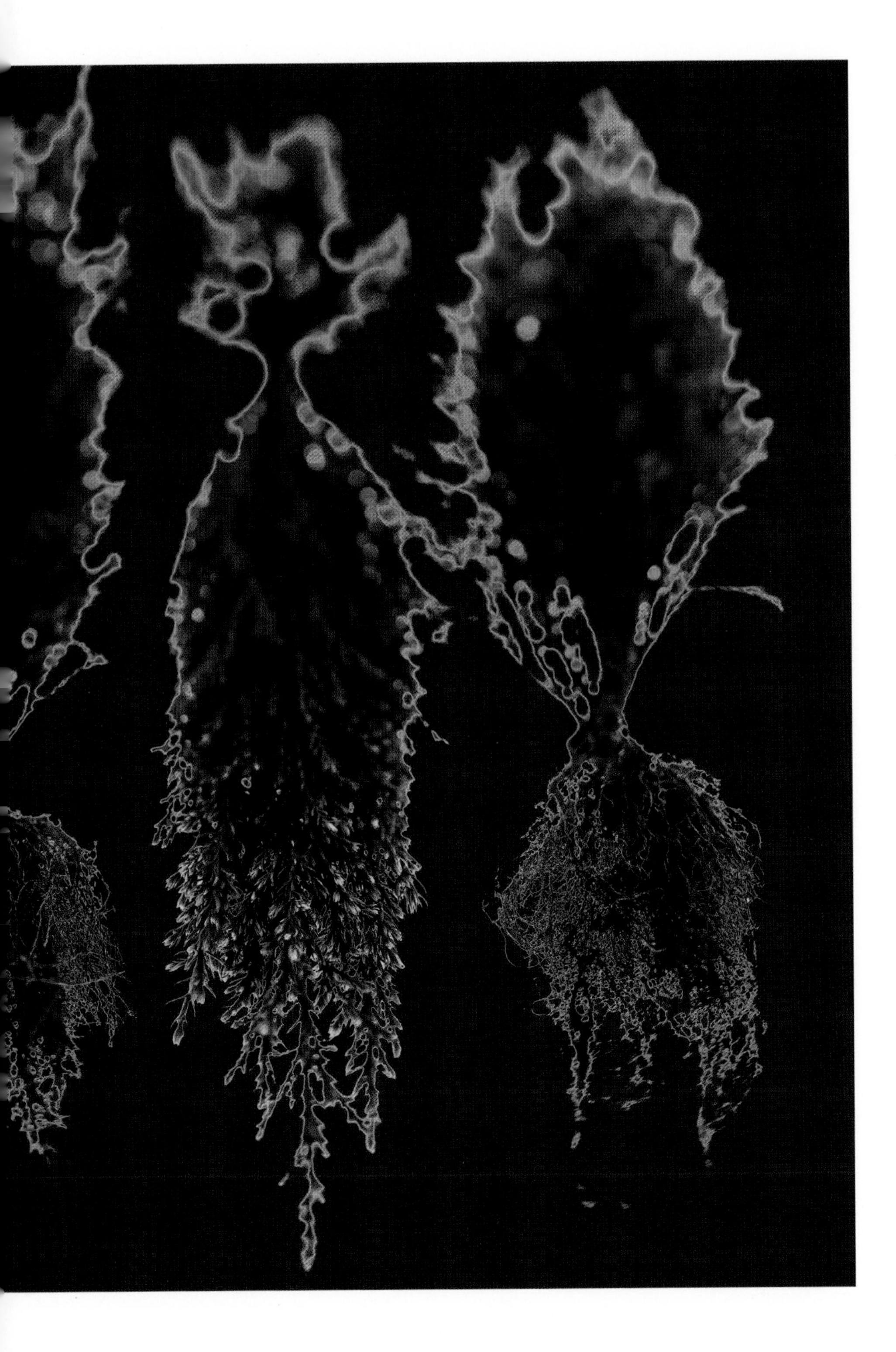

Chapter 9

Realising New Value Creating System Innovations[1]

Box 9.1. Chapter 9 at a Glance

This chapter recounts some of the main challenges of thinking about, analysing, designing, prototyping, piloting and realising new value creating systems (VCSs) — or making changes to existing ones. The challenges are based on research — our own and that of others — and on the experiences of strategists with whom we have worked. The chapter also offers guidance on how strategists can effectively handle these challenges.

We discuss seven different challenges to realise a new VCS:

1. Letting the design vision guide, but not define the design.
2. Redirecting management attention into VCS thinking.
3. Creating organisational ownership of VCS changes.
4. Step-by-step realisation of a new VCS.
5. Understanding value creation as multiple and contingent.
6. Learning as a stepping stones process.
7. Avoiding value chain push backs.

This chapter is about making designs into real offerings and real VCSs.

Designers imagine, build, and test models and prototypes to enable new offerings to be realised. Their work is iterative (for example, see

[1]Björn Ålsnäs, Global Brand Innovation Manager, Service, SCA Hygiene Products, co-authored parts of this chapter.

Smith & Eppinger, 1993). The seven challenges thus may not happen sequentially; instead a tentative finding regarding one challenge may bring the designer to revisit another one that has already been engaged with. While all seven matter, they do not need to take place in practice in the order we present them in this chapter.

Design complements — but differs from — the assessment practices we overviewed in Chapter 7, where guidelines to assess the viability of a design with the help of scenario planning were surveyed (Selin *et al.*, 2015; Bhatti *et al.*, 2015).

1. Letting the Design Vision Guide, but Not Define the Design

However well-thought through an initial VCS concept might be, one can be almost sure that just now it is wrong. What do we mean by this?

It is one step — an early step — in a design and realisation process, and as such, it is iterative in its stages, from the exploring of historical basis for the business, to ideation to realisation. Once one starts on a path for realisation, unforeseen things typically happen along the way, and that will bring new learning and possibly reveal new obstacles to consider. New actors or technologies may come into sight, enabling new developments.

As an interviewee expressed so well, when Arvidsson and Mannervik (2009) were studying how a new VCS paradigm had been brought about in the signal processing field of telecoms: "innovation may look neatly ordered in hindsight, but it is often an iterative process between different stakeholders' gradually evolving complementary visions and an emergent enacted reality."[2]

A large medical technology firm that we studied in a research programme on strategic renewal at the University of Oxford was a good illustration of this approach to designing a new VCS. In an early stage of redesigning their VCS, they started a vision-led design journey. This would lead value creation towards more individualised healthcare,

---

[2] See http://www.nusap.net/sections.php?op=viewarticle&artid=13 (Accessed December 2015): Our colleague Jerry Ravetz considers that in post-normal times, this too is what scientific research consists of.

enabled by bespoke technologies and more system-based offerings. Initially, they did not have a definitive view of what the system of solution offerings would be. The visionary top management were convinced individualised healthcare was the right direction and that they had comparative advantages that could afford them the opportunity to develop a configuring offering, and to enrol those they needed to mobilise. The top management spent a lot of effort communicating this vision inside and outside the organisation, inviting views to iterate the VCS design. The vision has today brought the firm into the business of connecting biological research with clinical therapy. They have managed to develop and orchestrate a VCS that enables better and more individualised therapies with lower costs through the provision of imaging, diagnostics, and bioprocessing.

Their basic belief that tomorrow's healthcare might be better targeted to the needs of the individual set a flexible but powerful vision to develop a new offering and to challenge big pharma incumbents. Their technologies and systems-based configuring offerings have evolved, as has their vision, but without having it constrained or limited by their initial conception.

So, in working with VCS thinking in designing configuring offerings and realising a VCS, it can be helpful to be guided by a broad and flexible VCS vision that can be easily modified, perhaps having to let go of some of the details in the initial concepts. Doing so is to take one's realising of the VCS as a process of change, where one recognises historical dependencies and shortcomings, embraces opportunities and threats in the present, actively navigates in the changing landscape, and wisely creates leverage of comparative advantages, so as to orchestrate activities and resources into realising the new or improved VCS.

2. Redirecting Management Attention into VCS Thinking

So how can one get started with developing a vision for the design or by initiating some pilots of the configuring offering for the VCS?

Some researchers, following the seminal work of Ocasio (2010), believe that senior management attention is one of the scarcest resources in modern organisations. Standing in a queue in Davos a few years ago in front of two CEOs, one of the authors overheard their conversation: they bemoaned that they no longer could attend any of the sessions (which they were interested in!) but were in Davos because they could meet so many more clients, suppliers, and partners — saving them, they said, 40 international trips each year. Intercontinental and international travel time savings measured in weeks/year enable the attention of these CEOs to be used far more effectively, but possibly at the cost of ideas for a new VCS.

A welcoming space for VCS-based work can be created by bringing it into another initiative, such as a "board away day" where new and explorative strategic thinking might be more accepted. Otherwise directing attention to a VCS initiative may not be very welcome, particularly if it is interpreted as "yet another thing to do" (or which one "must" do). Nor is dedicating attention to considering alternative VCS designs very welcome if that were to "interrupt" what one must "already" do.

A VCS design or redesign initiative is more compelling if it "reframes" what is already going on in more helpful ways (Normann, 2001; Ramírez & Wilkinson, 2016). VCS design needs to be seen as having immediate business relevance. An illustration: one of the authors worked with colleagues from a Scottish university on a project on the future of whisky for a major firm there. The bulk of their offering was 12 year old Scotch. Of course some degree of freedom existed — one can blend more of the single malts, or make more "premium" (older) bottles that are 15 or 18 or more years old. But the bulk will be sold — and consumed — in 13 years' time. The Scottish colleagues had persuaded the executives of this firm that considering in advance who might buy it and who might drink it might be helpful. One of the authors was invited to the workshop by these colleagues precisely because of our VCS thinking. This thinking turned out to be truly essential to rethinking the business. By applying the analysis of the offering in Chapters 5 and 6, we helped the executives discover, as the CEO put it, that they "are being had". What transpired was that, in VCS language, their suppliers and main clients had managed to have the firm in question carry far more risk than was their role to do. The company took action — it changed warehousing and logistics massively, and then did very well. A sad but important aspect of what happened is that while the company did very well, the CEO who had envisioned the reframed VCS by putting in crucial new support offerings was ousted in the changes that his insight brought about.

Similarly, several years ago we worked with a large global publishing group on a strategy away day. The focus was on digitalisation, and how it could impact its current business model and business portfolio — as threats or opportunities. Using VCS as a strategic exploration framework enabled them to explore different designs in a small set of contrasting scenarios that laid out how their business environment might change and their business be transformed. This led to new strategic priorities for their business planning. The VCS strategy framework enabled them to break out of their up to then more linear thinking, which was mainly defined by competitive strategy within existing industry boundaries. Thinking about strategy as designed VCSs helped them to identify both strengths and vulnerable parts of their business model and portfolio, including the strength of their local agent networks, vulnerabilities in terms of pricing models ill fitted to digitalisation, or whether a given division could withstand devastating competition in the next 4–5 years. The assessment helped them to define actions to meet some of the threats and seize the opportunities before they materialised. So they were better prepared when some of these digital and low cost entry developments started to emerge and impact their business two years later.

As the Scotch whisky and publishing house examples illustrate, VCS is a strategic framework and a form of thinking that can be taken as part of another initiative that seeks to redirect scarce management attention. It helps to do something practical about future profitable revenue streams — in a strategy away day, a scenario planning initiative, an executive development programme, a portfolio review, a due diligence assessment, an exploration of emerging markets, a business development effort, a new country entry initiative, etc. But it can also be the central framework used in strategic innovation as we have seen in several examples in this book. What we want to illustrate here is how space for VCS design thinking can be created, by enabling the effectiveness of another existing or planned initiative.

3. Creating Organisational Ownership of VCS Changes

The third challenge we describe is related to creating the organisational ownership, so that the likelihood of successful realisation is increased.

Take the example of a "repeat innovator" company like W. L. Gore,[3] the company behind the well-known "Gore-Tex"-branded fabrics, and of other applications of their invention of highly versatile polymers.

W. L. Gore ensures its innovation teams contain a variety of professional profiles. Perhaps they would include a product specialist, a technology specialist and a marketing professional. They are also keen to recruit such people from their typical customer contexts, and in doing this, they build also customer context intimacy into the teams. In addition they are excellent at field studies, using anthropological approaches as they spend time at user sites to observe and eventually also identify new business opportunity areas — sometimes in quite unexpected fields. For example, the dental floss Glide is a Gore innovation that emerged from one such field study. A Gore researcher observed heart surgeons at work, using Gore's synthetic blood vessels. In a pause, the surgeon casually used the vessel to floss his teeth, commenting that he never had come across any material that was so good for flossing. The Gore researcher brought back this unexpected insight, which they designed as a new offering with considerable market success. That offering was developed, brought into venturing and eventually sold off to a global company within the fast moving consumer goods space that floss fits into.

W. L. Gore extends the teams' perspectives beyond cross-disciplinary insiders to also extend into the customer and customer's customer organisations and their contexts. This bringing in of others into offering design is good for innovation, and is also excellent for building the internal credibility of an emerging new VCS so it gets supported and not killed off.

Doubts about VCS thinking or a new VCS are often there for good reasons, and these must be acknowledged and addressed, and may be the source of changes to the original VCS offering design that improve its efficacy. Or attending to such issues may lead one to stop a VCS design effort at a stage before it starts to cost serious money, either because it will not fly — or because it could cause too severe countermeasures by VCS actors who benefit in the existing VCS (see Ramírez *et al.*, 2013). W. L. Gore illustrates how team composition can help from early stages in the

---

[3]We thank G. Lechner, previously an executive at W. L. Gore, for helpful comments regarding this case.

VCS design process to address organisational ownership challenges for new innovations.

A lesson is that one way of engaging the expected sceptics in a VCS initiative is to make a representative of them part of the team, or at least — and in some cases, better — in a reference group that is brought in at key stages. It may be a sales director who is successful in the existing business logic and the current VCS design who opposes a new design. If the team can make this individual see benefits — and engage in creating the innovation — it can help in building organisational ownership and with that less resistance at stages of realising the VCS. It may also result in a better VCS design, with a good base in the company's existing comparative advantage, while leveraged into a next growth stage. Involving sceptics, and heroes in the existing business logics, can enable VCS configuring offering designers to surface tensions and address them in the work, instead of having them cause trench wars in late stages of realising a new VCS — which if one is an incumbent often means that one is, to some degree, changing an existing business and VCS, in which one may have high stakes. We analyse more about this issue below, under governance.

Another helpful way to enhance organisational ownership is to represent the current business in VCS terms. We saw this in Chapter 6 with the EDF example. Representing the current business in VCS terms helps strategists to surface issues such as: How has the current VCS emerged? What are its roots, forces at play, dependencies, biases, bastions, inefficiencies? Are these growing or not? How have the company's distinct competences and comparative advantage — and role in the existing VCS — emerged? What are these? How are external forces thought to shape the VCS and its business context tomorrow? Why is there a perceived need for change now? In what direction might this change be advisable, how quickly, where, by whom, and why? And, important in an organisational perspective, have there been similar initiatives in the past? What happened with these — what was done well and what was done less well? What were the obstacles encountered? Were these overcome, and if so, how? If not, why?

A round of interviews on such questions across the organisation — and beyond it, with key suppliers, investors, partners, customers, regulators — provides valuable information concerning internal and external pitfalls as well as criteria of success. Sharing views while preserving anonymity can contribute positively to organisational ownership by helping people reflect on implications, become involved in tests, and even perhaps feel more like getting involved.

4. Step-by-Step Realisation of a New VCS

The realisation of a new VCS often involves a gradual realisation process, including "translations", as Actor-Network Theory (ANT) scholars put it (see Appendix B), of the design vision into an enacted reality as a VCS. This realisation is accomplished through problematisation, intéressement, enrolment and mobilisation (see Chapter 6 and Appendix B) in negotiation with various stakeholders; it is accompanied by exploring moves and countermoves, seeking reconciliation of different values and motives, building alliances, and countering external and internal forces that do not welcome the changes. This iterative design process is important to keep in mind for the VCS innovator, but also for those wanting to avoid being surprised by new collaborative VCS models in which the incumbent may eventually find itself in a difficult situation. The story about the leasing company Ryder[4] (see Normann & Ramírez, 1994) is a great illustration of this.

Ryder, in late 2015 describing its role as "the trusted fleet partner", used what we in this book call a stepping stone approach to define a VCS in the North American truck and trucking (transportation done with trucks) markets, which it then replicated in "translated" forms in many international locations. Before Ryder came on their radar, truck manufacturers saw themselves as truck companies, whose core job was making and selling trucks. They would talk to truck experts in transport companies about truck performance. Then, from the point of view of the truck companies, one day a new type of customer appeared — Ryder. It did not see itself as a trucking company, but as "a leasing and logistics company". It bought trucks and then leased these to trucking companies. As a leasing company, it talked much more about money with finance people on the customer side, than about trucks with the customer's truck experts. Ryder

[4] See http://www.ryder.com/en/about-us/history.aspx (Accessed December 2015).

did very well, and became an important and big customer for the truck manufacturers. They considered it a "key account", while the "competitors" were the other truck manufacturers.

Over time, based on its deepening understanding of the trucks in use and challenges of running them, Ryder (step-by-step) integrated new services into its offering, which they provided themselves or arranged for third parties to provide. These support offerings included leasing trailers, HR services to help manage driver staffing, insurance, and back office administration. The logic was simple: Ryder could buy these services in bulk and pass on some of the savings to customers, who got a better deal buying through Ryder than directly with their suppliers (not only trucks, but also trailers, drivers, insurance, and payroll and accounts receivable). As Ryder's customer pool grew, its buying power grew, making itself a more competitive supplier for customers, whose numbers grew too. They also relieved customers of the need for managerial skills in either performing these other services or purchasing them on the market.

Then Ryder did some imaginative things. It had started with offering network and logistics-improving services to individual fleet operators. It then found operators who were not direct competitors and offered to put their fleets together (rather like airlines do with code sharing) so each could have more filled trucks in each route, lowering costs and increasing their capacity. It made the pie bigger for many of the actors in its VCS, enabling more and better value creation among those it enrolled.

At first Ryder was considered a top customer by the truck manufacturers, because it bought a lot of trucks. But the truck manufacturers' relationship with the trucking transport companies, and the interaction with these customers, representing quite a big customer group, started to erode as Ryder's offering took hold. Eventually things got nasty for the truck manufacturers — Ryder had for some time operated workshops for repairs and maintenance as one of the activities in its offering. They then started to sell spare parts as part of their expanding offering, but sourced them from other equipment manufacturers than the truck manufacturers. This hit truck manufacturer's business model — and profitability — hard, as their business model depended on clients "destroying" parts of the trucks (by wearing them out through use), and then selling them spare parts at good margins.

A calculation at the time was that if one bought the whole truck, new, at spare parts prices it would cost forty times the original price. For the trucking company clients at that time, trucks represented about 10–15% of overall costs (of course this would depend a lot on the fleet, the network served, and fuel and insurance prices) — the rest went on fuel, labour, administration, logistics, IT, insurance, trailers, maintenance, financing, etc. Helping them improve performance and creating value in that other 85% of overall costs enabled Ryder to make the pie bigger for many actors in the larger trucking system.

At the time, the heavy automotive company executives typically thought of value in chains, and comparing their position in terms of competitiveness with others holding similar chain positions. Yet they discovered that their "customer" Ryder had with its newly redesigned configuring offering become a "competitor" (taking away a substantial proportion of the business of each of its customers). This particular "customer" had intruded itself between them and the other customers in a new VCS. But at this point, Ryder was itself a big customer for the truck manufacturers, and could not easily be rejected.

The stepping stone iterative configuring and support offering design approach Ryder used enabled it to realise a novel VCS, moving a critical actor (i.e. the truck manufacturers) into a support role that would have rejected it early on had they seen its late stage version and full implications.

5. Understanding Value Creation as Multiple and Contingent

An aspect that is important to consider for successful realisation is that values in different parts of a VCS are often contingent upon each other. So when some actors, in interacting with others may gain from changes to support offerings in one part of a VCS, actors interacting in other support offerings may lose — as demonstrated in the Ryder case above.

Letting go of value as "added" and dropping the view of it arranged along "value chains" has important implications that need to be taken into account for strategists who design configuring offerings as systems of relations, and not as linear ones. Normann and Ramírez (1993a, 1994); (Ramírez & Wallin, 2000; Normann, 2001) had realised that in a co-creation world, one value manifested in a first interaction would be con-

Figure 9.1: Value in Configuring Offerings

Note: Value 1 is contingent on how much it contributes to the co-creation of value 2

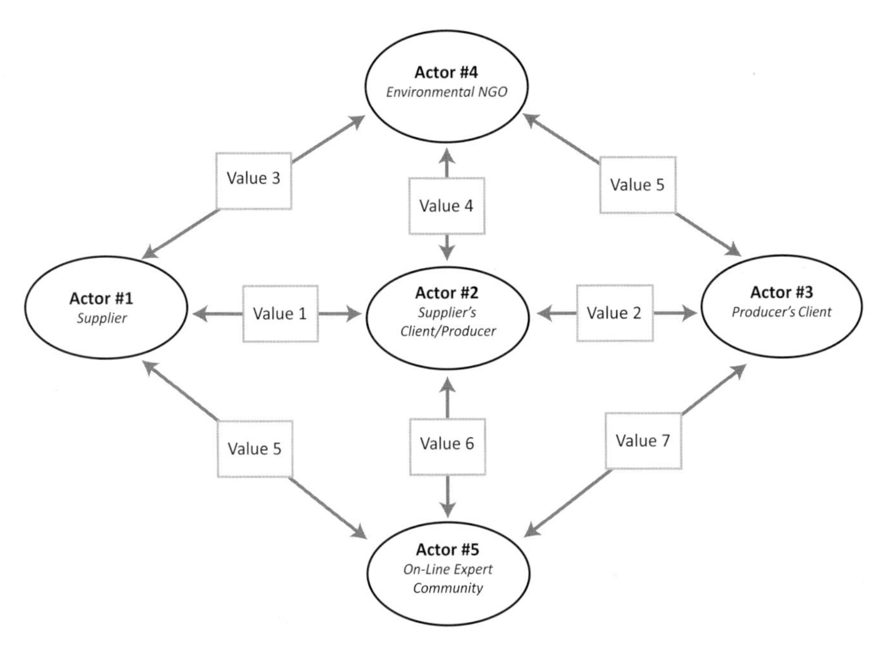

Figure 9.2: Value and Values Considerations in Designing Configuring Offerings

Note: Any one value is contingent on how much it contributes to the other values

tingent on how it enables the co-creation of a second value. This is represented graphically in Figure 9.1.

This is a simplified case of a more complex set of contingencies that the designs of all VCSs have to take into consideration. For VCSs operate as systems or webs, not as lines or chains. This is graphically illustrated in Figure 9.2.

As we saw in Chapter 6, EDF offering designers had to reconcile multiple values to enact the VCSs that linked people to electricity. What was good for community governance might not work for the initial funders; what politicians sought had impacts on the choice of technology, etc.

We noted above that it is important to consider who in the intended VCS might welcome change and who might oppose or reject it, perhaps even refusing to take on an intended role. One can do so by assessing how a value created in each intended support offering might impact the value creation for other interacting actors, in other parts of the VCS — for better or worse. Those insights may have implications for adjustments to be made in the configuring offering or its support offerings.

6. Learning as a "Stepping Stones" Process

Stepping stone approaches to learning are useful for realising new configuring offering and a new VCS. This is because they allow learning and adjustments of the configuring offering and support offerings to be done, over time, through experimentation — through trial, error, and redesign. They involve a series of steps that manifest the unfolding vision of a VCS, steps which are tuned along the journey of a design of the configuring offering and the related support offerings (and thus of the VCS they bring forth). As a step into a new stone follows a prior step, perhaps stepping back a few times, one progresses in the realisation.

The step approaches can be useful in avoiding early countermeasures by VCS actors who may reject the enrolment (see Chapter 6 and Appendix B) desired for successful mobilisation. They can enable early wins and build credibility, proving concepts, and getting acceptance for moving in the direction of more developed versions of the VCS.

There can of course be various numbers and types of steps in such an approach. It would all depend on the situation at hand. The whole point is to iterate and ensure that from the start learning gets going in real user settings, which leads to adjustments along the way. Early successes help to secure buy-in from both external and internal actors. Hostile countermeasures, if such can be expected from some actors, need to be anticipated early.

This approach can be easier if started at a small-scale, but this does not mean that companies cannot try to start with a larger scale effort — as long as processes are in place for learning and adjustment.

A "stepping stones" approach is centred particularly on the enrolment stage of ANT methodology, where potential counterparts or actors in a VCS are negotiated into their roles in an envisioned VCS. The illustration below provides an example of what a stepping stones approach can look like, from the viewpoint of a company aiming at transforming its VCS and role.

The first stepping stone in this example involves acting on short-term opportunities and creating early wins within an existing business or VCS logic, yet in the direction of the long-term VCS design intent. One might simply extend an existing offering with some new activities, such as sourcing and adding new ancillary products and interactions to an existing customer base. This extends the offering in the direction at which the strategic intent is aimed. It may be possible to take the first step with the existing internal organisational set-up, with products sold by the existing sales-force, through the existing distribution channels and within the existing incentive structure. Inappropriate incentive structures can be a big innovation killer. Do not expect an organisation to embrace a VCS change, if it is incentivised not to. This may include monetary incentives such as what aspects of performance are measured and rewarded, but also other organisational incentives such as promotions and career paths.

The second stepping stone here realises changes to the VCS that imply business growth or transformation opportunities. These may be substantial, such as adding a new offering — or less substantial, such as only extending an existing VCS slightly. The forestry, tissue, and hygiene company SCA (see Chapter 8) shifted its strategy from serving the incontinence product market to having a wider role in the broader hygiene business, including specific care services. In its successive offering design steps, SCA sourced and added care related products that would benefit actors in its VCS. It experimented with various care supporting concepts — service and product combinations — through care initiatives, in various VCS constellations. These included a joint venture with a home nursing company in a dynamic emergent market as well as close collaboration with public health actors in mature markets. Guided by its vision of being a company enabling VCS in care, SCA is pragmatic in the way and pace to realising the vision. It is guided also by innovation initiatives that have developed various VCS concepts for different care segments in different parts of the world. Some of these could be realised as part of creating new growth in the direction of the vision. Others helped build up understanding about the forces shaping the market, and included actors who played roles in it or could be invited to enter and to change it, bringing strategic clarity by broadening and deepening the internal knowledge and thinking around the company's increased understanding of its comparative advantages: understanding of care and how care may change. The second step involved an explorative business prototyping stage, which saw them experiment and prototype early versions of the intended VCS. This is well beyond step one, where a business is only "dipping its toe in the water".

The third step in the stepping stones approach used here for illustration was the realisation of the full intended VCS offering. This step was where the full shift from enrolment to mobilisation can be said to have taken place, and where the ambition of the design was first realised. This stage implied enacting a full business model with supporting offerings, including ensuring the organisational prerequisites were in place. These included creating separate units to manage this new part of the business — and could lead to transforming the existing business as well so it comes to be more in tune with the new VCS.

Development of a new VCS is most often not a neat linear process — it is not just project management and executing a plan. Instead, as the VCS emerges, it might look quite different from what was first envisioned. Each step's design must attend to the competences, resources and activities required — and how these requirements are felt across many co-creators with different values. Through the process of mobilising these, and trying to enrol different actors and their value co-creation and values into the unfolding and growing VCS, the offerings will take on a different shape.

In some cases successful VCS designs may be expected to be very different from existing VCS on the market. They may redefine what the market is — as Napster, Apple, or Spotify did with online music. A new design can be a creative stroke that may fit neatly into the customer context from a very early stage, as did Sidewalk Express. But it may also entail a more gradual build-up of the new VCS and defining of the market, eventually getting actors to align and join in the VCS. Spotify really took off once it had signed collaboration contracts with the four major music labels in North America, after years of negotiations. At first the record labels saw Spotify as a threat, but they eventually found that its VCS could be tuned to be aligned with their interests too. Spotify also brought the social media site Facebook into the VCS in the customer context, as a login route and a way to share play lists. As the VCS became more established, some of the actors, who initially perceived it as hostile, joined in. Better value was enabled for the actors in the VCS — including users who in the "freemium" streaming service had several options of accessing and sharing music and to build meaning by creating "soundtracks" for their own specific lives.

Of course, some actors who did better in the pre-existing VCS may become worse off, such as some music artists who now get far lower monetary compensation. It is inevitable that when new VCSs displace old ones there might be losers too — not only winners. Those actors (users) who consider that the new VCS gives them a "free" service are often themselves the product — monetised in terms of user information produced for sale to others. Therefore, it is important to analyse carefully who would win and who would lose in each step of the VCS offered for realisation; and to attempt to compensate the losers if at all possible, as Ciborra (1995) found worthwhile when studying how new IT systems installed had to work with the incumbent IT systems (see Section 7).

A further consideration in the stepping stones approach involves geographic scope: where will different steps be launched? The choice of markets, and the order in which one enters them or creates them, can be decisive for success — or failure. Some VCSs are global from the start. Mojang's online computer game Minecraft,[5] the digital "sandbox" where online players could shape their worlds and also play with others on their own servers or on multiplayer servers, was entirely web-based from the beginning. It was global from day one, as were its stepping stones in realising the VCS. The offering was released and sold as soon as it was playable even though it was in a very early development ("beta") version. This VCS is under continuous development, as this book is written, with forthcoming developments such as allowing new ways for players to connect or bringing in third parties and hosting them.

Other VCS offerings are more limited to geographic markets, even if they may be IT-enabled to some extent. Most of the companies we have

[5]See https://minecraft.net/ (Accessed December 2015).

researched and worked with as advisors are global or international; but like many internet-based companies geographical limitations matter e.g. due to language, intellectual property rights or distribution capabilities, or regulation or government policy (e.g. Alibaba versus Google).

Many factors are in play in the choice of which geographical markets are to be used in the different steps, and in what order. One of these may be market research feedback, where customers and users have responded well to the stepping stones, including the third step version of the VCS offering. But there are many cases of false negatives and false positives with market research to beware of.

Another factor that affects choice of geographic market can involve assessing where the new offering design appears to be less likely to trigger fierce countermeasures from established incumbent actors who may resist change. For instance, if today one has one part of the business going through a distributor that may be threatened by the new VCS design, that may not be the ideal market to launch in the early stages — or at all. One may be able to bring in the changes at a later stage, when one has developed the VCS design further in other markets and created alliances with other actors who may want to bet on the new design and join forces to promote it.

A third factor that can play a role is favourable internal capabilities; for example, a sales-force with a mind- or skillset that would be very suitable, a suitable organisational situation including managers who really would like to push for the VCS change, or a business situation — where one's attention is not overwhelmed by constant firefighting. Another favourable internal situation could be that there is recognition that the current VCS and its business model are under pressure, e.g. if it is moving towards commoditisation with margins squeezed, and for that reason that there is an appetite for VCS change. Such conditions are not always "given" and can be "manufactured" at least to some extent by re-setting expectations.

7. Avoiding Value Chain Push Backs

Even with stepping stones lined up, a go-to-market approval in hand, and piloting and business prototyping ready to go, including a solid and attractive business case on expected costs and returns, the most promising VCS innovation candidate can fail to get out of the starting blocks or may quickly derail along the race.

This is likely if one has failed to design the governance to be fit for supporting change. The research of our late friend Claudio Ciborra (1995, 2000) on how new IT systems need to be hosted within IT systems that still lived on documents — how a new design needs to be "hosted" within an established one — if it is to do well. This is also true with new VCSs in established companies, for a while at least they have to cohabit the premises (and managers' minds) with the old established players in the firm — the example of Shell Global Solutions International within Shell surveyed in Chapter 5 is an excellent example of the issues involved. This is at the core of Christensen's (1997) famous "innovators dilemma", where the next business — which will ensure survival — has to live alongside an old business that refuses to die, and often refuses the new business also.

Then, how can the new VCS be hosted within an established company? One well-established approach, made famous by Tracy Kidder's book, *The Soul of a New Machine* (in HP), is the "skunkworks" option in which the new VCS is separated out into premises and operations that are far away from those where ongoing operations are housed and managed. One of our clients in the Netherlands has done exactly that: after describing an opportunity area and creating a new VCS, they allow promising VCSs to be "promoted" to become an Emerging Business Area (EBA), after which it will become a self-standing Limited Company. Another approach, championed by Hamel (1999), was to "bring Silicon Valley inside" big firms, with venturing budgets supporting entrepreneurship by employees ("intrapreneurship"). Yet others, championed by firms such as Cisco, are to let the innovators innovate and then buy them in at the right time.

Yet another approach was pioneered by Shell, which in the mid-1990s, following a massive reorganisation that transformed 200 CEOs in a 3D matrix into a centralised company with only 5 CEOs, had to reconsider how to feed its Research and Development (R&D) funnels. Starting with the biggest division (exploration and production) and then spreading out to other divisions before reaching the corporate centre, a separate stream for innovation was established, named "GameChanger". It created new gates and criteria for passing through ideation and build-up or spin out. Technologists and experienced innovators, not line managers, could peer review new ideas and fund them up to a certain development and stepping stones stage. This proved to be a big success, which generated new businesses, extensions to existing businesses, and spin outs through venturing.

When working with the Shell GameChanger team in the mid-2000s, we supported them with what we here describe as VCS offering innovations. One of the important elements introduced to manifest VCS thinking in developing new businesses was strategic innovation domains (Ramírez *et al.*, 2011), which are "mini-VCSs" made up of technologies, technologists, projects, functional and line professionals, who together seek to establish new businesses — such as growing oil from algae. These domains grew up step by step, interaction by interaction. They may graduate as a whole (new business) or they may spin off parts of themselves as new business elements or wholes and remain in operation. They focus and attract attention, as well as resources and people. They are both experiments and houses of experiments. GameChanger, together with strategy, sought to promote and accept ideas that fit into domains, and to kill ideas that didn't. They could promote and kill domains if one of their future scenario worlds became implausible due to developments in the larger world. This enabled more return on investment for the ideas that were promoted, yet all in a stream preparing for radical innovation.

While GameChanger and the domains structure were managed separately from the business and from traditional R&D funnels, with a separate budget, they were also governed and measured on a longer time scale than the current businesses. The GameChanger team reported directly to the Board and also enjoyed visible support from the CEO, which helped it survive in the internal politics.

IBM and their Emergent Business Opportunities (EBO) model was a similar initiative, which has been well described by O'Reilly *et al.* (2009). In an assessment of why IBM had missed many big opportunities for new businesses, top management concluded that though the company was good at innovation for the existing business, and even at new growth market initiatives, it failed to innovate for new emergent areas, which were not yet defined as businesses or markets. In our words, its VCS had not yet been defined. IBM's CEO launched the EBO initiative in 2000, differentiating the approach between innovation for mature business, growth business, and future business. These had different foci for innovation, different expected outputs and success factors, and were measured on different metrics. To improve effectiveness in innovation for future businesses, IBM safeguarded these in a way similar to the GameChanger. After some years, as EBO grew, it was realised that the safeguarding by top management had become a bottleneck. In response, specific criteria were created for the gate controlling the passage from future businesses to growth businesses. These included having a strong leadership team, a well-defined strategy for how to make money, some early market success, and a proven customer value proposition. If the EBO met the criteria, it became a business in its own right to avoid being undermined or killed by the existing business.

It is unfortunately not unusual to find VCS initiatives killed off early, simply because companies treat them as one-off pet projects favoured by this or that small group of executives. There can be a failure to realise that making a novel VCS succeed requires not only treating it as a design and learning processes, but also sustaining it through several rounds of the stepping stones development approach. One must also ensure management and governance support for effective progress on terms suited for each organisation — no design fits all — and for the innovation type and stepping stones stage at hand.

Chapter 10

The Growth of VCS Thinking

Box 10.1: Chapter 10 at a Glance

In this chapter, we review how value creating system (VCS) thinking is steadily growing and replacing the obsolete value chain thinking. Although the early optimism of Normann and Ramírez (1994) has taken some time to be realised, obstacles are now being overcome. We can understand the delays by analysing why the older system could persist. First, the value chain idea is still useful in many situations. Also, the new forms of business practice have come to widespread importance only quite recently. Even now, most managers have been trained on the old tools and do not easily abandon them. However, with the realities of our current business environments, it is now time to change thinking, from structure to process, and from chains to systems. With this book, we hope to help that happen.

1. A Networked World of Business in a Value Chain World of Management

Our colleague Richard Normann used to differentiate between World of Business (WOB) concerning the organisation's interactions with its external context — and World of Management (WOM), or what happens inside the organisation. While in an ideal world WOM supports WOB, in the real world WOB often shifts faster than WOM in established companies and in established societal processes, and WOM becomes a prison or obstacle for new WOB possibilities, preventing WOB to develop as fast as one would hope.

Nevertheless, when Normann and Ramírez published *From Value Chain to Value Constellation* in 1993 and *Designing Interactive Strategy* in 1994, they felt that the WOB insights they manifested were so blindingly obvious that the world (WOM as well as WOB) would quickly embrace what they suggested.

As we have argued throughout this book, 20 years later the ideas of strategy as interactive design and of value co-creation are not only still in good currency (Ramírez gets invitations to keynote on the ideas still today) but growing. Yet value chain thinking is still a major conceptualisation of value creation in an ever more networked world.

There are certainly strong signs that the WOB forms Normann and Ramírez imagined over 20 years ago are becoming more central in thinking about, and for designing systems to create value. In this book, we have explained at length why this is happening now, and we have expressed the benefits of implementing a collaborative systems approach to strategy.

The transition for established companies away from value chain thinking to VCS thinking, which Normann and Ramírez outlined in the early 1990s, has been happening since and is still happening now.

The central issues we explore in this chapter are (a) why has it been so hard to make this transition before (and why is it still difficult for some today)? And (b) why is it so hard to remain in a VCS world? We suggest there are three main causes explaining these difficulties, and that strategists and strategy teams who want to gain comparative advantage by utilising the VCS strategic framework would be well advised to understand these causes to enable successful governance of VCSs.

2. The Concept being Replaced (The Value Chain) is Still Considered to be Largely Valid and Useful in Many Places

The situation is as if one is aware of Quantum physics but one uses Newtonian physics to get from home to work. Or as if one is aware the earth is round but one uses flat earth coordinates to travel from work to home.

3. The VCS View of Business Has Grown to Have Widespread Importance to Most Businesses *Only* Over the Last Part of the 20 Year Interval Mentioned Above

While the world is now more networked, only in these last few years has the Internet become ubiquitous, broadly available, and mobile. The iPhone 6 put more computing power in the hands of each of the consumers who bought one in the September 2014 launch weekend than the whole world had available in 1995, but the first iPhone was only released on 29 June 2007.

It is in the last few years, then, that the VCS mode of strategising has started to become a tangible, common, and palpable reality for the many, and not a leading edge for the few.

Highly distributed computing power in smartphones, tablets, and "ultraportable" PCs is one highly visible manifestation of the reconfigurations of the business landscape that brought about the rise of the Internet and the way that this has enabled everybody to participate much more intimately and interactively with every business provider.

Also, systemic forces not in the Porterian "five force" analyses also began disrupting businesses — be it ageing populations, climate change-induced unusual weather patterns, water-stressed basins, instability in the financial systems upon which those businesses depend, cybercrime, or shale oil and gas, which has transformed the energy value equations that underpin much of business (Dale, 2015).

So it is only in the last few years that business after business has found that they too are well advised to shift their view of what is a "consumer", "client", and "user" — and indeed a "supplier", "2nd tier supplier" and other "stakeholders" — from a value chain view to a value system one. These businesses have come to realise that it is no longer possible to pretend that any one actor holds only one of these roles in all circumstances.

All actors, understood as having multiple roles as co-creators of value, increase their strategic options in order to create more value. But this realisation, this understanding, also complicates governance. This is

Box 10.2: A Networked World Makes Value Chains Ever More Obsolete

Before the Internet became so important, only a few significant VCSs were being designed in ways that made it evident that the relevance of the value chain was decreasing — FedEx, OneWorld, VISA, and IKEA being good examples. This is now changing massively — networked complexity is ubiquitous, and value is co-created almost everywhere in the system. Here, the old mapping technique — the value chain — no longer provides guidance. Thus, some 90% of foreign exchange trading is now carried out by semi-automated networked platforms; and about 30% of marketing investments are now directed to online formats, increasingly relating many to many among each other rather than in 1:1 dyads.

Paraphrasing the old poem, we might say that now, no business is an island. Business ecosystem language, originating in the IT sector, is now finding its way into broader use as the web-enabled interactions take hold.

because the new WOB is very much at odds with established WOM.[1] The networked WOB lives in a WOM that: accounts for and taxes value as "added", implicitly assumes that customers have the role of destroying value (depreciation, amortisation), does not count the value of customers or customer relations on balance sheets, and has antitrust laws (for very good historical reasons) that play against cross-sectoral partnerships that could stabilise turbulence, as we saw in Chapter 7.

The changes we are now witnessing and which were heralded by Normann and Ramírez over 20 years ago are quite substantial, and they have substantial implications for governance. As a result of this unprecedented situation, there is not yet a commonly accepted nomenclature in current business vocabulary that carries the new meanings and roles in a widely accepted form. Concepts without well-accepted, stable names are

[1] A salient governance complication is that it is now impossible to pin down responsibilities and accountabilities to someone as if they still held only one role. Thus, for example, the "end user" label and role no longer captures effectively how those individuals and organisations who held that role (and rights to complain) in value chain conceptualisations relate to the other counterparts in value creation.

hard for people to use. Also, the names used by accountants, analysts, fund managers, regulators (and courts) to sanction conduct refer the established value chain business logic, not to the emerging new logic.

As was anticipated in the original work, the pervasive adoption of the possibilities of IT has resulted in many more businesses finding that their offerings are constructed much more dynamically, with many more counterparts, in patterns of interaction for which linear models of governance and accounting are inadequate. Linear models can no longer encompass the multiple and often paradoxical roles that a configuring offering designer has in relation to the enrolment of counterparts.

The design of dynamic configuring offerings — which involves relating many interlinked interactors with each other — requires a different way of thinking about strategy. For example, in a recent high-level conversation, senior officers of a University were considering how digital options might disrupt established research and pedagogic formats (and the relations between them), and it became clear that the very way of strategising in an "analogue" world — with fact-finding research preceding strategy definition, execution or implementation and finally assessment — is incompatible with strategising in a "digital" context. In a digital strategising context, many of the activities above interact with each other synchronically rather than being done independently, one after the other sequentially, and also involve multiple loops and levels of engagement among them. The dynamic experimentation that a VCS world requires of strategy, with short feedback loops, bootstrapping, bricolage, and so on, sits uncomfortably with established governance systems, authority protocols, roles, and procedures — even of and in strategic planning!

4. The Conventional "Value Chain"-Based Tools Have Shaped the Minds of Managers, While VCS Tools are in Emergent Stage

A third challenge now is to develop practical, usable heuristics that will help managers develop the systemic awareness that is needed to work effectively with the three basic ideas that this book explores: values, value co-creation, and VCSs (articulated through designed offerings). This creates a very different set of challenges for the next generation of leaders. Thus, the CEO Report research conducted between Saïd Business School researchers and Heidrick and Struggles professionals on the basis of 152 interviews with CEO's in 2014 found that "Anticipating how, when, and why different contexts may interact to disrupt an organization requires leaders to develop "ripple intelligence", as well as the ability to harness doubt more effectively in order to improve decision making."[2]

Even where co-creation is understood as fundamental to business (for example, in any business that relates to its co-creators using a form of interactive network), the linear conceptualisations of the processes of delivery of the offering, and of the operations that sustain it, tend to dominate the management mindset. This is perhaps because of the professional training these managers were educated with, and the processes that have been put into their organisations (both important WOM components). With such training and processes, linearity trumps the appreciation of the relational and systemic understanding of value creation that these processes enable. Attention is drawn to the linear: the co-creation is implicitly taken to be someone else's concern. The common use of words such as "channels" (or "pipelines") of "delivery" to "end users" "downstream" demonstrates that the transition to another way of thinking about value creation not only requires learning a new language, but also becoming familiar with a foreign culture.

Thinking based on value chains is supported by considerable and interdependent systems — including most of the available tools for strategy analysis, as well as the means and methods for the assessment of these strategies. A new way of thinking is not just about having new thoughts. New thinking also challenges established uses and practices — and practitioners. Based on studies of navigational cultures in Papua New Guinea and the US navy, both enabling expert navigation but navigated in profoundly different ways, cognitive anthropologist Edwin Hutchins (1995) suggested that thinking co-evolves with, and is closely linked to, the development of tools, practices and practitioners.

---

[2] http://www.sbs.ox.ac.uk/faculty-research/entrepreneurship-centre/global-shapers-community-collaborates-sa%C3%AFd-business-school/ceo-report-0.

If one follows this line of argument, then as one advocates practitioners' need to learn new thinking, one must acknowledge its relations with tools and practices. This is consistent with "strategy as practice" research.[3] One must thus recognise all the implicit stakes linked to these dependencies, such as a massive strategy consulting business with many established firms, several of which each employ thousands of professionals, whose offerings and tools are largely based on value chain thinking, with their activities — with those of their clients — resting on operating and learning models that employ value chain concepts.

Attending to "the medium that is the message" for strategy formulation is important for understanding the persistence of value chain thinking. Research shows that the medium used for communicating the message affects how the message is perceived. McLuhan (1964) was the first to proclaim this explicitly. People working in offices use two-dimensional media such as paper and screens, and tools such as Excel tables to communicate. This reduces the complex topology of business possibilities and contexts that need to be interacted into a two-dimensional, flat space. Conceptual boxes live happily in these two dimensions which box-in the thinking of those using such media to work together. Although Tapscott (2013) suggested that Facebook would replace email as more collaborative work would be needed, a point also made by Adler and Heckscher (2006), this has not yet happened.

Three-dimensional (3D) sharing media, such as 3D printers and PC screens with two thin layers that allow for users to perceive data in this manner, may provide a richer medium to share more complex phenomena. Tufte (1983) has studied how it is possible to help our mind "escape" from the 2D media prison through imaginative renderings — more of this will need to be deployed to help the transition that this book explores. Given the power and economy of IT graphics, it is possible to imagine the creation of interactive displays in which both structures and quantities can be represented and also manipulated by crowdsourcing.

The rise of publications and courses relating design in business with business strategy, championed by the likes of Roger Martin, until recently

---

[3] See http://sap-in.org/.

Dean of the Rotman School in Toronto (Moldoveanu & Martin, 2001) and Robert Austin of the Copenhagen Business School (Devin & Austin, 2012) is also encouraging. Designers can think "out of the" (2D) box more easily than conventional managers and are lending renewed perspectives to how strategy is imagined, shaped, defined, and communicated. When designers realise that in designing offerings they are not only working for the design team, or the product development team, or the marketing team, but for the company's strategy, then the argument this book proposes will have taken hold.

One must also consider the personal discomforts and risks that managers may put themselves into when they suggest a new way of thinking. This will be particularly so if the novel option they propose is more difficult to translate into a well-known method, such as those taught at business schools. We believe that herein lies a challenge, and an important contribution of this book: Those who want to pursue this route need to show not only what VCS thinking is, but also how it can be used in strategy work, and not only in envisioning possibilities but also in enacting change.

Structure and process reinforce each other, but in the value chain era attention has been on structure. Since its beginning, systems thinking (Emery, 1970) has underlined that structures support and host processes, and processes support and shape structures. Yet in Western management, even if "processes" have taken hold, the attention of senior executives has been predominantly on structures. To change firms and even whole economic sectors these managers restructure: buying and selling divisions and subsidiaries, redoing organograms, hiring and laying off staff, taking layers away, closing down manufacturing facilities, announcing joint-ventures and mergers, and merging departments. In fact, even much of so-called business "process" reengineering (BPR) in vogue a decade ago was about structuring companies to be process friendly.

Our work invites strategic managers to do a "background/foreground reversal" in what they attend to. We seek to help them overcome the challenge that for many people value remains embedded in value chain world views. Even when this foregrounding reversal is successfully achieved, it is now mostly only done away from the everyday structure, as in "away days". Then the "back in the office" environment brings structure to the foreground and pushes process back into the background. Instead, we would expect to see the reversal to be done — not only in away days but also in the everyday of strategising.

Process is also harder to foreground because feedback loops change over time — and in relation to each other. These dynamics mean that process is more demanding for what our mind attends to. This contrasts with structures, which are (apparently) frozen and fixed and visible over time. Appreciating and using structure can more easily fit into limited time and limited attention spans than is the case with process.

Processes manifested with loops are often considered to be more difficult to grasp than structures manifested with hierarchies of boxes. Even those who have been trained to look at feedback loops have trouble making this vision their dominant foreground. This is one of the things that came loud and clear from Senge's work at MIT and manifested in his *Fifth Discipline* (2014). A major contribution of this present book is to show how attention to the offering, and to the interactions that it configures, brings both the process and structure of a VCS into a natural focus of attention for the managerial mind.

Of course companies pay a lot of attention to product design, to pricing, and so on. In that sense what the book offers is a "natural" extension of design from a focus on things and services to instead focus on offerings and strategy and the VCSs they bring forth. It remains to be seen how counterintuitive the approach is to a culture (managerial, professional culture) that foregrounds things, structures and actors, and not connections, feedback processes and interactions. Because new thinking requires new tools, we have presented a first set of design and analyses tools (some of which have been around for decades) that together help this attention foregrounding to be more easily grasped and kept there.

5. How to Think and Act Differently

A challenge that we explore in this book is how to invite managers in companies whose business they consider to be distant from communication and information technologies to embrace thinking about their businesses as designed VCSs or to think of them as systems that can be redesigned: by them, or by others, and possibly in ways that may not benefit them, if they are too late to see and take initiatives.

To do so we have spelled out our thinking and provided examples from real world firms and settings as well as methodologies they can take up.

We are proposing that managers in any company can profit from thinking as if their businesses were intimately connected to spheres of interactivity. While there are "industry associations" where one meets others in one's industry, there are far fewer occasions when one can gather those in one's VCS — across industries — in win–win collaborations such as those that this book espouses. More cross-sectoral partnerships (Selsky & Parker, 2005) are edging their way up the priority list of issues boards must consider.

Perhaps because the most influential strategy academic in the last 50 years — Michael Porter — posited that strategy was about competing against peers (Porter, 1985), and not about co-creating superior value with stakeholders (clients, employees, investors, owners, suppliers), strategy has been mostly understood to be about competing. Competitive strategy is about getting a bigger share of a finite pie. Competitive strategy is not focused on making the pie bigger, by collaborating.

In retrospect, this is odd. It is so odd that recently even Michael Porter has started to talk about what he calls "shared" value (2011). We prefer, as did Normann and Ramírez (1993), to talk of co-created value. To co-create, one has to collaborate and co-design, not just share.

While writing and research on systems appears to have leveled off and in some places even declined, two of Normann and Ramírez's suggestions seem to have taken root: the rise in services as co-created value in a much more richly interconnected world, and the rise in "business ecosystems" manifesting much of what they called "value constellations".

We take heart in these developments and propose they signal that the time has come to further test and prototype the underlying logic of business that was proposed some 20 years ago. In the field of marketing they have gone further, with Vargo and Lusch (2008) claiming that a "service dominant" logic must replace the "goods"-based dominant logic of the past. Online communities such as Facebook are being tapped to make enterprise more collaborative, as has the "open innovation" field.

6. In Conclusion

We hope this book provides clearer concepts, clearer definitions, clearer terms, a clearer methodology — and a number of tools — that will help more managers to see the benefits of switching from an "industry" and "value chain" and "position" strategic thinking to one centred on "offerings", "VCSs" and "interactively designed".

Attention is a scarce resource — it appears costly to expend it on complicated things, and comforting to expend it on well-known and boxed in, structurally clear, ones. Our book suggests that efforts to dedicate economic, staff, and attention resources to VCS thinking should not be seen as "expenditure", but as worthwhile "investment" producing handsome returns and avoiding costly mistakes.

Strategists can choose what strategy frameworks and approaches to use, but the contextual business environment, they cannot choose. As we have argued in this book, the systemic, networked, turbulent, ambiguous and uncertain business environments of today require a strategic framework that is effective to do well in such conditions.

Appendix A

Origins of Value Creating Systems

Box A.1: Appendix A at a Glance

Many of the ideas we present and relate to each other in this book have long pedigrees, often stretching over several hundred years.

We believe it is of help to readers who want to use these ideas to know where they came from, and what "baggage" in the forms of connotations and relations they carry with them.

So this appendix overviews the historical development both of "value creating system (VCS)" thought and of "offerings".

In doing so, the appendix proposes to situate the book as another step in an unfolding story — a story that is still being written, alongside several other intellectual initiatives described and analysed in this book.

So another purpose of this appendix is to acknowledge the building blocks from which our thinking is derived, and to help practitioners who want to use our proposed approach to develop business to be capable of relating them to other practices, traditions, and approaches.

A.1. A History of the Thinking of Value as Co-Created

Ramírez (1999) found that the understanding of co-creation is at least 300 years old. Key builders of the notion included the following:

- De Boisguilbert (1707) worked out an economic model based on interdependence.
- Storch (1823) proposed that services require cooperation and enable capital accumulation; and developed the notion of "internal benefits".
- Bastiat (1851) took value "to be the result of a many-sided exchanges of services".
- Mill (1852) for whom "utility" was embodied in objects, and/or in people, or was not embodied.
- Colson (1924) for whom "production consists of nothing else than to arrange combinations and transformations which are useful to us".
- Sauvy (1949) and Naville (1963) who thought of services not as a given form of output of production, but as a distinct type of productive activity.
- Fuchs (1965) who proposed that the consumer is a factor of production.
- Bell (1973) who underlined the important role that the organisation of science, technology, and intellect has on value creation.
- Gershuny (1978) whose work highlighted the importance of self-service in the economy.
- Stanback (1980) and Brender, Chevalier and Pisani-Ferry (1980) who proposed that goods and services are complementary.

A.2. A More Recent History of Value and the Concept of Offerings

Based on the ideas concerning value co-creation, Normann and Ramírez began developing ideas on the design and architecture of offerings in the 1980s. Updated and refined views on these ideas are found below and in Chapter 5. In 1989, they suggested that value co-creation means that what one economic actor (let's call their role in this interaction to be that of a "supplier") makes available to another economic actor (holding the role of "customer" or client' or "buyer" in this interaction) is an "offering",[1] always consisting of work by at least two parties, of goods, and of information.

But this 1:1 relationship of value co-creation was of course seen to be too simplistic in reality — any one offering relationship connecting two

[1] We are aware that in many cultures and religions, an "offering" is brought by the believer to a temple or other setting for a "God". We do not in any way suggest that the term "offering" as used in this book involves any of the spiritual or religious connotations in that other use of the term.

economic actors was seen to be inescapably embedded in much broader, and often more complicated relationships — which in turn are linked to yet other relationships, and so on. So the supplier in turn related itself to others from whom it buys offerings such as advertising and storage (its "suppliers" in those relationships), to those it gets money from (its "investors", "lenders", "owners"), to those it employs (its "employees", "contractors", "partners"), to those it pays taxes to and which regulate it (the "government" and its various departments and functions), to those who help it to promote its activities (its "advertisers", "marketers", "competitive intelligence researchers", "journalists"), etc. and so too for the client — who was seen as never being in isolation and whose value creating with the DVD offering (see p. 250) depends to a large extent on how it improves relations — with others, and indeed, with oneself (i.e. the music calms one down and helps to concentrate and write better letters).

So co-created offerings thus came to be seen as inextricably embedded in relations, and also in systems of relations. These systems of relations are networks of relationships — not just networks of actors — and they are understood to have emergent properties. Emergent properties arise through "unintended consequences" (positive or negative) of relating, and they emerge in particular strength when several relations become interlinked. Emergent properties of systems have been studied in various ways, as in the examples shown in Box A.2.

Box A.2: Different Ways in Which the Emergent Properties of Systems Have Been Studied

Emergent properties have been studied in many ways. Two that are particularly intriguing are what biologists Maturana and Varela called "autopoesis" (1980) — a form of evolution that involves emergent self-organisation and cannot be entirely planned for in advance. Normann (2001) related this to organisations which have the capability of renewing themselves over and over again, in a purposeful reemergence in interaction and co-emergence with the context they are in. Another set of insights of emergent systems were discovered by Nobel prize winning chemist Ilya Prigogine in what he called "dissipative structures", popularised in his book with Isabelle Stengers (1984) and linked to thinking by Mary Bernard (2008).

A good example of the way that a new relationship can bring about unintended consequences is how the reintroduction of wolves into Yellowstone National Park in the USA (a new offering for those visiting it, as well as for those inhabiting the park!) changed not only the deer population and the vegetation they ate (and then stopped eating), but also the river banks of the park and the quality of the rivers themselves (Monbiot 2014).

This embeddedness of any one offering in wide sets of relationships is inescapable — it obeys to the relational ontology that is at the core of Schatzi's (2001) description of practice theory. In strategy terms it means that in designing offerings, one has to both (a) be attentive to the context of relations in which the designed offering relation will be embedded — often, as we see in this book, by designing (for) the other offerings that of necessity support the new design or redesign; and (b) that the designer must inescapably also determine how far within the wider system the designing will go, what it will include, and what it will exclude and when it stops. One cannot (re)design the whole world. That which the design "bounds" is just a small part of value creation.

The role of the offering as a design approach to organise co-creation was extensively discussed in Normann (2001), who built on the Normann and Ramírez (1989), (1993), and (1994) publications where they had suggested that the roles that goods, people's activities, and information play in a given offering can be exchanged for each other when the offering is redesigned. In the DVD example, for instance, when MP3 players enabled iTunes to emerge, the special value of the DVD was eliminated. Instead of a DVD player one bought an iPod or a mobile phone (for a while Nokia, when it integrated music into its mobile phones, was the biggest seller in the world of MP3 players). This individualised music changed who did what and when, and also made it more portable — changing where and when music could be listened to. iTunes became a big information source and storage system. Spotify in turn then transformed things again, when the web became widely accessible through Wi-Fi. These examples illustrate that redesign of the offering is also the redesign of the whole set of relationships and roles that come together to co-create a VCS.

Normann and Ramírez also distinguished *relieving* value ("I do this for you") manifested more in goods-centred offerings from *enabling* value

("I help you to do this yourself") manifested more in service-centred offerings. The role any one actor pays is constituted by the offerings that they are involved in. In one offering I may act as client, in another as supplier. Many redesigns of offerings transform enabling into relieving value or the other way around. In the DVD example, iTunes stores things for the user, so the user no longer needs to store physical DVDs; and iTunes and MP3 players together enable the music to become mobile, allowing listening while commuting or exercising.

We develop the concepts of offerings and of value co-creation in systems further in Chapter 5. Having outlined the main features of these concepts here, we turn to the history of value co-creation in marketing.

A.3. Strategy, Marketing and the History of Value Co-Creation Thinking

Our late friend and colleague Richard Normann (1943–2003) was a "reflective practitioner" as articulated by his and our friend Donald Schön (2005). He was a management consultant with academic connections. The consultant role formed the arena on which he — using his clinical approach to reflective practice — created actionable and innovative insights.

Normann started his consulting career in Scandinavian Institute for Administrative Research (SIAR), which Mintzberg considered an important school in the development of 20th century strategic thinking.

> "SIAR led to a kind of golden age in Swedish management writing, to my mind one of the richest we have ever seen in the field. … SIAR stimulated deep probes into serious and critical issues, offering rich and creative theory. … Proponents of this Swedish "school" of management were not afraid to theorize. As Richard wrote to me earlier this year "SIAR was a kind of protest movement against academia with (its) traditional methods, and (for) the idea that research and intervention could be united." (Henry Mintzberg, in the introduction to Normann, 2001)

From understanding the crucial role of the interaction between the organisation and its context, SIAR professionals were among the first ones to detect what is now generally well known: that it is possible for a social system to influence itself by choosing which parts of the environment to interact with (Normann, 2001). Normann manifested this already in his doctoral dissertation and the English version of this, which was published as *Management for Growth* (1977). Normann developed the SIAR ideas further in his *Service Management Model*, first published in Normann *et al.* (1978), and then in Arndt and Friman (1982). The service management model got wider publicity in Normann's 1983 *Service Management — strategy and leadership in service business*. The important notion of viewing the customer not only as a part of the market segment to approach, but, and more importantly, as a *co-creator* in the service delivery process, was a cornerstone of his conceptual development.[2]

The insight of the many innovative roles customers can have which allow companies to engage them in many different ways and relate them with other external resources, led Normann and his colleagues to invent the breakthrough concepts of "value constellations" and interactive strategy as a design process, first presented in Normann and Ramírez (1993, 1994) and further developed by Normann in 2001.

> "The crucial competence of business companies today is exactly this: the competence to organise value creation. ... The new paradigm ... also implies a dramatic conceptual change and a very real shift in how we view customers. The customer is no longer just a source of business, but now actually a co-creator, and a co-designer, of value creation." (2001: 24–25)

Normann and Ramírez (1993) based their analysis on an in-depth understanding of three cases — IKEA, Danish pharmacists, and French water utilities. They concluded that successful businesses do not just create value, they reinvent it. Such companies, Normann and Ramírez concluded in 1993, focus on

> "the *VCS* itself, within which different economic actors — suppliers, business partners, allies, customers — work together to co-create value. Their key strategic task is the *reconfiguration* of roles and relationships among the constellation of actors in order to mobilise the creation of value in new forms or by new players."

---

[2]His colleagues Eiglier and Langeard (1977) came up with a compatible view in their book on "servuction", where those served were involved in production.

This might imply new roles for actors in their interactions in systems, and also a reframing of roles internally within an organisation. For example, several years ago we did some strategic consulting work for a very large organisation with world-class professionals supported by a very large database and a highly sophisticated set of processes and staffs. The professionals in their value creation thought of what the staff did as "back office" support. As a result, they thought of the staff members as second class citizens. It was thus a huge shock to these professionals when the boss of the staff team brought in a marketing manager — why did the back office think it needed to market itself? The response was that as online technology came in, the way value was produced, and hence, the business, had been becoming ever more digital-intensive. As digitalisation took hold, what had been the "back" office had become the "front" office for those whom the organisation served. Indeed, as orders and inquiries and relationships moved online, the interface with users changed, as indeed did criteria for timeliness, quality, traceability, and of the effectiveness of the whole organisation. In the terms of this book, the offering was being transformed, and its transformation changed the interfaces and the systems of co-creations involved in serving customers. The power and relative status of different departments within the organisation were themselves transformed. Some of this change had been designed, other parts just emerged — and the professionals and staff and their managers scrambled to redesign the offering.

Ramírez and Paltschik (2013) assessed how the field of marketing has developed its thinking of co-creation, with similarities to the value co-creation systems thinking. Below we survey some of their assessment.

A.3.1 The Nordic School

Paltschik and Ramírez (2014) reviewed how service marketing scholars studying industrial relationships also generated views of more complex relationships. An example they furnished is as follows:

> "The IMP Group was originally formed in the mid 1970s, as a research project on "Industrial Marketing and Purchasing", by a group of researchers representing five European countries and universities; the Universities of Uppsala, Bath, UMIST, ESC Lyon and the Ludwig Maximilians

> University (Munich). A dynamic model of buyer-supplier relationships, the Interaction Model, was developed and (it was) used in comparative empirical studies of industrial marketing and purchasing within and across a number of European countries (France, Germany, Italy, Sweden and UK). A common experience from these early investigations of about 900 business relationships was that business exchange cannot be understood as series of dis-embedded and independent transactions of given resources — but rather as complex relationships between buying and selling organisations, where what is exchanged is created in interaction. The result of this first IMP Group study was published in the books *Industrial Marketing and Purchasing of Goods*, Håkansson (1982) and *Strategies for International Industrial Marketing* Turnbull and Valla (2013, see also 1986) (pp. 229–238)."

Paltschik and Ramírez related how Grönroos and Gummesson established what they named "the Nordic School" of service marketing, which started by studying the links between a service company and a customer. The key insight of Grönroos's work, as expressed in Fisk *et al.* (2000), was the observation in 1976 that "a service firm has no products, only interactive processes". It was only later that the Nordic School moved on to study value constellations such as those studied by Normann and Ramírez (1993a). An example is the work of Heinonen *et al.* (2010) who sought "to introduce a new perspective on the roles of customers and companies in creating value by outlining a customer-based approach to service".

A.3.2 The Service-Dominant Logic School

The Nordic School, as well as Normann's earlier work on service management, helped to spawn the highly influential Service-Dominant Logic (S-D) approach developed and popularised by the American marketing academics Vargo and Lusch in many highly cited papers, perhaps the best known of which was titled the "Evolving to a New Dominant Logic for Marketing" (2004). S-D has been elaborated by the same authors either alone, together, or with others in a very significant number of publications, notably (2005) and (2008). The concept got a first institutional "home" when the *Forum on Markets and Marketing* was held in 2008 at the University of New South Wales in Australia, now a biennial event. As with the Nordic School, the original S-D concept was focused on the exchange between a seller and a customer, and then expanded to include networks. The original 8+2 S-D "foundational premises" included four that appear to be viewed as the core ones. These four principles were (a) service is the fundamental basis of exchange, (b) the customer is always a co-creator of value, (c) all social and economic actors are resource integrators, and (d) value is always uniquely and phenomenologically determined by the beneficiary.[3]

A.3.3 Service Science

Another related development has been the so-called "service science" approach promoted by large IT companies, headed by IBM. It has been a well-funded interdisciplinary attempt to bring service thinking to bear upon the design and operation of large scale complex systems. Service Science has sought to relate computer science, cognitive science, economics, organisational behaviour, human resources management, marketing, operations research into a coherent whole.

A.3.4 Actor-Network Theory

Finally, the development of actor-network theory (ANT) in the sociology of innovation, which we analyse in detail in Chapter 6 and Appendix B, has been an important development that parallels and influences our thinking. It offers both a view of actors that is well in line with our thinking, and a methodology to effectively map and develop an understanding of the historical evolution of specific actor systems and their design.

A.4. Historical Roots of the VCS Construct and the Situation Today

Each of the theoretical initiatives in marketing, IT, and the sociology of innovation described above includes insights that are manifested in the

---

[3](c) and (d) were not, however, included in the original set of premises.

designing of VCSs as we understand it today. VCS thinking and practice builds on these ideas and insists that the core of the design effort is the offering, which is a feature that distinguishes our approach from these other perspectives.

As companies such as Airbnb and Uber design innovative offerings that transform the existing hotel (or accommodation) and the taxi (or urban transportation) businesses, they not only replace value but also create new value creating possibilities. *The Economist* (Graphic Detail 2015) reported that while Uber has indeed taken some of the market in NYC from taxis, it has also created a market that taxis did not serve. These companies did not enter an existing value creating configuration only by analysing strengths and weaknesses in the existing offering; they designed new offerings by accessing and mobilising capabilities of information and communication technologies that — bundled into newly designed configuring offerings — help to mobilise what had been dormant assets (unused rooms, unused cars, unworked hours in households) to make them available to users seeking to create value (travellers). The economics work partly because the offering is designed to use the marginal value of these resources; and thus the offering works from marginal cost, not average cost. Sidewalk Express, which is described in Chapter 5, is another good example of this.

Airbnb and Uber executives may not be aware of the view of offering design we articulate in this book — but the ideas that underpin their business's offerings design have a long history to which they have contributed a new step, and which will underpin further ideas in the future. This book's core aim is to explain the strategic aspects of what is involved in such strategies and to propose actionable ways to make them happen.

Appendix B

Actor-Network Theory

Box B.1: Appendix B at a Glance

This appendix gives a more extensive description of Actor-Network Theory (ANT), which we use to explore the emergence of an existing value creating system (VCS) design, as described in Chapter 6.

ANT started out in France as the so-called "sociology of translation" (Callon, 2001; Latour, 2005; Law, 2009).[1] Its proponents sought to understand how the managers in one company (or "actor" as sociologists would call it) attempt — and often succeed — to "translate" the role of any one other "actor" with whom they interact to develop what these sociologists refer to as an "actor-network" — composed in effect of many such enrolments with several actors. Their "actor-network" is what we call a VCS in the strategy terms of this book.

B.1. Introduction

The idea of an "actor-network" (from a sociological perspective) is that any one actor that is simultaneously both a member of a network and an actor, so that the "actor" sustains the network while the "network" sustains the ongoing stability, role, and identity of the actor. We, in this appendix, relate

[1]Their key term, "translate", combined both senses of "change place" and "change form"; it is fertile but sometimes confusing.

their "actor-network" concept to our "VCS" one. The sociological perspective on actor-networks was developed into a theory — "ANT". However, as we shall see, ANT is for our purposes perhaps better understood as a method for tracing the actions of actors and their interrelatedness with others, rather than something to be thought of primarily as a sociological theory (Latour, 2005).

For example, Michel Callon studied how the French electric utility EDF failed to "translate" Renault's role from being a car manufacturer in Europe into a role as — in effect — a second-order builder of vehicle chassis, in their effort to create an electric car systems in the 1970s.[2] Much later Renault created its own electric vehicle actor-network with Nissan and got other actors with whom it worked to translate their roles accordingly. This example shows that power relations are important in the ANT analysis.

An actor — in this case the EDF company — aiming to build a new actor-network, will attempt to (re) define the necessary roles and seek to enrol others (like Renault at the time) into them (Callon, 1986). Some actors will comply. Others will refuse the necessary roles, and instead of accepting a role offered, they may seek to enrol others into their own system (Callon, 1986). In other words, while some actors will comply and join a new actor-network or VCS, others will resist (as did Renault), trying to redefine roles and relationships according to their own interests. This set of those possible and alternative power configurations highlights the importance of association, power, and compliance in the ANT sociological analyses (Latour, 2005).

ANT built on the idea that actors and networks cannot be separated from each other and are two sides of the same coin. Thus any actor, such as a company, and indeed other entities with actor-type roles like technological objects,[3] are taken to be inextricably embedded in, and sustained by, networks of relations with other actors and entities, which in turn are part

[2]The innovation was referred to as the VEL (véhicule électrique), see Callon (1986) for a more detailed account.

[3]ANT famously extended the notion of "actor" to include not only living entities such as individuals, groups, and organisations, but also inanimate ones such as technologies (which "act upon", constrain, and enable, other actors with whom they interact) and things, and manifestations of information such as maps and inscriptions. Here, we also understand that such relationships are necessary for the proper functioning of a VCS.

of other networks (Callon, 1986). In Chapter 1, we saw how well Facebook and the World Economic Forum understood this.

If it was not for the networks that make up a VCS, the actors and entities it joins would disintegrate, as they would lack their necessary sustaining relations that make their role — and in that sense, their identity as a supplier or consumer or partner or producer, etc. — viable and sustainable. This means that in order to understand organisations and VCSs, one needs to be able to trace and understand the interactions and more or less stabilised relations that constructed them, that developed them, and that co-define them (Callon, 2001; Latour, 1987; 2005) — and which continue doing so, and in doing so sustain their identity and value creating roles.

What the VCS framework adds to the ANT methodology is the construct of the offering, which is analysed in depth in Chapter 5. Thus we distinguish a major enrolment (as an offering) that configures the system of others' roles (we call this the "configuring" offering, as was seen in Chapter 6) from the individual "support offerings" (still important but less central) that support the coming about of a new VCS.

Utilising the ANT methodology invites one's mind to be open to "seeing" a wider network of potential actors and interactions, not confined to the conventional descriptions of business and business networks (customers, suppliers, producers, etc.) or groups of these labelled differently — such as "industries" or "markets".

With ANT, strategists should not be satisfied with listing the usual suspects *a priori* when doing a VCS analysis. As the 1970s case on EDF's electric vehicle showed, the complex actor world of electric cars included not only electricity producers, electric powertrain engineering firms, car-body builders, cities, and consumers, but also unruly "accumulators, fuel cells, electrodes, electrons, catalysts and electrolytes" (Callon, 1986) that did not perform their intended functions as envisioned at the time by the EDF engineers. This recalcitrance contributed to the collapse of that VCS project, which aimed to create the new electric vehicle actor-network.

All this means that the strategist must have a broad view on who are relevant actors and must explore how they interact. A lesson from ANT is moreover that, even though the strategist can aim at orchestrating a VCS, the VCS can never be fully controlled: at some point someone else may come in and change and redefine the configuration. Famous examples of such "redefinitional invasions" are Microsoft to IBM, Apple to Microsoft (and perhaps, sometime in the future, someone else to Apple).

ANT was in its beginnings used as a description and as an analytical construct or conceptual framework by the sociologists. Thus ANT methods were developed as methods for describing and analysing actor-networks and how they had been established — not as a method to design or create them (Law 2009). However, as we show in this book, ANT methods can also be useful for analysing an existing VCS, for redesigning it, or for designing new VCSs. A VCS in this book is an actor-network that is designed to co-create value, with the central attention of design being the configuring offering and a secondary support focus of attention being the support offerings.

In the English-speaking world, ANT's intellectual home of origin was not the sociology of innovation (as was the case in France) but science and technology studies (STS), which since the 1970s became interested on how scientific facts and technical artefacts are produced (Callon, 1986, 2001; Latour, 1987; Latour & Woolgar, 1979, 1986).[4] Other famous sociological

[4]A common argument in the STS research field is that facts are shaped by interests and ideologies. STS researchers suggested that science does not "mirror" nature as it "discovers" it (as positivist researchers would hold) but instead the social construction of science contributes to constructing the parts of society's conceptual edifice which are labelled "nature" (Latour, 1987). As provocative as this may sound, the origin of the word "fact" actually comes from Latin *facere*, which means "to make" (Knorr-Certina, 1980) — facts are then taken not as "given" data (from the Latin "datum") but as made and inscribed (recorded) by people and their instruments — that in turn were made by other people. In an often cited STS ethnography of scientific laboratory life, Latour and Woolgar (1979) traced how beheaded rats were (as they say) transformed by the people society calls "scientists", via apparatuses and inscription devices, into the points, traces, histograms, numbers, and diagrams used in writing scientific papers. These moves by individual scientists and teams of individual scientists in time and space take place in a process of translation, where entities are transformed when the action and intervention/observation and inscription are moved by these people from one time and place and actor, to another (Latour, 1986; Czarniawska & Sevón, 1996). As Latour (1987) argued, translation of rats to scientific findings and findings to facts, and facts to the development of other technologies such as drugs means that the spread of anything is at the hands of people, who may act to modify, deflect, betray, add to, or appropriate that which they translate.

ANT analyses have considered how strawberry markets (Garcia-Parpet, 1986/2007) and the fishing of scallops (Callon, 1986) and the translations they involve took place.[5]

B.2. Actor-Network Theory Methods

As we stated above, Callon (1986b) and then Harrisson and Laberge (2002) developed and used an ANT-based analytical grid to understand how actors have come together in more or less well-defined networks over time. That was the grid Denis *et al.* (2007: 185) utilised in studying strategy in what they termed "pluralistic" contexts — in contexts such as those of universities or hospitals where multiple forms of legitimacy, diffused centres of power, numerous objectives and diverse performance indicators co-exist.

In the language of this book, their analytic grid helped to

(1) reveal the shape, nature, and boundaries of networks of actors involved in making and renewing VCSs;
(2) identify interests and power structures among actors or firms involved in each new VCS, and to assess how each of these actors (people, things, technologies) engages the interest of others, enrols, and mobilises them;
(3) understand the processes through which irreversible links are sought and established;
(4) highlight the situations where this creating of a VCS might be maintained, reversed, broken up or broken down.

In our work, we have found this STS grid to be a practical, flexible, and useful analytical method. It has helped us to identify, investigate, and

[5]We do not here, however, provide extensive comments on these interesting cases, as this appendix is about utilising ANT's *descriptive* insights to appreciate how VCSs are *strategically designed and manufactured.* In ANT terms, we ourselves are "translating" ANT methods and tools in developing an understanding of the design and enacting of VCSs. We do this for pragmatic reasons, since we wish to utilise the insights from ANT as a descriptive and analytic tool and transform them into an interactive strategy design method (Normann & Ramírez, 1993).

exhibit what Foucault called "diffused" power (c.f. Picket, 1996). It has helped to make a given interpretation of the objectives being sought in creating a new VCS understandable to those who hold a different perspective on these objectives. It also helps them appreciate how their views can be at odds with the "dominant logic" (Prahalad & Bettis, 2000) of the larger ecosystem in which the new VCS wants to live.

While innovation research has attended to technology as an actor, strategists have tended not to do so. We have found that inviting technology as an actor in the creation of a new VCS is conceptually and practically helpful for strategic planners — and that is one thing that ANT does well. In short, the work of Callon, Harrisson and Laberge; and Denis *et al.* have provided us with a consistent terminology to compare what otherwise appeared to be very heterogeneous cases.

We found that Harrison and Laberge's approach resonated with our own purposes, as their research sought to understand "*actions of creating and putting the actors' arguments into actions...* (constructed) *with the aim of diffusing innovation among workers whose support was essential to the project's success*," (2002: 497).[6] We adopted the four elements they proposed in their analytic grid: problematisation, "intéressement" (a French term for getting others interested), enrolment, and mobilisation, which we describe below. We found these constructs to be directly geared towards the construction of innovation networks, similar to VCSs, and thus suitable for analysing existing VCS designs.

While Harrison and Laberge (*ibid.*) described these four moments as stages, they already allowed for some degree of relationship among them as cycles, and they accepted that they might possibly occur together, as activities and actors shift and change (Knights *et al.*, 1993). In the EDF example that we and our EDF clients together describe in Chapter 6, we found that the four moments were not entirely distinct from one another, but were often overlapping and intertwined.

---

[6]These four elements originally come from Callon's (1986) seminal article on scallop farming in the St. Brieuc Bay in France, where he referred to them as the four moments of translation.

In our work, we also found that these four moments did not always take place in a linear fashion; instead they quite often involved a number of tries where those enrolled did not become mobilised, others who were aware of the problem and could have been potentially interested were not, so the initial problem had to be reformulated, and so on.[7] From our work, we have learnt that VCS design and building appears to be a matter of persistence and reframing possibilities until the four moments all fall into place and a new VCS can be enacted.

Each of the four moments can be described as follows (this was the use we put them to in analysing EDF, as written up in Chapter 6).

1. Problematisation involves identifying and/or discovering, then formulating and defining some situation into one that can become coalesced as a "problem". This may or may not already entail exploring possible "solutions". This "problem-solutions" set-up can articulate the raison d'être of a project to create a new VCS. Harrisson and Laberge considered that problematisation actors can include technologies, market contexts, HR managers, workers, ideologies of excellence, and professional standards.
2. Intéressement includes the actions of a designer of a configuring offering, which Callon (1986a) and Normann and Ramírez (1993) called a "prime mover". In their analyses at the time he is the "focal" individual actor who tries to enrol others. He takes these actions in order to interest other actors as stakeholders in an innovation initiative. If intéressement is successful, then motives of different actors are coherent so that interests can be aligned to contribute to the proposed solution. The configuring offering designer persuades those it is attempting to interest to accept its own definition of the situation and to join in with their translated roles and identities

[7] Callon (1986) also discussed the possibility of re-problematisations and iterations moving between the four moments of translations. This means that the four moments remain fluid and dependent on the inputs of many different actors, until circumstances and relationships create the necessary conditions for change. However, the ANT literature has generally not focused on such iterations.

(Callon, 1986b). The configuring offering designer makes promises on relevant benefits that "interest" the different actors. To do this, the configuring offering designer needs to include and understand the issues of concern for each actor, and how to establish a suitable complementarity of interests.

3. Enrolment is the process whereby the proposed role to be played by the actor is defined, negotiated, and accepted. Enrolment typically results from successful intéressement. Enrolment is not considered to be only an individual process, but also a networked one, where arrangements for tying different actors into the collective means of producing solutions within a new actor-network (Latour, 1997, 2005) structure are developed. Enrolment often results in adjustment of support offerings.
4. Mobilisation involves having the allies in the actor-network that is being formed, which the configuring offering designer orchestrates, to begin to actually work together as a coherent new structure, where the innovation project they co-constitute (also designed and orchestrated by the configuring offering designer) becomes reality. If successful, mobilisation may also become irreversible and sustainable, preventing the actor-network from falling apart. In mobilisation, configuring offering designers get the interested, enrolled actors to move away from their initial positions to commit to the new venture. This is achieved through meetings, training, information, granting of privileged status, contracting and resource allocation, and possibly also through forms of institutionalisation.

At the risk of repeating this too much (but too little would run the risk of being unhelpful!) — problematisation, intéressement, enrolment, and mobilisation are not entirely exclusive of each other; they are somewhat ambiguous, interdependent and partly overlapping moments. In practice the transition from the one to the other may be difficult to distinguish. Yet despite these limitations, the four moments have proved helpful as a method to understand and analyse how strategists interactively design a VCS — not only a "brand" new VCS but also those VCSs that renew large incumbent firms.

Bibliography

Adler, P. S. & Heckscher, C. C. (eds.) (2006). *The Firm as a Collaborative Community: Reconstructing Trust in the Knowledge Economy (pp. 11–105).* New York, NY: Oxford University Press.

Ahrne, T. & Brunsson, N. (2008). *Meta-Organizations.* Cheltenham: Edward Elgar Publishing.

Akrich, M., Callon, M. & Latour, B. (2002). The key to success in innovation, part I: The art of interessement. Translated by Adrian Monaghan. *International Journal of Innovation Management*, 6(2), 187–206.

Alexander, C. (1964). *Notes on the Synthesis of Form* (Vol. 5). Massachusetts: Harvard University Press.

Alexander, C. (1965). City is Not a Tree. *Architectural Forum (Vol. 122: 1), April 1965, 58–62 (Part I), (Vol. 122: 2), May 1965,* 58–62 (Part II), (Vol. 122: 1).

Alexander, C., Ishikawa, S. & Silverstein, M. (1977). *A Pattern Language: Towns, Buildings, Construction (Vol. 2).* Oxford: Oxford University Press.

Amado G. & Ambrose, A. (eds.) (2001). *The Transitional Approach to Change.* London: Karnak Books.

Anderson, C. (1995). A survey of the Internet: The accidental superhighway. *The Economist.* 1 July. p. 10.

Arndt, J. & Friman, A. (1983). *Intern marknadsföring.* LiberFörlag.

Arthur, B. W. (1996). Increasing returns and the new world of business. *Harvard Business Review*, 74(4), 100–109.

Arvidsson, N. & Mannervik, U. (2009). *The Innovation Platform.* VINNOVA report, VR 2009:25.

Ashby, W. (1958). Requisite Variety and its implications for the control of complex systems, *Cybernetica (Namur)*, 1(2).

Austin, R. D., Devin, L. & Sullivan, E. E. (2012). Accidental innovation: supporting valuable unpredictability in the creative process. *Organization Science*, 23(5), 1505–1522.

Baines, T. S., Lightfoot, H. W., Evans, S., Neely, A., Greenough, R., Peppard, J. & Wilson, H. (2007). State-of-the-art in product-service systems. *Proceedings of the Institution of Mechanical Engineers, Part B: Journal of Engineering Manufacture*, 221(10), 1543–1552.

Barney, J. B. (1986). Organizational culture: Can it be a source of sustained competitive advantage? *Academy of Management Review*, 11(3), 656–665.

Bason, C. (2014). *Design for Policy.* Retrieved from Series: Design for Social Responsibility. http://www.ashgate.com/isbn/9781472413529. (Accessed December 2015).

Bastiat, F. (1851). *Harmonies Economiques.* Paris: Guillaumin.

Bell, D. (1973). *The Coming of Post-Industrial Society: A Venture in Social Forecasting.* New York: Basic Books.

Bernard, M. (2008). New Forms of Coherence for the Social Engagement of the Social Scientist: The Theory and Facilitation of Organizational Change from the Perspective of the Emery-Trist Systems Paradigm and the Ilya Prigogine School of Thought. In Ramírez, R., Selsky, J. & Heijden, v. d. (eds.), *Business Planning in Turbulent Times: New Methods for Applying Scenarios* (65–84). London: Earthscan.

Bettis, R. A. & Prahalad, C. K. (1995). The dominant logic: retrospective and extension. *Strategic Management Journal,* 16(1), 5–14.

Boisguilbert, P. I. (1697). Le Détail de la France. In *Boisguilbert* (1966) (581–662).

Boisguilbert, P. I. (1704, 2000). Dissertation de la nature des richesses, de l'argent et des tributs, où l'on découvre la fausse idée qui règne dans le monde à l'égard de ce trois articles, *translated with an introduction by Peter Groenewegen as A Treatise of the Nature of Wealth, Money and Taxation, Sydney: Centre for the Study of the History of Economic Thought, Reprints of Economic Classics,* Series 2(10).

Boisguilbert, P. I. (1707). Traité de la Nature, Culture, Commerce et Intérêt des Grains, tant par rapport au public, qu'à toutes les conditions d'un État. In *Boisguilbert* (1966) (827–878).

Boisguilbert, P. I. (1966). Pierre de Boisguilbert ou la Naissance de l'économie politique, Jacqueline Hecht (ed). Paris: Institut National d'Études Démographiques.

Brandenburger, A. M. & Nalebuff, B. J. (2011). *Co-opetition.* New York: Crown Business.

Brantley, P. (2008, April 23). *Dilbert Embraces User-Generated Content.* Retrieved from http://toc.oreilly.com/2008/04/dilbert-embraces-usergenerated.html (Accessed 4 December 2015).

Brender, A., Chevalier, A. & Pisani-Ferry, J. (1980). *Etats-Unis: Croissance, Crise et Changement Technique dans une Economie Tertiaire.* CEPII — La Documentation Franceaise, Paris.

Bucki, J. & Pesqueux, Y. (1995). *Le Systéme de Valeurs et sa Dynamique.* Cahier de recherche *533/1995, Groupe HEC.* France: Jouy-en-Josas.

Callon, M. (1986a). The Sociology of an actor-network: the Case of the Electric vehicle. In Callon, M., Law, J. & Rip, A. (eds.), *Mapping the Dynamics of Science and Technology* (19–34). London: Macmillan Press.

Callon, M. (1986b). Some Elements of a Sociology of Translation: Domestication of the Scallops and the Fishermen of Saint Brieuc Bay. In Law, J. (ed.), *Power, Action and Belief: A New Sociology of Knowledge?* London: Routledge.

Callon, M. (1991). Techno-economic Networks and Irreversibility. In J. L. (Ed.), *A Sociology of Monsters? Essays on Power, Technology and Domination. Sociological Review Monograph,* 38 (132–161). London, Routledge.

Callon, M. (2001). Writing and (Re)writing Devices as Tools for Managing Complexity. In Law, J. & Mol, A. (eds.), *Complexities in Science, Technology and Medicine.* Durham: Duke University Press.

Castells, M. (2015). *Networks of Outrage and Hope: Social Movements in the Internet Age*. New Jersey: John Wiley & Sons.

Chatman, J. A., Caldwell, D. F., O'Reilly, C. A. & Doerr, B. (2014). Parsing organizational culture: How the norm for adaptability influences the relationship between culture consensus and financial performance in high-technology firms. *Journal of Organizational Behavior*, 35(6), 785–808.

Checkland, P. & Scholes, J. (1999). *Soft Systems Methodology in Action Chapter 9.* Chichester: John Wiley and Sons.

Cheng, J. (2009). *Google-Apple Board Ties Severed; Collaboration Next to Go?* Retrieved from http://arstechnica.com/apple/2009/10/google-apple-board-ties-severed-collaboration-next-to-go/ (Accessed 2 December 2015).

Chevalier, M. (1968). *A strategy of interest-based planning,* unpublished doctoral dissertation, University of Pennsylvania.

Christensen, C. (1997). *The Innovator's Dilemma.* Boston: Harvard Business School Press.

Churchman, C. (1968). *The Systems Approach.* New York: Dell Publishing.

Churchman, C. (1972). *Design of Inquiring Systems.* New York: Basic Books.

Ciborra, C. (1995). The platform organization: recombining strategies, structures, and surprises. *Organization Science*, 7(2), 1–16.

Ciborra, C. (2000). *From Control to Drift: The Dynamics of Corporate Information Infrastructures*. Oxford: Oxford University Press.

Coulson, C. (1924). *Cours d'Economie Politique.* Paris: Gauthier Villars & Alcan.

Cusumano, M. (2010). *Staying power — Six Enduring Principles for Managing Strategy and Innovation in an Uncertain World.* Oxford: Oxford University Press.

Czarniawska, B. & Hernes, T. (eds.) (2005). *Actor-Network Theory and Organising.* California: Sage Publications.

Czarniawska, B. (2001). Anthropology and Organizational Learning. *Handbook of Organizational Learning and Knowledge*, 118–136.

Czarniawska, B. & Sevón, G. (eds.) (1996). *Translating Organizational Change* (Vol. 56). Germany: Walter de Gruyter.

D'Aveni, R. A. & Gunther, R. (1994). *Hyper-Competition: Managing the Dynamics of Strategic Maneuvering.* New York: The Free Press.

Daft, R.L., Sormunen, J. & Parks, D. (1988). Chief executive scanning, environment characteristics, and company performance: an empirical study. *Strategic Management Journal*, 9(2), 123–139.

Dale, S. (2015). *New Economics of Oil.* Society of Business Economists Annual Conference, *13 October 2015, London.* Retrieved from http://www.bp.com/content/dam/bp/pdf/speeches/2015/new-economics-of-oil-spencer-dale.pdf New Economics of Oil (Accessed 4 December 2015).

Damasio, A. (2000). *The Feeling of What Happens: Body, Emotion, and the Making of Consciousness.* New York: Vintage Books.

Davis, S. (1987). *Future Perfect.* Reading, MA: Addison-Wesley.

Denis, J. L., Langley, A. & Rouleau, L. (2007). Strategizing in pluralistic contexts: Rethinking theoretical frames. *Human Relations*, 60(1), 179–215.

Devin, L. (2012). *The Soul of Design: Harnessing the Power of Plot to Create Extraordinary Products.* Palo Alto, CA: Stanford Business Books.

Dineen, J. (2010). *Healthymagination Investor Update.* GE Healthcare, June 24.

Dineen, J. (2013). *Presentation at Global Industrials Conference.* GE Healthcare, March 19.

Dorst, K. & Cross, N. (2001). Creativity in the design process: Co-evolution of problem–solution. *Design Studies*, 22(5), 425–437.

Eiglier, P. & Langeard, E. (1977). Services as Systems: Marketing Implications. *Marketing Consumer Services: New insights* 83–103. Cambridge, MA: Marketing Science Institute.

Elahi, S. (2008). Conceptions of fairness & forming common ground. In Ramírez, R. & Seisky, W. (eds.), *Business Planning in Turbulent Times: New Methods for Applying Scenarios* (232–242). New York: Earthscan.

Emery, F. (1970). *System Thinking*. London, UK: Penguin Books. Retrieved from http://www.amazon.com/Systems-Thinking-Penguin-management-readings/dp/0140800719 (Accessed December 2015).

Emery, F. (1976). *Futures We Are In*. Leiden: Martinus Nijhoff.

Emery, F. (1977). Active Adaptation: The Emergence of Ideal-Seeking Systems. In Trist, E., Emery, F. & Murray, H. (eds.) *The Social Engagement of Social Science.*

Emery, F. E. (1969). *Systems Thinking: Selected Readings*. London, UK: Penguin Books.

Emery, F. E. & Trist, E. L. (1965). The causal texture of organizational environments. *Human Relations*, 18(1), 21–32.

Finkelstein, S., Whitehead, J. & Campbell, A. (2009). *Think again: why good leaders make bad decisions and how to keep it from happening to you.* Harvard Business Review.

Fisk, R. P., Grove, S. J. & John, J. (eds.) (2000). *Contribution to Services Marketing Self-Portraits: Introspections, Reflections, and Glimpses from the Experts*. (71–108) Chicago, IL: American Marketing Association.

Fogelman Soulie, F. (1991). *Les Théories de la Complexité: Autour de l'Oeuvre d'Henri Atlan*. France: Seuil.

Freeman, R. E. (1984). *Strategic Management: A Stakeholder Approach*. Boston, MA: Pitman.

Fuchs, V. (1965). *The growing importance of the service industries, occasional paper #96,* National Bureau of Economic Research, Washington, DC.

Fuchs, V. (1968). *The Service Economy*. New York: Columbia University Press.

Garcia-Perpet, M.-F. (2008). La construction sociale d'un marché parfait/Le marché au cadran de Fontaines-en-Sologne. *Idées économiques et sociales 2008/1 (N°151).*

Gawer, A. & Cusumano, M. A. (2002). *Platform Leadership: How Intel, Microsoft, and Cisco Drive Industry Innovation.* Cambridge: Harvard Business School Press.

Gershuny, J. (1978). *After Industrial Society? The Emerging Self-Service Economy*. London: Macmillan.

Gillette, F. (2011, June 23). The Rise and Inglorious Fall of Myspace. *Bloomberg Businessweek*. Retrieved from http://www.businessweek.com/magazine/content/11_27/b4235053917570.htm (Accessed 23 June 2011).

Grant, R. (2003). Strategic planning in a turbulent environment: Evidence from the oil majors. *Strategic Management Journal*, 24, 491–517.

Håkansson, H. E. (1982). *IMP Group. International Marketing and Purchasing of Industrial Goods: An Interaction Approach.* Chichester: John Wiley & Sons.

Håkansson, H. & Snehota, I. (1989). No business is an island: the network concept of business strategy. *Scandinavian Journal of Management*, 5(3), 187–200.

Hamel, G. & Prahalad, C. K. (1990). Corporate imagination and expeditionary marketing. *Harvard Business Review*, 69(4), 81–92.

Hamel, G. & Prahalad, C. K. (1990). The core competence of the corporation. *Harvard Business Review*, 68(3), 79–91.

Hanssen-Bauer, J. & Snow, C. (1996). Responding to hypercompetition: the structure and processes of a regional learning network organization. *Organization Science*, 7(4), 413–427.

Harrisson, D. & Laberge, M. (2002). Innovation, identities and resistance: The social construction of an innovation network. *Journal of Management Studies*, 39(4), 497–521.

Heckscher, C., Maccoby, M., Ramírez, R. & Tixier, P. E. (2003). *Agents of change: crossing the post-industrial divide*. Oxford University Press.

Heifetz, R. A., Grashow, A. & Linsky, M. (2009). *The Practice of Adaptive Leadership: Tools and Tactics for Changing your Organization and the World.* Boston: Harvard Business Press.

Heinonen, K., Strandvik, T., Mickelsson, K. J., Edvardsson, B., Sundström, E. & Andersson, P. (2010). A customer-dominant logic of service. *Journal of Service Management*, 21(4), 531–548.

Herhausen, D., Trumann, M. & Schogel, M. (2011). Learnings from "healthymagination" — how GE provides better care to more people at lower cost. *Marketing Review St. Gallen*, 28(6), 26–33.

Hirschhorn, L. (1984). *Beyond Mechanization: Work and Technology in a Postindustrial Age.* Boston, MA: MIT Press.

Hutchins, E. (1995). *Cognition in the Wild.* Boston, MA: MIT press.

Huxley, A. (1931). *Brave New World.* First Edition, London: Chatto and Windus.

Kerfoot, D. & Knights, D. (1993). Management, masculinity and manipulation: from paternalism to corporate strategy in financial services in Britain. *Journal of Management Studies*, 30(4), 659–677.

Kidder, T. (2011). *The Soul of a New Machine.* New York: Back Bay Books.

Kim, W. C. & Mauborgne, R. (2005). *Blue Ocean Strategy: How to Create Uncontested Market Space and Make Competition Irrelevant.* Massachusetts: Harvard Business Review Press.

Kjellberg, H. (2001). *Organising distribution: Hakonbolaget and the Efforts to Rationalise Food Distribution 1940–1960.* Published PhD dissertation. Stockholm: The Economic Research Institute.

Klamer, A. (1995, September). The value of culture. *Boekmancahier,* 7, 298–310.

Knights, D., Murray, F. & Willmott, H. (1993). Networking as knowledge work: A study of strategic interorganizational development in the financial services industry. *Journal of Management Studies*, 30(6), 975–995.

Langeard, E. (2000). *Servuction — Le Marketing Des Services.* Paris: Dunod.

Latour, B. & Woolgar, S. (1979, 1986). *Laboratory Life: The Construction of Scientific Facts.* Princeton: Princeton University Press.

Latour, B. (1987). *Science in Action: How to Follow Scientists and Engineers Through Society.* Massachusetts: Harvard University Press.

Latour, B. (1997). *The Trouble with Actor-Network Theory.* California: Sage Publication.

Latour, B. (2005). *Reassembling the Social: An Introduction to Actor-Network-Theory.* Oxford: Oxford University Press.

Latour, B. & Woolgar, S. (1979). *Laboratory Life: The Social Construction of Scientific Facts.* California: Beverly Hills.

Lavén, F. (2008). *Organizing Innovation. How Policies are Translated into Practice.* Sweden: University of Gothenburg.

Law, J. (2009). Actor network theory and material semiotics. In Turner B.S. (ed.), *The New Blackwell Companion to Social Theory*. Oxford: Wiley-Blackwell, pp. 141–158.

Lesourne, J. & Stoffaes, C. (eds.) (2001). *La prospective stratégique d'entreprise: De la réflexion à l'action.* Paris: Dunod.

Levy, S. (2011). *In the Plex: How Google Thinks, Works, and Shapes Our Lives.* New York: Simon & Schuster.

Lusch, R. F., Vargo, S. L. & Wessels, G. (2008). Toward a conceptual foundation for service science: contribution from service-dominant logic. *IBM Systems Journal*, 47(1).

Marx, K. (1974). *Théories sur la Plus-value.* Paris: Editions Sociales.

Maturana, H. R. & Varela, F. J. (1973). *De Máquinas y Seres Vivos: Una Caracterización de la Organización Biológica.* Santiago, Chile: Editorial Universitaria.

Maturana, H. R. & Varela, F. J. (1980). Autopoiesis and Cognition: The Realization of the Living (No. 42). Springer Science & Business Media. In Wartofsky, R., Cohen, S. & Marx, W. (eds.), *Boston Studies in the Philosophy of Science*, Springer.

Maturana, R. H. &Varela, F. J. (1987/1998). *The Tree of Knowledge.* Boston & London: Shambhala.

McLuhan, M. (1964). *Understanding Media* Toronto: W. Terrence Gordon.

Meyer, J. W. & Rowan, B. (1977). Institutionalized organizations: formal structure as myth and ceremony. *American Journal of Sociology*, 83(2), 340–363.

Michlewski, K. (2015). *Design Attitude.* Retrieved from http://www.ashgate.com/isbn/9781472421197.

Mill, J. S. (1852). *Principles of Political Economy* (3rd edn.). London: John W. Parker.

Millard. (2012, February 13). *When Giants Meet.* Retrieved from Healthcare IT News.

Milnere, S. (2015). Retrieved from https://twitter.com/#!/rupertmurdoch/status/157719858904174592 (Accessed October 2015).

Moldoveanu, M. & Martin, R. (2001). *Agency Theory and the Design of Efficient Governance Mechanisms.* Canada: University of Toronto.

Monbiot, G. (2014). How Wolves Change Rivers. [Online video]. 13 February 2014. Retrieved from: https://www.youtube.com/watch?v=ysa5OBhXz-Q (Accessed November 2014).

Morgan, G. (1983). *Beyond Method: Strategies for Social Research.* London: Sage.

Moss-Kanter, R. (2002). Strategy as improvisational theatre. *MIT Sloan Management Review, Winter*, 76–81.

Murdoch, R. (2012). Retrieved from https://twitter.com/#!/rupertmurdoch/status/157719858904174592 (Accessed 20 November 2015).

Myspace. (2015). *Wikipedia, article 'Myspace', section '2008–2011'.* Retrieved from 'Decline and sale by News Corp'. (Accessed 20 November 2015).

Naville, P. (1963). *Cahiers d'études des sociétés industrielles et de l'automatisation #5, #7.* Paris: Centre de Recherche d'Urbanisme.

Normann, R. & Ramírez, R. (1989). A theory of the offering: Toward a neo-industrial business strategy. In Snow, C. C. (ed.) *Strategy, Organization Design, and Human Resource Management.* (111–128). Greenwich, CT: JAI Press.

Normann, R. & Ramírez, R. (1993a). From value chain to value constellation: Designing interactive strategy. *Harvard Business Review*, 71(4), 65–77.

Normann, R. & Ramírez, R. (1993b). Strategy and the art of reinventing value (Perspectives section). *Harvard Business Review*, 71(5), 50–51.

Normann, R. & Ramírez, R. (1994). *From Value Chain to Value Constellation: Designing Interactive Strategy.* Chichester: John Wiley & Sons.

Normann, R. (1977). *Management for Growth.* Chichester: John Wiley & Sons.

Normann, R. (1978). *Development strategies for Swedish service knowledge.* Stockholm: report from multi-client study, Scandinavian Institute for Administrative Research.

Normann, R. (1984). *Service Management, Strategy and Leadership in Service Business.* Chichester: John Wiley & Sons.

Normann, R. (1991). *Service Management* (2nd edn.). Chichester: John Wiley & Sons.

Normann, R. (2001). *Reframing Business: When the Map Changes the Landscape.* Chichester: John Wiley & Sons.

Ocasio, W. (1997). Towards an attention-based view of the firm. *Strategic Management Journal* 18(1), 187–206.

O'Reilly, C. H. (2008). Organizational ambidexterity: IBM and emerging business opportunities. *California Management Review*, 51(4), 75–99.

O'Reilly, C., Tushman, M. & Harreld, J. B. (2009). *Organizational Ambidexterity: IBM and Emerging Business Opportunities.* Stanford Graduate School of Business, Working Paper No. 2025.

Ocasio, W. (2010). Attention to Attention. *Organization Science,* 22(5).

Ouzeau, R. (2014, January 14). *Unlock the Power of User-Generated Content on Instagram.* Retrieved from Instagram Marketing: http://blog.iconosquare.com/unlock-power-user-generated-content-instagram/ (Accessed 4 December 2015).

Pahnke, E. C., Katila, R. & Eisenhardt, K. M. (2015). Who takes you to the dance? How partners' institutional logics influence innovation in young firms. *Administrative Science Quarterly*, 60, 596–633.

Paltschik, M. & Ramírez, R. (2014). An Essay on Christian Grönroos's Contributions through the Lenses provided by Richard Normann's work. In Lindqvist, L.-J. (ed.) *Festschrift for Christian Grönroos.* Hanken University, Helsinki, Part of the series 'Legends in marketing' edited by Jagdish N. Sheth: Vol. 8(16), 229–238. California: Sage.

Pickett, B. L. (1996). Foucault and the politics of resistance. *Polity*, 28(4), 445–466.

Pigman, A.-S. (2007). *The World Economic Forum: A Multi-Stakeholder Approach to Global Governance* (1). London: Routledge.

Piketty, T. (2014). *Capital in the 21st Century.* Cambridge: Harvard University Press.

Porter, M. (1980). *Competitive Strategy.* New York: Free Press.

Porter, M. E. (1995). The competitive advantage of the inner city. *Harvard Business Review*, 73(3), 55–71.

Porter, M. & Kramer, M.R. (2011). *Creating Shared Value.* Boston: Harvard Business Review.

Porter, M. (2015). Retrieved from https://www.sharedvalue.org/partners/thought-leaders/michael-e-porter (Accessed 4 December 2015).

Postma, T. & Liebl, F. (2005). How to improve scenario analysis as a strategic management tool? *Technological Forecasting and Social Change*, 72(2), 161–173.

Powell, W. W. & DiMaggio, P. J. (1991). *The New Institutionalism in Organizational Analysis.* Chicago: University of Chicago Press.

Prahalad, C. K. & Bettis, R.A. (2000). The dominant logic: A new linkage between diversity and performance. *Management Journal Volume*, 7, 485–501.

Prigogine, I. & Stengers, I. (1984). *Order out of Chaos: Man's new dialogue with nature.* London: Flamingo.

Ramaswamy, V. (2009). Leading the transformation to co-creation of value. *Strategy & Leadership*, 37(2), 32–37.

Ramaswamy, V. & Ozcan, K. (2014). *The Co-Creation Paradigm.* USA: Stanford University Press.

Ramírez, R. & Mannervik, U. (2006). Customer Value Co-Creation And Co-Innovation. In Gummerson, E. (ed.), *Involving Customers in New Service Development.* London: Imperial College Press.

Ramírez, R. & Mannervik, U. (2008). Designing Value Creating Systems. In Kimbell, L. & Seidel, V. (ed.), *Designing for Services — Multidisciplinary Perspectives: Proceedings from the Exploratory Project on Designing for Services in Science and Technology-based Enterprises.* Saïd Business School, 2008, University of Oxford.

Ramírez, R. & Paltschik, M. (2013). Seizing the opportunities opened by the 'peak oil effect to reorient' 'services' and 'systems' research towards 'value co-production systems' scholarship. *Systems Research and Behavioral Science*, 30(5), 548–560.

Ramírez, R. & Selin, C. (2014). Plausability and probability in scenario planning. *Foresight*, 16(1), 54–74.

Ramírez, R., Selsky, J. W. & van der Heijden, K. (eds.) (2008). *Business Planning for Turbulent Times: New Methods for Applying Scenarios.* USA: Earthscan.

Ramírez, R., Selsky, J. W. & van der Heijden, K. (eds.) (2010). *Business Planning for Turbulent Times: New Methods for Applying Scenarios* (2nd ed.) UK: Taylor & Francis.

Ramírez, R. & Selsky, J.W. (2014). Strategic Planning in Turbulent Environments: A Social Ecology Approach to Scenarios. *Long Range Planning*. Retrieved from *http://dx.doi.org/10.1016/j.lrp.2014.09.002*.

Ramírez, R. & van der Heijden, K. (2007). Scenarios to develop strategic options: a new interactive role for scenarios in strategy. In Sharpe, B. & van der Heijden, K. (eds.), *Scenarios for Success: Turning insights into Action.* Chichester: John Wiley & Sons.

Ramírez, R. & Wilkinson, A. (2016). *Strategic Reframing: The Oxford Scenario Planning Approach.* Oxford University Press.

Ramírez, R. (1999). Value co-production: Intellectual Origins and implications for practice and research Strategic Management. *Strategic Management Journal*, 20, 49–65.

Robles, P. (2015). *Microsoft, Google, Apple, and Mozilla Collaborate On Game-Changing Web App Tech.* Retrieved from Programmable Web. June 22: http://www.programmableweb.com/news/microsoft-google-apple-and-mozilla-collaborate-game-changing-web-app-tech/2015/06/22 (Accessed December 2015).

Rothbard, M. (1995). *Economic Thought before Adam Smith: An Austrian Perspective on Economic Thought* (444–448). Aldershot, UK: Edward Elgar.

Sauvy, A. (1949). Progrès technique et repartition professionelle de la population. *Population*, 1–2.

Schatzki, T. R. (2001). Introduction: Practice Theory'. In Schatzki, T., Knorr Cetina, K. & von Savigny, E. (eds.), *The Practice Turn in Contemporary Theory* (1–14). London: Routledge.

Schön, D. A. (2005). *The reflective practitioner: How professionals think in action.* New York: Basic Books.

Schwab, K. (2010). *A Partner in Shaping History. The First 40 years 1971–2000.* Retrieved from weforum.org — World Economic Forum: www3.weforum.org/docs/WEF_First40Years_Book_2010.pdf (Accessed 1 December 2015).

Scott, S. D. & Ofori-Dankwa, J.C. (2008). Toward an integrative cartography of two strategic issue diagnosis frameworks. *Strategic Management Journal*, 29(1), 93–114.

Segall, L. (2011, June 29). *News Corp. sells Myspace to Specific Media.* Retrieved from CNN: http://money.cnn.com/2011/06/29/technology/myspace_layoffs/ (Accessed 1 December 2015).

Selin, C., Kimbell, L., Ramírez, R. & Bhatti, Y. (2015). Scenarios and Design: Scoping the Dialogue Space. *Futures*, 74, 4–17.

Selsky, J. W., Ramírez, R. & Babüroğlu, O. N. (2013). Collaborative capability design: redundancy of potentialities. *Systemic Practice and Action Research*, 26(5), 377–395.

Selsky, J. W., Goes, J. & Babüroğlu, O. N. (2007). Contrasting perspectives of strategy making: Applications in 'hyper'environments. *Organization Studies*, 28(1), 71–94.

Selsky, J. W. & Parker, B. (2005). Cross-sector partnerships to address social issues: challenges to theory and practice. *Journal of Management*, 31(6), 849–873.

Selznick, P. (1957). *Leadership in Administration: A Sociological Interpretation.* California: Berkeley.

Sempels, C. & Hoffmann, J. (2013). *Sustainable Innovation Strategy: Creating Value in a World of Finite Resources.* London: Palgrave-Macmillan.

Senge, P. (1990). *The Fifth Discipline Fieldbook.* New York: Doubleday.

Senge, P. M. (1990). *The Fifth Discipline: The Art and Practice of the Learning Organization.* New York: Doubleday.

Simmel, G. (1977). *Philosophie de l'Argent.* Paris: PUF.

Sivak. (2013). *Has Motorization in the US Peaked? Report No. UMTRI-2013–17.* Transport Research Institute, University of Michigan.

Stanback, T. M. (1980). *Understanding the Service Economy.* Baltimore, MD: Johns Hopkins University Press.

Storch, H. (1823). *Cours d'Economie Politique ou Exposition des Principes qui Déterminent la Prospé rité des Nations.* Aillaut, Paris.

Tapscott, D. (2013). *Introducing Global Solution Networks.* Canada: Martin Prosperity Institute.

Thuriaux-Alemán, B. and Rogers, S. (2012). *The Projects, Technology & Procurement Organization: The Emergence of a New Organization Form in E&P*. Arther D. Little Energy Utilities. Retrieved from: http://www.adlittle.com/downloads/tx_adlreports/Energy_Utilities_2013_Emergence_of_the_Projects.pdf.

Toffler, A. (1970). *Future Shock*. USA: Random House.

Trist, E. L. & Murray, H. (eds.) (1990). *The Social Engagement of Social Science: A Tavistock Anthology (Vol. I) The Socio-Psychologic Perspective*. Philadelphia, PA: University of Pennsylvania Press.

Trist, E. L. (1981). The evolution of Socio-Technical Systems. In van de Veb, A. & Joyce, W. (eds.), *Perspectives on Organizational Design* (19–75). New York: Wiley.

Tufte, E. (1983). The Visual Display of Quantitative Information. Connecticut: Graphics Press. Retrieved from: www.edwardtufte.com/tufte (Accessed 1 December 2015).

Turnbull, P. W. & Valla, J. P. (eds.) (2013). *Strategies for International Industrial Marketing*. London: Routledge.

Turnbull, P. W. & Valla, J. P. (1986). Strategic planning in industrial marketing: An interaction approach. *European Journal of Marketing*, 20(7), 5–20.

van der Heijden, K. (1996/2005). *Scenarios — The Art of Strategic Conversation*. Chichester: John Wiley and Sons.

Vargo, S. L. & Morgan, F. W. (2005). Services in society and academic thought: an historical analysis. *Journal of Macromarketing*, 25(1) *June*.

Vargo, S. L., Maglio, P. P. & Akaka, M. A. (2008). On value and value co-creation: A service systems and service logic perspective. *European Management Journal,* 26.

Vargo, S. L. & Lusch, R. F. (2004a). Evolving to a new dominant logic for marketing. *Journal of Marketing*, 68 (January), 1–17.

Vargo, S. L. & Lusch, R. F. (2004b). The four service marketing myths: Remnants of a goods-based, manufacturing model. *Journal of Service Research*, 6(May), 324–335.

Vargo, S. L. & Lusch, R. F. (2008). From goods to service(s): divergences and convergences of logics. *Industrial Marketing Management*, 37(May), 254–259.

Verloop, J. (2004). *Insight in Innovation*. New York: Elsevier.

Vickers, G. (1968). *Value Systems and Social Processes*. Middlesex, England: Penguin.

WEF. (2010). *The First 40 Years*. Retrieved from http://www3.weforum.org/docs/WEF_First40Years_Book_2010.pdf.

Weiszfeld, M., Roman, P. & Mendel, G. (1993). *Vers l'entreprise démocratique: le récit d'une expérience pionnière.* Éd. La Découverte.

Winnicott, D. (1965). *The Maturational Process and the Facilitating Environment.* London: Hogarth Books.

Wissema, J. G. (2009). *Towards the third generation university: Managing the university in transition.* Cheltenham: Edward Elgar publishing.

Woolgar, S. (1986). On the alleged distinction between discourse and praxis. *Social Studies of Science*, 16(2), 309–317.

Glossary

ANT — This is a way of describing how actors such as people and organisations are inextricably joined with others and get others to join in their efforts. The acronym stands for Actor-Network Theory — explained in Appendix B. In this book, ANT is used as a fruitful descriptive framework. The creation processes of very different sorts of VCS can be described and studied by this framework — see Chapter 5.

Offering — The offering is the core unit of analysis in this book. It is a rich construct, both conceptually and in terms of practice, and it is also paradoxical. The offering manifests the relationship of co-creation between actors, and in joining them, distinguishes them from each other in terms of roles and — typically — also in terms of values created.

Configuring Offering; Support Offering — There are two kinds of offerings: configuring offerings that organise the VCS, and support offerings between two actors within the system.

TUNA — An acronym for a condition of business landscapes in unstable times: Turbulent, Uncertain, Novel, Ambiguous.

Value/Values — This is the other core idea of this book. The idea itself has a very rich history — see Appendix A. Its meaning depends strongly on the culture and setting in which it is used, ranging from the bravery of a knight to the price of a financial instrument. In this book, we break with the prevalent way of thinking about value, which is to see it as a quantity, added to objects in a chain of phases of production, and then destroyed by "consumers". We conceive value as interaction, as co-created, and as plural: comprising many values (plural) rather than only one type of value.

VCS — This acronym stands for "value creating system". It expresses the insight that value is co-created in a system, in businesses and societies today. The VCS framework for strategy considers value and values from an outcomes-in-use (or expected-outcomes) perspective. This is always from the point of view of an actor who is acting to create value — for the self, and for others — and using what other actors do to help create value.

WOB, WOM — These abbreviations were used by Richard Normann to characterise two different but related worlds. The World of Business (WOB) is the space of strategy interactions where organisations enable or relieve others in order to create value, and what is done to do this. The World of Management (WOM) depicts the intra-organisational arrangements which are meant to (but often fail to) support WOB.

Index

S

T